T0301630

Narrowing the Channel

Chicago Series on International and Domestic Institutions

Edited by William G. Howell and Jon Pevehouse

OTHER BOOKS IN THE SERIES

Narrowing the Channel

The Politics of Regulatory Protection in International Trade

ROBERT GULOTTY

THE UNIVERSITY OF CHICAGO PRESS   CHICAGO AND LONDON

The University of Chicago Press, Chicago 60637
The University of Chicago Press, Ltd., London
© 2020 by The University of Chicago
Published 2020
Printed in the United States of America

29 28 27 26 25 24 23 22 21 20   1 2 3 4 5

ISBN-13: 978-0-226-66922-9 (cloth)
ISBN-13: 978-0-226-66936-6 (paper)
ISBN-13: 978-0-226-66953-3 (e-book)
DOI: https://doi.org/10.7208/chicago/9780226669533.001.0001

Library of Congress Cataloging-in-Publication Data

Names: Gulotty, Robert, author.
Title: Narrowing the channel : the politics of regulatory protection in international trade / Robert Gulotty.
Other titles: Chicago series on international and domestic institutions.
Description: Chicago : University of Chicago Press, 2020. | Series: Chicago series on international and domestic institutions | Includes bibliographical references and index.
Identifiers: LCCN 2019035333 | ISBN 9780226669229 (cloth) | ISBN 9780226669366 (paperback) | ISBN 9780226669533 (ebook)
Subjects: LCSH: Protectionism. | Trade regulation. | Trademarks. | Globalization.
Classification: LCC HF1713 .G946 2020 | DDC 382/.73—dc23
LC record available at https://lccn.loc.gov/2019035333

Contents

Preface

The ideas in this book were first developed at the Economic Research and Statistics Division of the World Trade Organization (WTO), then headed by Patrick Low. There I benefited greatly from interactions with the WTO's team of trade economists and lawyers, particularly my supervisor, Michele Ruta. It was these interactions that convinced me that there was more to be understood about the politics of regulatory barriers to trade.

During the waning years of the Doha Round, the WTO produced a bevy of statistics and reports showing the importance of global supply chains and multinational firms in international commerce. The then director general of the WTO, Pascal Lamy, argued that because traded goods and services carry with them inputs from all over the world, globalization of production eliminates the traditional rationale for protection. The hope was that if governments were made aware of their stake in globalization, they would return to the negotiating table to address the rising tide of regulatory protection. The argument and evidence in this book show that the governments' stake in globalization is more the cause than the cure. Globalization enables a new form of entangled mercantilism, where governments shift profits toward their connected firms.

This book benefited from the community of scholars at Stanford University. My greatest intellectual debt is to Judith Goldstein, who patiently advised my doctoral studies and provided outstanding levels of professional support and guidance. Judy encouraged my participation in a workshop on the economics of dispute settlement at the WTO, which introduced me to Alan Sykes, Robert Staiger, and Kyle Bagwell, pioneers in the political economy of trade cooperation. My thanks also go to my graduate committee—Mike Tomz, Phillip Lipsy, and Kyle Bagwell—for their help and guidance. I am especially indebted to Kyle for introducing me to the WTO secretariat and for his help on the theoretical aspects of this project.

At Chicago I have benefited from an astounding community of political scientists, particularly the International Relations group: Robert Pape, John Mearsheimer, Paul Poast, Paul Staniland, and Austin Carson. Robert Pape was particularly insightful in helping me frame the project for a broader audience. Paul Poast ably led a book workshop, funded by the Center for International Social Science Research, where I received helpful and critical reactions from Sonal Pandya, Jeffry Freiden, J. Lawrence Broz, and, again, Michele Ruta.

This book has also profited from discussions at workshops and conferences and in classrooms and coffee shops. I am particularly grateful for conversations with and comments from Justin Grimmer, Mariya Grinberg, Xiaojun Li, Rebecca Perlman, Matthias Staisch, Gary Herrigel, and Haichao Wu. I thank Chuck Myers, the two anonymous reviewers, and the editorial team at the University of Chicago Press for their support in helping finish this book. Finally, this project would also not have been possible if not for research assistance from Ipek Cinar, Zuhad Hai, Minju Kim, Nikita Coutinho, Alexander Nye, and Maximiliano Verjares.

Finally, I thank my family, my parents, and my amazing wife, Katie Malone, for her love and support.

PART I

A Theory of Regulatory Protection

CHAPTER ONE

Introduction

In the late summer of 2007, US regulators were alerted that 1.5 million children's toys contained dangerous levels of toxic lead. These toys were designed and sold by the American toy giant Mattel but manufactured by a network of affiliates and subcontractors in China. One of these Chinese manufacturers used neurotoxic lead paint on toys featuring characters from *Sesame Street* and *Dora the Explorer*. The defect went unnoticed by Mattel's internal testing and audits, allowing toxic toys to spread across the world.[1] By the end of the year, product defects, including other lead paint incidents, had forced companies to recall 44 million children's products. Consumers, legislators, and safety advocates were outraged, and within a few months of the first incident, the US legislature passed the Consumer Product Safety Improvement Act (CPSIA) of 2008, overhauling the regulatory regime for children's clothes, books, and toys across the supply chain.[2]

The new legislation made two major changes to the regulation of children's products. The first was to provide additional funding and authority for inspectors, a natural response to Mattel's detection failures. The second was to slash the level of lead allowed in technical standards for children's products. The new standard moved the allowed level of lead down from 600 parts per million to 100 parts per million, the technical boundary of reliable testing.[3] This level of sensitivity would have made no difference to the 2007 lead crisis. Tests of the faulted toys revealed lead levels as high as 50,000 parts per million, more than 80 times higher than the existing legal limit.[4] Nonetheless, one of the sponsors of the legislation, Bobby Rush of Illinois, boasted that only the holy ground of Mount Horeb, where Moses received the Ten Commandments, would meet the new standard.[5] The effect was a steep increase in testing costs: all children's products sold in the United States would be required to undergo independent laboratory tests at a cost of tens of thousands of dollars.

The new standard reshaped the American toy industry. Most producers of children's products are small, surviving by producing niche products at relatively low volume. In the United States, crafters of handmade goods and other small-batch producers struggled to cover the costs of sending each version of their craftwork to laboratories for testing. As one producer put it, "The CPSIA wants our company to sell 50 items, not our current 2,000, and wants us to sell them in lots of 50,000 units, not 500–10,000 as we do currently" (Woldenberg 2009). Companies were forced to reduce variety, raise prices, or exit the market entirely. Before the CPSIA, there were 770 firms producing children's toys in the United States, but by 2012, that number had fallen to 559.[6] The survivors passed on the costs to consumers—toy prices rose dramatically. The outcome was industrial concentration: in a period when the value of domestic toy shipments rose from $28 billion to $44 billion, the tonnage of shipments dropped by 7 percent.[7]

While these domestic effects were severe, the impact of the CPSIA was magnified abroad. Many small exporters were unable to charge 50 percent more to cover testing costs for their products and were forced to abandon the American market.[8] In China, where 80 percent of toys are manufactured, access to the US market is sine qua non for survival.[9] After the CPSIA came online in 2009, the number of toy manufacturing companies in Guangdong Province plummeted from 8,000 to 3,000.[10] Small and independent producers bore the brunt of the losses, decimated by the 10-fold increase in testing costs under the CPSIA (Huang 2011). These smaller firms lacked American headquarters or affiliates and US Congress could safely enact regulations at their expense.

Nonetheless, the CPSIA garnered support from the largest toy manufacturers. Mattel spent millions lobbying to support the legislation, twice as much as on all other issues in the previous eight years. The other major toy manufacturers followed suit. Hasbro, the second-largest US toy company, hired a lobbyist for the first time in the company's history to push for the bill (Carney 2009). Anne Northup, the commissioner of the US agency tasked with enforcing the CPSIA, testified to Congress that these companies pushed the legislation *because* of its high costs.[11] By ensuring higher prices and less competition, regulations benefited a small number of the most productive firms while "the backbone of [the US] economy, small businesses—from screen printers to manufacturers of chemistry sets for schools—are being forced to cut jobs or take other drastic measures due to the cost of compliance" (United States 2010). Meanwhile, multinationals saw import value from China rise by 11 percent and profits nearly triple.[12]

This book argues that the political dynamics of regulatory measures such as the CPSIA reflect a transformation in commercial politics. Governments are increasingly setting stricter regulations to advantage their large firms. Regulatory barriers such as the requirements to test and label children's products raise fixed costs that exclude smaller and less productive producers from the market. Those firms exit, lowering the variety of products available and raising the prices of those that remain. Larger, more productive firms thereby have fewer competitors, can charge higher prices because they can cover the costs of the more onerous regulation. This simple account of firm preferences, typical of past theories of regulatory capture, is transformed when applied to international commercial relations.

While theories of regulatory capture have long identified beneficiaries of restrictive government actions, this book contributes to understanding when these interests would be acted on by governments. What interest do national governments have in the foreign ownership of imports? I argue that the connection lies in the development of a new kind of international commercial politics, *entangled mercantilism*, where national interests flow through the global production networks operated by multinational corporations.[13] Governments seek to shift value toward large firms abroad because such firms have local operations that contribute to the local economy. By helping governments internalize the profits of regulatory protection, global firms promote the use of regulatory barriers to trade. Regulatory power is still bound by national borders, but profits, and so national interests, need not be.

1.1. International Conflict over Regulatory Protectionism

Regulatory protectionism originates in economic conflict among firms and results in political conflict between nations. Governments value the interests of their exporters as sources of revenue, engines of growth, and employers. Just as the largest exporters benefit from regulatory protection and smaller firms lose, there are national consequences to regulatory protection. To address these concerns, governments have tried to use the global trade system to limit regulatory protectionism—but to no avail. For instance, smaller exporters convinced Beijing to deploy diplomatic resources to oppose the CPSIA at the World Trade Organization (WTO). Chinese diplomats formally submitted a specific trade concern (STC) objecting to the CPSIA as a technical barrier to trade (WTO 2009). At the same time, Chinese regulators initiated an informal counteroffensive, rejecting imports of millions of dollars of frozen pig kidneys from the US (Beamish and Bapuji 2008).[14] Both efforts failed. This case is only one of hundreds of new regulatory barriers being submitted to the WTO. Addressing the trade effects of programs like the CPSIA is high on the agenda in Geneva, where governments now raise STCs at a rate of 20 per month. Yet going from an agenda item to concrete negotiations has remained an elusive move, and regulatory barriers were left largely unaddressed in the Doha Round of multilateral negotiations, and today even cooperation on tariffs is beginning to unravel (Cho 2007).

The rise in regulatory protection and the absence of meaningful international rules addressing regulatory matters stand in stark contrast to the success of global agreements on tariffs. Even the global economic crisis did not cause governments to reverse their commitments on tariffs, and the system appears to be remarkably robust to challenge, but the prospects for new agreements on regulatory matters have, if anything, moved further out of reach with the failure of the Doha Round of negotiations at the WTO.

Some scholars and analysts would argue that the absence of rules addressing regulatory protection relative to tariffs is less a failure of international cooperation and more a consequence of the domestic trade-offs inherent in regulatory protection. From a national welfare perspective, even if a regulation reduces the number of varieties and raises prices, a regulation can serve consumer interests by ensuring that goods are safe and of high quality. This has led some scholars to argue that the adoption of regulatory barriers has little to do with international externalities and more to do with the competition between firms and consumers (Vogel 2012). The CPSIA would never have been written if not for real consumer demands for safe children's toys. The consequences for foreign businesses, such as the small Chinese firms that cannot produce up to US standards, are an unintended side effect of meeting legitimate consumer demands. On this account, rising regulatory barriers around the world reflect the spread of democracy and accountable government and not some protectionist coalition of import-competing industry groups.[15]

However, even if governments around the world have become increasingly accountable to citizens, the public is too fickle and regulatory protection is too widespread to be caused solely by domestic public-policy demands. The variety of licensing requirements, labeling rules, and registration fee structures are too complex for even an attentive public to dictate. Consumer activists are ill-equipped to determine what sorts of tests would be technically feasible or what kind of fee structure is appropriate for a registration scheme. In addition, the behavior of Mattel, Hasbro, and the other major toy companies suggests that there is more to regulatory politics. It appears that the fight over the character and extent of regulatory protection is less about the consumer versus industry and more about the conditions of global competition. Paradoxically, this competition-driven regulation may have the effect of undermining support for commercial cooperation more generally by undercutting the tools of international cooperation.

These international competitive dynamics are central to understanding contemporary commercial politics, but they can also shed light on drivers of economic inequality within countries. Across a wide variety of developed economies, inequality is at levels not seen since the Gilded Age, and corporate profits have hit historic highs (Piketty 2014). Scholars and advocates have variously sourced these effects in campaign finance rules, international competition for capital, and captured governments (Lindsey and Teles 2017). However, as markets are becoming concentrated everywhere, no market is as concentrated as the global market for goods.[16] In a landmark study, Freund and Pierola (2015) show that across a sample of 32 countries, the top 1 percent of firms are responsible for more than half of that country's exports. Moreover, new microdata on firms and workers have found a tight connection between rising inequality and these firm-level differences in access to global markets (Helpman et al. 2017).

As I show, the concentration of global trade has implications for the political decision-making on regulatory barriers to trade. Rather than opposing these measures, the interests of large exporting firms, combined with the political access generated by multinational production, have conspired to create a new form of protectionism. The very large, more productive firms that benefit from fixed-cost regulations are those that are most engaged in global production. As testing, labeling, and registration requirements increase profits, they bring benefits that spill over national borders. Governments share in these profits when large firms organize production abroad, as local affiliates bring shared benefits from profits earned from trade. In sum, the interests of large multinational firms are a general cause of a new form of protectionism, one that seeks not to eliminate trade but rather to shift its ownership away from small foreign firms toward a limited set of concentrated global producers.

In the following section, I discuss the role of firms in international trade and how differences among firms play out in commercial policy-making (Kim 2017; Osgood et al. 2017). A growing international political economy literature finds that large and productive exporting firms are the primary advocates for lower trade barriers. On this account, the concentration of trade would empower large firms that benefit from and promote international trade openness. As large firms are increasingly operating across national borders, their dependence on international trade expands, and so too does their interest in lower tariffs. For regulatory barriers, this concentration will likely have the opposite effect. The following section places these results into the broader context of interdependence theories of international political economy. I then show how my argument recasts the effect of globalization as reinforcing rather than undermining mercantilist interests. I conclude with an overview of the research design and a preview of the forthcoming chapters.

1.2. Firms in International Commerce

Recent advances in economics have highlighted the role of firms in determining the patterns of international trade. More than product or industry characteristics, it is the character of the individual company, particularly its productivity, which determines the content of trade and its volume. Innovative studies have used US census data to show that only a very small subset of firms trade at all, and among that small subset, trade is further concentrated in a handful of giant firms (Bernard et al. 2003, 2009; Freund and Pierola 2015). In the following, I briefly describe the heterogeneity of firms that exist within sectors, differentiating three major classes of firms: small domestic firms, larger exporting firms, and internationally organized multinational firms. Each plays an important role in contemporary understandings of commercial cooperation.

While economists have only recently begun incorporating the extraordinary concentration of economic activity into trade models, the phenomenon is hardly new—trade has long been dominated by a few

TABLE I.I **Home and foreign firm organization**

Actors	Production location	Prevalence (%)	Min. productivity	Export share (%)
Domestic	Home	95	Low	0
Exporter	Home	4	Moderate	10
MNC	**Home and Foreign**	**1**	**High**	**90**

Source: Bernard, Jensen, and Schott (2009).

large firms. As far back as 1914, the largest firms accounted for almost 90 percent of American manufactured exports (Becker 1982, 48).[17] Eighty years later, firm-level census data reveal that this concentration is in the hands of multinational corporations (MNCs). Table 1.1 displays firm-level estimates of US trade activity in 2000, created by joining customs transactions with data from US enterprises (Bernard, Jensen, and Schott 2009). These data show that 95 percent of American firms did not record any international transactions. Among trading firms, approximately three-quarters are based solely in the United States. Together, these domestic-only firms are responsible for only 10 percent of exports. The remaining quarter, or 1 percent of all firms, are MNCs or affiliates of them that produce value both in the United States and abroad. The small subset of businesses that are organized globally is responsible for 90 percent of total export volume.[18]

These patterns in US exports hold for other countries—trade is a rarified game around the world. Canada, for instance, has thousands of firms exporting textiles and clothing, but the top 5 percent of firms are responsible for more than 60 percent of the export value (Chen and Yu 2010). The same applies outside of highly developed economies. In China, for example, the top 2 percent of exporters are responsible for more than 40 percent of the value of exports in electrical equipment, food, and machinery.[19] That is to say, firm-level characteristics, more than industry or national differences, drive international commercial activity, and the profits of this trade accrue to a tiny subset of giant firms.

To explain this consistent pattern of inequality, trade economists have borrowed from studies of industrial organization that theorize heterogeneity in productivity across firms. In these theories, firm-level productivity differences explain both size and behavior. Productive firms are larger in the sense that they have more employees, sell more goods, and have higher profit margins. Firms that participate in international trade do so because they are productive enough to overcome the fixed costs of

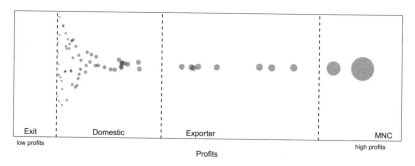

FIGURE I.I. The distribution of profits across firms

export. Among trading firms, a few are sufficiently productive to form foreign affiliates and engage in multinational production. Where most companies are at the mercy of national commercial policy, multinationals can choose how to engage in commerce abroad. They can join other exporters in finding foreign purchasers for their goods, or they can produce abroad via their foreign affiliates. This option is both a function and a source of the economic power of multinationals; it provides the ability to overcome the fixed costs of foreign production, the opportunity to leverage their foreign partners.

Figure I.I depicts the relative size and number of these firms in a single market. The least productive firms expect not to make profits and therefore immediately exit the market. Those that enter the market can choose whether to sell solely in the domestic market or attempt to export. Finally, the most productive firms can export and organize production abroad as MNCs. Only the largest and most productive firms can pass all three hurdles: entry at home, sales abroad, and organization as multinationals.

In the following, I describe how firm characteristics, particularly firm size and the distribution of production across borders, generate political preferences over commercial policy. Although there is debate over the political efficacy of industrial interests, the broad consensus is that trade liberalism is strongest within the largest businesses and that these interests derive from the association between size and productivity. As shown below, that assumption finds support from the commercial policy debates of the twentieth century, which centered on the tariff (Hiscox 1999).[20] However, when it comes to regulatory barriers, the opposite holds.

1.2.1. Small and Large Firms and International Commercial Policy

Despite clear expectations from theory, scholars have struggled to find evidence of systematic cross-firm political divisions over the tariff. In 1954, Raymond Bauer, Ithiel de Sola Pool, and Lewis Dexter commissioned a survey of 1,000 leaders of small, medium, and large firms and found little support for an association between size and protectionism.[21] They found that perhaps large firms preferred free trade, but so did small firms that ought to have felt disadvantaged. Table 1.2 reproduces the original survey responses from the 1954 study. Among the 903 respondents, only 14 reported support for raising "most tariffs," and there is no statistical difference between the responses across categories. This survey motivated Bauer, de Sola Pool, and Dexter (1963) and a generation of subsequent scholarship to reject simple notions of economically driven interests.

Attention to the broader conditions of competition challenges a straightforward interpretation of these statistics. The sampling strategy for the survey was to recruit respondents from firms with more than 100 employees that appeared in the Old Age and Survivors' Insurance list of employers in 1954 (Bauer, de Sola Pool, and Dexter 1963, 108). With this sample of already large firms, the study was forced to classify firms with fewer than 1,000 employees as "small." Contemporary evidence suggests that assessment is misleading. In 1958, the US Census Bureau began collecting enterprise statistics based on the same list of employers. Of the three million companies in operation in 1958, 99 percent fall below the survey cutoff of 100 employees.[22] Only 223 companies in the United States would be classified as large by the survey, amounting to 0.007 percent of all operations (US Bureau of the Census 1963). Surveys of large

TABLE 1.2 **Tariff attitudes of businessmen by size of firm, 1954**

Attitude	Large firm (%)	Medium firm (%)	Small firm (%)
Favors raising most tariffs	2	7	5
Favors reducing most tariffs	41	41	37
Favors leaving most tariffs at present levels	32	34	31
Does not know	17	11	24
Refuses to generalize	8	7	3
Total	166	404	333

Source: Bauer, de Sola Pool, and Dexter (1963), 115.

firms—such as Bauer, de Sola Pool, and Dexter's—inevitably draw from the top 1 percent of firms, obscuring a full picture of the market.

Even given the interests of large and productive firms in exporting, their role in domestic tariffs is not as straightforward. Governments and firms have long been united in favoring exports and opposing imports. Rationalizing export interests in low tariffs at home raises the international dimension of trade politics, the strategic problem of tariff protection, and the role of reciprocity. The problem for exporting firms is that foreign governments will respond to high domestic tariffs with their own protectionist measures (Bagwell and Staiger 2002a; Grossman and Helpman 1995; Johnson 1953). This strategic environment produces a prisoner's dilemma and a socially inefficient outcome of mutually high tariffs.

One way for governments to facilitate the connection between local and foreign tariffs is through the negotiation of trade agreements (Gilligan 1997). An agreement extends the shadow of the future, allowing exporters to be reassured that politicians will not renege on their promises to keep markets open. Insofar as tariff reductions are made reciprocally, negotiations are balanced in a way that allows trade without disproportionately affecting one or another partner's exporters. Kyle Bagwell and Robert Staiger argue that these provisions, as instantiated in the global trade regime, work because as governments reduce tariffs in concert, neither party faces a loss in relative market access (Bagwell and Staiger 1999, 2002a; Bagwell, Mavroidis, and Staiger 2002).[23] Exporter interests are also at play in the enforcement of trade agreements. The General Agreement on Tariffs and Trade (GATT) includes provisions that allow governments to withdraw concessions in response to a partner's failure to uphold the agreement. If a foreign state raises a barrier, the GATT legally authorizes the offended state to retaliate by imposing tariffs. This motivates exporters to oppose violations of agreements and encourages sustained cooperation.[24]

This norm of nations trading reciprocal market access to the benefit of exporters characterizes much of the history of trade politics. It is essentially an enlightened form of mercantilism, accepting imports as a price for exports, and done in the service of a few giant national corporations and in the interests of consumers. In theory, large exporters can push for lower tariffs at home to purchase reductions from the foreign government, as long as the effect does not give an advantage to one nation or another. In practice, as I show in chapter 6, these bargains break down in the face of regulatory protection.

1.2.2. Multinationals and International Commercial Policy

Firm-level data reveal that among the largest exporters are MNCs. Just like other exporters, MNCs are highly dependent on international trade for their sales. Unlike other large exporters, MNCs have invested in the control of a foreign entity. Such investment, referred to as foreign direct investment (FDI), enables MNCs to manage production, source inputs, and access foreign markets. In the last decade of the twentieth century, trade openness grew by two-thirds, but FDI flows doubled and doubled and doubled again.[25] These flows have established global production networks that are utterly dependent on foreign markets and, as a result, are assumed to have even stronger preferences for trade liberalization than even large exporters (Milner 1988a, 1988b).

Given their dependence on foreign markets, multinationals are assumed to be the most stalwart advocates for free trade. As Richard Baldwin (2016) explains, for an MNC, a tariff is like erecting a wall in the middle of a factory. Governments are thought to seek to take advantage of MNC sensitivity, raising tariffs on MNCs in order to manipulate their investment decisions. This is what Ralph Ossa (2011) calls "profit shifting." By making imports more expensive, domestic consumer expenditure might shift toward local production and increase the incentive for tariff-jumping investment. The United States famously deployed targeted protectionist measures to coerce Japanese automobile companies to produce in the United States.[26] MNCs are thereby doubly exposed to the costs of protectionism.

MNCs, although exposed, have a political advantage over other exporters. The distribution of production across national borders offers foreign governments a direct stake in the profits of firms that produce both at home and abroad. Policymakers often treat the affiliates of MNCs as local employers, investors, and constituents and internalize the interests of the dispersed company (Blanchard 2010). The result is that MNCs do not need to rely on reciprocity for foreign influence; they instead can rely on the fact that politicians care more about local employment and investment than they do about the national character of the employer.

All this is to say that we would expect exporting firms in general and MNCs in particular to advance the cause of free trade. Exporters are interested in foreign market access and are willing to advocate for low tariffs at home in hope of reciprocal reductions abroad. Multinationals may be able to produce abroad to jump tariffs but are also dependent on foreign markets for inputs and exports. The interests of multinationals, in particular, are important for trade liberalization, as their foreign affiliates give governments a direct stake in their profits. Trade protection would seem like a throwback to a world in which the revenue of large MNCs had not yet reached a quarter of the global GDP and more than two-thirds of world trade. How can governments seriously consider adopting new trade barriers when the "foreign" exporter is so tied into the domestic economy? Ought we not see governments lowering regulatory measures at the behest of foreign capital? Why is it that we do not see the race to the bottom?

1.3. The Character of Regulatory Protection

Regulatory barriers, for the purposes of this book, have two defining characteristics. The first is that they can have a public-policy motive. Regulatory barriers can serve to promote product quality, inform consumers, or even keep dangerous neurotoxins out of the mouths of toddlers. The second is that regulatory barriers impose fixed costs on firms. Tariffs work like a tax, raising costs by a percentage of the value of the traded good. Regulatory barriers act as a fixed cost, requiring firms to rework their product and then register, test, and label it before sale. A fee to register a company or to pay for a test is paid once, and firms are free to sell at any volume.[27] The requirement to test a product for lead applies whether 1 or 1,000 items are sold. This makes regulatory barriers much more damaging to smaller producers.

Regulatory protection is not limited to sensitive consumer products such as children's toys. Even important inputs have faced high barriers since the financial crisis. Between 2008 and 2012, more than 50 governments imposed regulatory barriers to trade on basic chemical products (Evenett 2013). These measures are raised on some of the world's most integrated markets. The members of the G8 and the G20 account for most of these new protectionist measures. On this metric, the G20 members are responsible for 65 percent of all protectionist measures imposed since November 2008.[28] At the same time, these countries maintain the lowest tariffs (Ederington and Ruta 2016).[29] Whereas the tariff peaks of the 1930s were at ad valorem equivalents of more than 50 percent, today the average applied tariff hovers below 5 percent. Yet in a recent survey of nontariff measures across nations, Josh Ederington and Michele Ruta (2016) find that nontariff measures are now more common than not. The median country in their sample applies nontariff measures to 66.9 percent of product categories or 70 percent of total imports.

The global trade regime formed at the Havana Conference in 1947 is utterly unprepared for these measures. Today, politicians and bureaucrats in Geneva and global capitals recognize that regulatory barriers are a problem, particularly for small and medium-sized exporters, but have yet to arrive at a solution. What is missing, I argue, is the correct diagnosis. The fundamental norms of GATT/WTO law, in use since the early decades of the nineteenth century, were developed in a context where productivity differences primarily varied across countries rather than firms. The legal operationalization of the reciprocity norm works well for promoting aggregate trade volume of a product, but it does not address the distortions created by regulatory protection, which operate across firms. The result is that the institutions that were effective in removing tariffs are ineffective at resolving the challenges posed by contemporary commercial relations and the policies passed at the behest of the largest and most internationally engaged firms.

I.4. Overview of the Argument

My argument proceeds in three steps, each corresponding to a part of the book. In this section, I reiterate why it is that large firms have an interest in regulatory protection, why governments with local affiliates of multinational firms would thereby adopt regulatory barriers at the expense of small foreign firms, and why it is that the current rules are unable to address this new form of mercantilism. Each step combines insights from economic theories that account for the varying size and multinational activity of firms with the differences between regulatory barriers to trade and better understood, but currently less troublesome, tariff barriers. It is the combination of market characteristics and policy effects that undermines trade cooperation today.

I.4.1. Firm Preferences over Regulatory Protection

Part 1 of this book lays out the theory of firm preferences over regulatory protection. I show that the conventional account of the aligned interests among exporting firms fails when it comes to fixed-cost type measures. Instead, the political interests of large exporting and multinational firms are for more rather than less regulatory protection. Globalized firms like Mattel can *benefit* from closing markets, so long as the instrument of that closure imposes *fixed costs*. By forcing small and medium-sized foreign exporters out of the market, prices and profits rise. In the cost-benefit calculations of regulators, the benefits include monopolistic rents alongside public-policy goals like protecting children. The costs are borne by consumers that must pay higher prices and by small and medium-sized firms that are forced to exit. The latter, however, are based in a foreign country. The fact that these businesses have no direct voice in regulatory matters gives governments an incentive to set stricter policies.

Chapter 2 develops a monopolistic competition model of trade with varying levels of regulatory protection. The stylized interpretation of that model generates predictions for the interests of six categories of firms, as displayed in table 1.3. Firms are distinguished by where they produce and where they market their goods. The former determines which government shares in the profits of the company; the latter is relevant for which government's regulations affect those profits. Domestic firms are entirely dependent on local production and the local market, whereas exporters and MNCs also can sell in foreign countries. Chapter 2 presents a formal analysis of the relationship between the interests of global producers, the choices governments have in making regulations, and the determinants of international cooperation in trade policymaking. As a result, larger, more productive firms benefit from regulatory barriers to trade in host markets. This is because unlike tariffs, regulatory barriers raise fixed costs that shift market share away from smaller, more marginal exporters. I then argue that when these large firms have local affiliates, their host government will adopt stricter regulatory policies to advantage these local businesses.

The final column of table 1.3 shows how foreign firms are divided on regulations in the home country. Foreign MNCs prefer stricter regulations, while foreign exporters and foreign domestic firms prefer lax regulatory standards. For those top producers, regulations that raise costs can nonetheless increase profits. Such costly regulations cause marginal firms to exit the market. If enough of these firms exit, prices will rise, which then increases the profits of the most productive firms that remain. Because foreign MNCs are systematically more productive than foreign exporters who lack local affiliates, foreign MNCs benefit from restricted

TABLE I.3 **Home and foreign firm regulatory preferences**

Actors	Production location	Market location	Ideal home regulation
Home domestic	Home	Home	Lax
Home exporter	Home	Home and foreign	Strict
Home MNC	Home and foreign	Home and foreign	Strict
Foreign MNC	Home and foreign	Home and foreign	Strict
Foreign exporter	Foreign	Home and foreign	Lax
Foreign domestic	Foreign	Foreign	Lax

entry. Smaller foreign exporters, on the other hand, are harmed by restrictive policies and are forced to exit the home market.[30]

As a political matter, however, the conflict between foreign exporters and foreign MNCs is only relevant for domestic governments if the MNC has a local affiliate. Governments prioritize local economic activity, including the operations of foreign multinationals that are engaged in local production and sales through their affiliates. Foreign-based exporters, such as the unaffiliated Chinese producers affected by the US lead regulation, lack local affiliation and thereby influence. To the extent that multinationals are more productive than marginal exporters, a regulatory barrier can shift the composition of trade and investment toward firms that are engaged in local research and development, hiring, and investment. So although regulatory barriers can be to the benefit of the top firms, they will come at the expense of smaller firms that lack political access to the regulating government.

To illustrate these dynamics, consider a stylized case of two markets, home and foreign, with an array of exporting firms and multinational production. Figure I.2 displays the two forms of economic engagement that entangle markets: trade and affiliation. The solid arrows indicate exports from foreign to home, and the thick dashed line indicates the profit sharing established by affiliation between the foreign MNC and local affiliate. As only the largest, most productive firms can survive the regulatory barrier, profits are shifted from unaffiliated foreign exporters and toward the MNC. The effect is to raise prices at home, lower the number of available varieties, and benefit the local affiliate. For example, while nearly all of Mattel's production occurs in China, an increase in toy export share toward the United States benefits employees at their El Segundo headquarters. For home country regulators, the choice between benefiting the MNC or benefiting one of the many unaffiliated foreign exporters is straightforward.

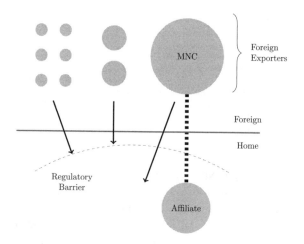

FIGURE 1.2. The distribution of imports across firms

The figure highlights the international economic consequences of regulatory protection, which favor stricter regulations. Governments must weigh these international incentives against a number of domestic benefits and costs. Unlike tariffs, regulatory barriers often apply on a nondiscriminatory basis, closing out small producers at home. Moreover, regulatory measures address a number of legitimate public-policy concerns. In either case, the government's problem is how to balance the costs facing domestic producers and the benefits that a government can extract from shifting profits toward the largest firms. Absent, however, are the interests of those smaller firms that lack local presence. Having described the main mechanism, the following section takes a step back to contextualize these ideas in broader international relations debates.

1.4.2. Interdependence Theory and Entangled Mercantilism

While there is widespread agreement about the key role of multinationals in contemporary globalization, there are diverging expectations about whether the connections between markets created by multinational production obviate or reinforce commercial conflict. The former position has roots in nineteenth-century liberal theories of interdependence: if national interests reflect those of domestic groups, governments will generally aim to promote national employment and revenue. While it is possible to achieve these interests at the expense of foreigners, the fact that the most powerful national firms now span borders will generate political pressure for commercial cooperation. For these theorists, multinationals tie nations together, just as the bankers and financiers of London formed the basis of Pax Britannica in the nineteenth century, and industrialists and corporate executives become the basis of contemporary commercial and political integration.[31]

There are reasons to be skeptical that the growth of multinationals would fundamentally alter the conflictual nature of international politics. The world has been integrated before, and in some ways, today's globalization is less impressive than that at the height of the British Empire. Noting this, state-centric and realist international political economy scholars argue that globalization need not override the more fundamental goals of states (Gilpin 1973; Kindleberger 1969; Krasner 1976). One of the pioneers of this perspective, Robert Gilpin, went further, directly challenging the idea that multinationals would promote cooperation. The very existence of the option to engage in foreign investment could make multinationals less reliable partners of their home state.[32] Moreover, given the substitutability of trade and investment, multinationals could be lukewarm or even opposed to free trade.[33] Writing in a moment when national governments were confronting rather than fighting to attract foreign enterprise and investment, Gilpin recognized the compatibility of multinational production and mercantilism. Governments would set commercial policies to benefit "their" multinationals at the expense of competing firms and other economies (1973, 219). As a result, these realist scholars argued that international commercial relations and decisions over openness or closure are driven less by multinationals than by national interests.

While not resolved, today the debate is less over the fact that multinationals have altered politics and more in trying to understand how governments navigate the benefits of attracting foreign investment against the costs to their national autonomy. Contrary to the assumptions that firms would pick either trade or investment, trade and investment are complementary, even at the level of the firm. Investment and trade increasingly follow global production networks, with multinationals on at least one side of each transaction. Contemporary scholarship in international political economy now largely adopts the interdependence position, arguing that multinational production limits international sources of commercial conflict. Political conflict arises between export interests that seek free trade at home in exchange for the same abroad and more domestically oriented firms that only compete with imports. In this environment, firms with foreign affiliates are distinguished by having an unconditional preference for free trade. When firms are multinational, governments set commercial policies in ways that avoid harming their partners abroad and are thus less likely to resort to old-fashioned mercantilism.

This book offers a mercantilist account of foreign policymaking that incorporates the assumptions of contemporary theories of interdependence—that markets and nations are entangled by multinational firms. Because of these entanglements, national governments have interests in targeted protection, in shifting profits toward locally affiliated multinationals. This entangled mercantilism generates a politics where states seek to advance a broader conception of national interests, one that includes the profits of foreign affiliates and comes at the expense of smaller and less connected polities.

Table 1.4 summarizes the shared and diverging assumptions across interdependence theory and entangled mercantilism. Both begin with a logic that globalization, and the overall reduction of tariffs, has produced a globalized environment dominated by multinationals. In addition, both theories model governments as instrumentally setting policies to maximize the national interest. Where the theories diverge is in whether that national interest is expanded to include the profits of foreign producers. This is akin to extending GDP to GNP. The former excludes foreign profits, as standard theories of interdependence assume that governments seek to enhance market access for their domestic firms and limit market access for foreign firms. In entangled mercantilism, governments seek opportunities to shift profits among foreign market

TABLE 1.4 **Connection between *Narrowing the Channel* and existing work**

	Theory	
	Interdependence	Entangled mercantilism
Market condition	Globalization with MNC	Globalization with MNC
Government interests	Promote revenue, employment and GDP	Promote revenue, employment and GNP
Goal of commercial policy	Promoting market access	Shifting profit
Predicted cleavages pro– free trade	All exporters	Marginal exporters
Protectionist	Nonexporters	Local affiliates of MNCs
State strategy	Free trade	Regulatory protectionism

players. They do so to advance a national interest that expands beyond purely local interests. The result is that states will have interest in uni-lateral reductions of tariffs and other barriers to expanding markets, as much of that expansion will involve their own firms. On regulatory mat-ters, however, states seek to narrow the channels of commerce toward affiliates.

In summary, regulatory protectionism is driven by the choices of governments to favor the imports of larger, more productive firms over imports from smaller companies. Domestically, governments can bal-ance the concerns of domestic small and large firms. Internationally, these interests are unbalanced; regulatory barriers to trade can arise from a new form of mercantilism, one where governments seek to ad-vance the interests of affiliated businesses over other firms. In the fol-lowing section, I describe the empirical strategy of part 2 of the book to substantiate this theory of regulatory protectionism.

1.4.3. Research Design

Entangled mercantilism predicts an association between the adoption of regulatory barriers to trade and sectoral and national conditions that facilitate international profit shifting. However, interpreting such an as-sociation as causal or as evidence of a particular political economy ac-count requires more than aggregate data. In general, it is important to avoid the *post hoc, ergo propter hoc* fallacy: assuming that the presence of beneficiaries of a policy is sufficient to establish the cause of the pol-icy. To establish this causal role of these firm interests, I deploy a num-ber of strategies, including the in-depth examination of policymaking processes. Combined, this evidence demonstrates that firm interests are present, recognized, and acted upon by governments.

This book takes two complementary approaches to establish evidence for the role of foreign interests, specifically the local affiliates of foreign firms, in regulatory politics and the consequences for international co-operation. My first strategy tests whether the presence of MNCs predicts the decisions of governments to adopt or not adopt regulatory barriers across products and time. Chapter 3, "The Determinants of Regulatory Barriers to Trade," focuses on a comprehensive data set of disputed mea-sures at the WTO—the kind submitted by China over the US lead safety law. These barriers have risen to the level of concern for governments but are not yet subject to dispute, avoiding some of the selection issues associated with either self-reported measures or the strategic interests of winning a WTO dispute. I find that regulatory barriers are substantially more common among governments with a shared interest in foreign firm profits and products where MNC activities are most concentrated.

My second approach uses in-depth case studies of the European chemical industry and the American food industry. These cases advance the argument in three ways. First, these cases circumscribe common explanations for stricter regulatory preferences among large firms. Second, the cases establish the role that small domestic firms play in government decision-making and how domestic regulators can incorporate their interests. Third, in both cases, I can leverage the fact that US and EU rule-making procedures require publication of the thousands of comments from various interest groups, firms, activists, and governments. Analysis of these comments reveals how regulations generate fixed costs and conflict between small firms and globalized producers.

Combining the evidence from these chapters helps rule out several prominent competing explanations for regulatory protection. One is that firms embrace regulation as a defensive measure. It may be that firms are attempting to forestall future regulation or to participate in the process in a way that limits the costs of regulations. The first possibility arises when limited efforts can forestall more severe and costly changes demanded by consumer activists. This is what David Baron and Daniel Diermeier (2007) refer to as "proactive measures." The second possibility is that firms advance regulations whose provisions they already satisfy, perhaps because of prior commitments incurred by selling in a high regulation market. This is what David Vogel (1995) refers to as the "California effect," where California sets a high standard and firms push other states to meet that standard so as not to suffer a competitive disadvantage for having paid the higher cost. In each of these accounts, regulators would find support among the largest firms to adopt stricter regulations than either the prevailing international standard or any standard yet adopted.

The case studies shed light on the plausibility of these competing claims. When European regulators initiated REACH (which stands for "Registration, Evaluation, Authorisation and Restriction of Chemicals"), they drafted standards well beyond those of any individual member state. As with US lead safety law, the member states of the EU found that expansive multinational production practices had outpaced the capacity of national regulators. At the same time, chemical registration programs are prototypical fixed-cost measures: all products must be labeled and their contents tested and reported at high cost. This came at the expense of small foreign firms, which broadly opposed the measure. Evidence from the statements of lobbyists and the behavior of firms suggests that a small set of the largest American chemical companies embraced the regulation, not in spite of its costs but in order to tighten them.

The food industry case also demonstrates the interplay of multinational organization and firm size. In chapter 5, "Regulatory Preferences in the Food Industry," I describe how a bioterrorism attack and a salmonella outbreak created the conditions for government action, but it was large foreign and domestic firms that sought strict and universal application of the rules. In this case, small domestic firms were able to acquire exemptions from the registration requirements, as these small firms had access to rulemaking. Small foreign producers had little say in the process, lacking channels of influence beyond the entreaties of their home governments.

These two cases, food safety in the United States and chemical regulations in Europe, demonstrate the intensity of lobbying by large and small firms, the presence of legitimate consumer concerns, and the fact that both were raised as regulatory barriers to trade at the WTO. These two cases also demonstrate the costs of regulatory protectionism. In neither case do regulators respond to the interests of the primary losers from regulatory protection: small and medium-sized firms located outside of the major industrial powers. A marginal exporter of food in Bogotá and the medium-sized chemical manufacturer in Ahmedabad can be devastated by what appear to be technical and well-meaning policies set by regulators in Silver Spring and Helsinki.

This political logic poses several challenges for the rule-based trade system. Regulatory protection breaks the traditional coalition for liberalization, with larger, more productive and internationally engaged firms advocating strict rather than lax regulations. The power of these firms in trade politics and the absence of a political voice for unaffiliated exporters pose a direct challenge to regulatory cooperation. More subtle, however, is the effect on trade cooperation. Before concluding this introductory chapter, I introduce the concerns of part 3 of this book, dealing with the problems that regulatory protection poses for the multilateral trade system and how governments might go about finding a solution.

1.4.4. Regulatory Protection in Multilateral Trade Agreements

The current trade regime is characterized by two central norms: reciprocity and nondiscrimination. Both are rooted in eighteenth-century commercial relations among European powers but are now widespread norms of commercial negotiations. Reciprocity requires that governments grant and maintain equal concessions in terms of import volume. For example, if the United States raises $3 billion in tariffs on Chinese steel, China may be authorized to raise $3 billion in tariffs on US soybean exports. The principle of nondiscrimination, also called the unconditional most-favored-nation rule, requires that concessions are de jure available to all parties of the agreement, making negotiations fundamentally multilateral.[34] Together, these principles are the basis for nearly all cooperative agreements on trade.[35]

The problem with using the norm of reciprocity for regulatory matters is getting the measurement right. Reciprocity demands the mutual exchange of exports for imports, what economists have termed *reciprocity in market access* (Bagwell and Staiger 2002a). This rule has worked to facilitate trade for almost 200 years but was designed for governments that preferred lower import trade volumes and higher export trade volumes, measured by quantity times price. However, regulatory barriers, insofar as they impose fixed costs, decrease the quantity but raise the price of imports. When China threatened retaliation against the United States for the CPSIA, they did so in response to policies with at best ambiguous effects on the volume of toy exports. Within China, some manufacturers saw sales and profits rise; others saw losses. Although China could raise the issue at meetings, without a clear loss in market access, they had little recourse under the law.

This book does not argue that the world should abandon the GATT/WTO system or the use of the reciprocity norm in international trade cooperation. Nor does it intend to criticize the choices of regulators or the strategic actions of firms in promoting their favored policies. Rather, the subsequent chapters aim to explain the difficulties in going beyond the tariff commitments that have been the mainstay of trade liberalization in the twentieth century. Rather than rooting the challenges of regulatory protection in the opacity of the measures or conflicts of national character and culture, I focus on the interests of globalized capital, a familiar but often misunderstood force in global economic policymaking. We cannot hope that the increasing power of multinationals will facilitate trade cooperation over the objections of protectionist governments, but we also do not need to abandon the enterprise of commercial cooperation.

Even given the challenges that governments face with regulatory protection, history has shown that they can create impressive institutional structures to govern trade and reduce barriers to it. But despite their complexity and apparent effectiveness in limiting tariffs, I argue that the rules inherited from the 1947 GATT fail to constrain governments with regards to regulatory barriers to trade. This is because the current trade regime centers on the use of two norms: reciprocity and nondiscrimination. These principles were combined with a far-reaching agenda in the Havana Charter of the International Trade Organization (ITO), which founded the multilateral trade system. While the charter was never ratified and the organization was abandoned, elements of the agreement were retained in the GATT, where nondiscrimination and reciprocity are understood in terms of the consequences of policy for aggregate trade volume. That perspective on trade cooperation, measured in trade volume, is rooted in practices developed during eighteenth-century commercial relations, and today governments depend on these rules both to structure the negotiation of trade agreements and to enforce their provisions. However, as it is becoming clear, these rules appear to be breaking down in the face of regulatory protection, as evidenced by the lack of progress in the multilateral system and the persistence of disputed regulatory measures.

The chapters in part 3 discuss international institutional design, beginning with the origins of the current system. Chapter 6, "The Design of Reciprocal Trade Agreements," argues that governments stumbled upon reciprocity in the nineteenth century in response to negotiating challenges specific to tariffs. Countries were unevenly capable of taking advantage of tariff reductions, and so they were tuned to allow equivalence in concessions. Today the problem is less national market access and more the exclusion of a subset of small firms. As a result, reciprocity-based institutions, including the GATT/WTO system, have seen failures in the presence of regulatory protection. In short, reciprocal trade rules, designed for the problems of prior centuries, have failed to balance the benefits of market access against the interest of smaller firms that remain excluded from the benefits of tariff liberalization.

Even if reciprocal trade agreements could account for the differential effects of regulatory protection across firms, a more fundamental question is whether governments ought to seek to constrain national regulatory autonomy. Is ensuring low prices and greater competition worth the effort when both consumer activists and multinational firms support stricter regulations? Chapter 7, "Designing Optimal Standards Agreements," takes a mechanism design approach to evaluate agreements on regulatory cooperation. In that chapter, I argue that perhaps the best that the world can hope for is not to eliminate regulatory protection or adopt internationally harmonized and fixed regulatory schedules but rather to limit its negative effects by specifying bounds on the costs that can be acceptably imposed on firms. Progress depends, however, on recognizing that these costs may be indirect and that reform will not come from industry leaders.

CHAPTER TWO

A Theory of Global Firms and Local Regulation

Protectionism has long been synonymous with nationalist and parochial interests. The losers from trade would form coalitions along class or industry lines, drawing from interests within national boundaries to promote tariffs. In the nineteenth century, tariffs were supported in Germany by a marriage of iron and rye—Prussian industrialists and landowners—and in the United States by a coalition of small manufacturers and farmers.[1] Businesses based outside the Zollverein or America had little to gain from tariff protection in these countries. Today, trade policy takes the form of regulatory regimes—regimes that draw support from firms across national borders. In this chapter, I argue that this is because regulatory barriers to trade limit competition in ways that profit a few large global firms and their partners. As governments initiate regulations to satisfy their public-policy needs, these profit considerations encourage the adoption of trade-restrictive regulatory designs.

Even in the absence of regulatory protection, international trade is prohibitive for many firms. A small set of firms are responsible for the lion's share of trade and investment in almost every sector.[2] To explain this concentration, Marc Melitz and Thomas Chaney developed models where firms have persistent differences in productivity. This heterogeneity produces substantial within-industry variation in market share, with more productive firms expanding production, sales, and export activity. To explain the coexistence of more and less productive firms, these models join "new trade theory" assumptions of consumer love of variety and monopolistically competitive firms with industrial organization theories of firm selection, entry, and exit.

These models were originally developed to explain the concentration of trade within nations. Trade activity can be divided along two dimensions: an intensive margin, or quantity of imports and exports, and an extensive margin, or number of unique varieties or firms engaged in trade. International trade raises the quantity and variety of goods available to consumers by shifting market share away from less productive firms toward larger, more productive businesses while expanding the selection of varieties. This selection effect can be dampened by tariff barriers to trade, as tariffs are designed to be proportional to the value of goods sold, applying as either a percentage of the unit price or a per-unit amount.[3] The largest and most productive firms are most disadvantaged by these policies. Fixed-cost regulatory barriers to trade, testing and labeling requirements, and licenses or registrations apply to whole lines of products, often independent of production volume. When the channel is narrowed, the number of exporting firms drops, aggregate prices rise, and firms that sell larger quantities profit. When governments set regulations on imported products, they shift profits toward large firms.

Governments have the ability to shift profits but only have an interest in doing so if some of those profits are local. Mattel's profits would not be a consideration in US lead regulation if not for the company's presence in El Segundo, California. While there is debate over the extent of business influence across politics, the profits of businesses that are organized across national borders, either as multinational corporations or at arm's length, can generate a variety of positive spillovers at home.[4] These businesses allocate profits across the global supply chain, hire local workers, pay local taxes, and purchase local inputs. By shifting market share toward top firms and away from smaller export-only shops, governments can assure that some stage of production remains at home. This is what produces what I term *entangled mercantilism*.

Below, I apply the Melitz (2003) framework to the case of endogenous fixed costs. By assuming a particular distribution of firm-level productivity, I can describe firm revenues and profits in terms of exogenous parameters: the elasticity of substitution across varieties and the degree of productivity dispersion among firms and fixed costs. I then show that regulatory protection, understood in terms of fixed costs of entry, affects consumer welfare and firm profits by forcing smaller firms to exit. The result is that there exists a level of productivity above which all firms benefit from higher regulatory barriers to trade.

The chapter proceeds as follows. Section 2.1 argues that large firms, both at home and abroad, benefit from the competitive consequences of regulatory protection. In that analysis, I distinguish regulatory barriers to trade from tariffs and other traditional trade barriers, arguing that the former take the form of fixed costs. I then formalize how regulatory decisions alter a firm's calculation of whether and how they should serve the international market. Under certain conditions, the largest and most productive firms gain from regulatory barriers in the export market, a competitive externality to regulatory barriers to trade. Section 2.2 examines two problems facing governments. The first is that when foreign firms are organized as multinationals, mercantilist governments can shift profits locally by adopting a policy of regulatory protection. Drawing on the political effects of foreign direct investment, I show that the interests of local MNC affiliates can align with that of the regulating state. The second problem is that governments will find it difficult to credibly commit to only using regulatory measures to address domestic public-policy concerns. Section 2.3 concludes that these material competitive interests in firm profits complement local regulatory concerns.

2.1. Firm Interests in Anticompetitive Regulations

Much of the economic benefit of trade liberalization comes from market selection toward productive firms.[5] Ideally, opening trade allows more firms to export (the extensive margin) and existing firms to expand sales (the intensive margin). Part of the reason they can do so is that less productive domestic firms close shop, freeing resources for the more productive enterprises. This is to say, when firms are unequally productive, the opportunity to trade moves business toward the more productive firms, creating welfare gains but exacerbating inequality in outcomes. The nature of trade liberalization, however, matters. Any change in "variable costs," such as a change in material input costs or a proportional tax like an ad valorem tariff, increases in incidence with productivity. If tariffs were to rise, it would lower the profits for the largest, most productive export-oriented firms, as any increase in variable costs disproportionately affects high-volume sellers. As a consequence, we would expect tariffs to be opposed by the largest and most internationally engaged firms.

However, regulatory barriers operate under a different logic, as they raise fixed rather than variable costs.[6] Increasing a fixed cost will raise the costs of every firm, and economic intuition would suggest that the main effect of such a cost would be negative for firm profits. However, rather than uniformly reducing foreign market access, fixed costs primarily influence the entry decisions of marginal firms. Small, unproductive firms may choose not to enter the market. As a result, the second-order effect of the fixed cost on competition overwhelms the first-order effect of having to pay the cost oneself, benefiting firms that are sufficiently productive and altering the composition of trade toward the most productive firms.

Prior work on regulatory barriers derives similar outcomes from models with sequential entry. Rogerson (1984) develops a model with an incumbent leader and a fringe of competitors whose entry decisions occur after the leader commits to a certain output. In that model, increasing fixed costs helps deter fringe entrants, increasing the profits of the leader. Below, I show that the advantage can accrue in the absence of a first-mover advantage when the only difference between firms is their productivity.

In the Melitz (2003) model, firms must pay fixed costs to enter and fixed costs to produce, and only firms that exceed an endogenously determined productivity can profitably participate in the market. In equilibrium, the distribution of firms that engage in a market will exhibit substantial inequality, with more productive firms capturing a larger share of profits. Subsequent work by Chaney (2008) simplified Melitz (2003) by introducing a particular power law distribution to describe inequality among potential entrants. These studies primarily focus on variable rather than fixed costs. I show that if the number of firms is governed by a *free entry* condition, increases in fixed costs of production can differentially affect lower productivity firms.[7]

The proposition developed below suggests the need for an alternative account of the motivations for trade policy. Under the canonical account of tariff policy, governments raise tariffs in ways that raise revenue from foreign firms and alter the world price in favor of domestic interests. Regulatory barriers shift the composition of imports from less productive firms to more productive firms. If governments were motivated by expanding tariff revenue, we might expect governments to *lower* regulatory barriers to trade and induce entry of marginal foreign exporters, who would then pay the border tax.[8] By contrast, if governments have preferences in favor of multinationals and their local affiliates, they would be likely to *raise* regulatory barriers, inefficiently closing out their domestic markets to foreign exporters in favor of connected and productive multinational firms. The following discussion raises this second possibility and shows how such a barrier to trade would operate differently than would a tariff.

2.1.1. Heterogeneous Firms in a Closed Economy

I begin by modeling the effects of regulatory protection in a closed economy consisting of consumers, entrepreneurs, and firms. While the number of firms and entrepreneurs is exogenous, the number of firms that attempt to enter the market, $M_e \geq 0$, is determined by market and policy conditions, including regulatory barriers to trade. To simplify matters, I assume that goods are freely differentiable and that each firm can only produce a single unique variety. That means that the overall number of producing firms is equal to the number of varieties. I shall refer to the number of varieties sold in a market with $\Omega \subset R$.[9]

Consumers are modeled as having identical preferences over their consumption of various goods. The degree of consumer utility derived from having a diverse basket of goods is inversely proportional to a constant elasticity of substitution (CES) parameter $\sigma > 1$. The higher σ is, the easier it is to substitute one variety for another and the lower the love of variety. Given these trade-offs, consumers can purchase goods of variety ω at price $p(\omega)$, and maximize their consumption subject to a budget constraint, which sets total expenditures to be no more than nominal income $R \geq 0$. As I show in the technical appendix, these conditions produce a market where demand for each variety, $q(\omega)$, and the amount of money spent on each variety, $r(\omega)$, are a fraction of overall demand:

(2.1)
$$q(\omega) = \frac{R}{P} \left(\frac{p(\omega)}{P} \right)^{-\sigma}$$

(2.2)
$$r(\omega) = R \left(\frac{p(\omega)}{P} \right)^{1-\sigma}.$$

The P in equations (2.1) and (2.2) is an aggregate price index, used to characterize the weighted prices of all the varieties in the market:

$$P \equiv [\textstyle\int_{\omega \in \Omega} p(\omega)^{1-\sigma} d\omega]^{1/(1-\sigma)}.$$

This P is a cost-of-living index, and R/P, or income divided by the prices of all goods, is a measure of aggregate economic welfare.

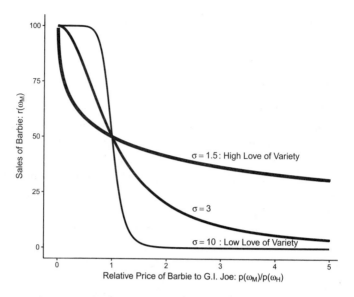

FIGURE 2.1. Amount spent on a single variety under CES utility (graphical representation of equation [2.2])

To see the relationship between the elasticity of substitution and consumer spending, consider the relative sales of two toys, a Mattel Barbie and a Hasbro G.I. Joe. In this case $\Omega = \{\omega_M, \omega_H\}$. Figure 2.1 displays how increasing the relative price of Barbie to G.I. Joe products would affect the sales of Barbie under different elasticities of substitution. So long as each doll is the same price, consumers evenly split their consumption, but as the relative price moves from unity, consumers with less love of variety, and higher σ, quickly substitute one good for another.

2.1.2. The Effect of Regulations on Profits and Prices

In the Melitz (2003) model, production decisions are made by firms subject to marginal and fixed costs. To account for regulatory protection, I disaggregate these fixed costs into an exogenous start-up cost, c, as well as a politically determined regulatory cost, η, set by the destination government, so that the total fixed cost $f \equiv c + \eta$.[10]

While fixed costs are the same for each firm, firms exhibit heterogeneity in their productivity, which here is modeled as the inverse of the marginal cost, $\varphi \in [\varphi_{min}, \infty)$. Firms that are very productive can produce more with the same amount of wage expenditure.[11] Each firm's total cost, TC, is a function of fixed costs, $f \geq 0$, and their productivity, $\varphi \in [\varphi_{min}, \infty)$.

Fixed-cost regulatory barriers on a variety do not directly affect the price of that variety. Instead, producers charge a constant markup over marginal cost, displayed in equation (2.3). Intuitively, if the love of variety is very low—σ is large—prices are equal to the marginal cost and profits are low; if the love of variety were high, firms would be able to exert market power, charge higher prices, and earn profits. Regulatory barriers to trade do not affect these pricing decisions:

$$(2.3) \qquad p(\omega) = \frac{\sigma}{(\sigma - 1)\varphi}.$$

While regulatory barriers do not directly affect product prices, firm profits depend on fixed costs in two ways. In the appendix, I show how the equations for prices (2.3), consumption (2.1), and expenditures (2.2) combine with firm profit maximization to generate an equation for firm profits as follows:

$$(2.4) \qquad \pi(\varphi) = \frac{R\left(P\frac{(\sigma-1)}{\sigma}\varphi\right)^{\sigma-1}}{\sigma} - f.$$

These profits increase with the size of the economy, R; the aggregate price index, P; and the firm's individual productivity, φ. Net of these other parameters, the effect of the fixed-cost regulatory barrier is an increase in total costs and a reduction in profits. However, there is an indirect general equilibrium effect on the price index, P, which is increasing in the fixed cost in a way that, for sufficiently productive firms, outweighs the increase in f.

2.1.3. Equilibrium Market Forces under Pareto Distribution

The price index (and thereby overall economic welfare) is affected by regulatory barriers in that it changes the entry and exit decisions of entrepreneurs and firms. To show this, we begin by identifying conditions where the firms enter and exit at equal rates. In such an equilibrium, the economy is fully characterized by the mass of entrants and the average productivity. To simplify the analysis, we will introduce an assumption about the distribution of firm profits to the Melitz (2003) framework and derive expected profits in terms of parameters of that distribution. In particular, I follow Arkolakis et al. (2008) and Chaney (2008) in imposing the Pareto distribution to simplify and analytically solve the model. We will then be able to derive a formal result showing the level of productivity necessary to benefit from higher regulatory barriers.

Entrepreneurs are forward-looking and make rational decisions about entry and exit. Upon paying a sunk domestic entry cost, $f_e > 0$, some number of entrepreneurs ($M_e \geq 0$) start a firm. Upon making the payment, each entrepreneur learns her productivity level, φ, drawn from a Pareto distribution with support over $[\varphi_{min}, \infty)$ and dispersion parameter $k + 1 > \sigma$.[12] Pareto distributions have long tails, which is in line with the extraordinary concentration of export activity in a few firms. As the dispersion parameter $k > 0$ approaches zero, the distribution approximates a uniform distribution. The Pareto distribution has two attractive features. First, as k rises, more firms draw low productivities, typical of the sorts of inequality observed among firms. Second, the Pareto distribution is mathematically convenient—a Pareto distribution with a cutoff is itself Pareto.[13]

Firms may learn that their productivity is too low to be profitable. This occurs if the expected value of the discounted stream of future profits v is smaller relative to the fixed costs of entry. Formally, the lowest productivity level that allows a firm to survive, the cutoff productivity, is $\varphi^* \equiv \inf\{\varphi : v(\varphi) > 0\}$. All firms with productivity below that cutoff will exit. In addition to this endogenous selection process, each firm faces a constant risk of forced exit, independent of productivity, at a probability $\delta > 0$. Melitz (2003) shows that in this dynamic process, the equilibrium is fully characterized by the mass of entrants (M_e) and the cutoff productivity (φ^*), which determines the average productivity. These two parameters are determined in the model by standard economic assumptions: φ^* is determined by a zero-cutoff-profit condition and a free entry condition, and M_e is determined by market clearing. Together, the resulting productivity cutoff productivity is

$$(2.5) \qquad \varphi^* = \left[\frac{f}{\delta f_e} \left(\frac{\sigma - 1}{1 + k - \sigma} \right) \right]^{1/k} \varphi_{min}.$$

2.1.4. Closed-Economy Comparative Statics

With the equilibrium mass of entrants (M_e) and (φ^*), we can study the general equilibrium effect of regulatory protection. I begin by showing that higher regulatory barriers raise the productivity cutoff for firms to survive. I then show that this raises average productivity by disproportionately excluding the marginal and less productive firms. Finally, I develop the main finding—that is, above a certain point of productivity, profits are increasing in the regulatory barrier.

Taking the partial derivative of equation (2.5), it is straightforward to show that the endogenous productivity cutoff (φ^*) increases in the fixed cost:

$$(2.6) \qquad \frac{\partial \varphi^*}{\partial f} = \frac{1}{fk} \left[\frac{f}{\delta f_e} \left(\frac{\sigma - 1}{1 + k - \sigma} \right) \right]^{1/k} \varphi_{\min} > 0.$$

Intuitively, this equation shows that less dispersed industries and those that have lower churn will be particularly affected by regulatory protection. Moreover, increasing this cutoff increases the average productivity in the industry.[14] It is not obvious what effect having a higher average productivity would have on profits. The following novel proposition relates the profits of individual firms and the fixed-cost regulatory barrier, finding that surviving firms benefit from the reduction in the extensive margin:

Proposition 2.1.1. *Given CES utility, a Pareto productivity distribution with dispersion parameter $k > \sigma - 1$ and lemma A.1, there exists a level of productivity $\hat{\varphi}$ such that all firms with higher productivity benefit from an increase in the fixed cost of production.*[15]

Figure 2.2 displays this effect graphically, showing the consequence of a change in the fixed cost on firm profits at various levels of productivity. On the x-axis is the productivity of the firm. The profits of such a firm are plotted on the y-axis. To the left of the critical threshold, $\hat{\varphi}$, we see that the profits of firms drop. Because $\varphi^{*\prime} > \varphi^*$, we know that some firms that would have produced profitably instead are forced to exit. Above $\hat{\varphi}$, we can see an increase in profits. Note that the higher the productivity, the larger the benefit to the rise in the regulatory barrier.

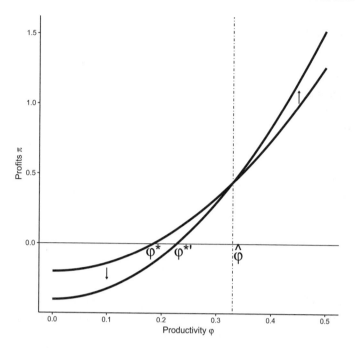

FIGURE 2.2. Effect of an increase of fixed costs (f) on profits (π) (graphical representation of proposition 2.1.1)

In contrast to the conventional wisdom, it is the smallest, most marginal firms that should be most opposed to regulatory protectionism.[16]

In the appendix, I extend these results to an open economy to show that in a model with two identical economies, a secular increase in the fixed cost of export similarly benefits the top exporting firms. Interestingly, this change in profits arises because increasing the fixed cost to exporting *lowers* the threshold for domestic entry. As f_x rises, new firms enter, but these new domestic entrants are inefficient relative to those that were driven out from exporting, improving the profitability of the firms at the top of the productivity scale. Furthermore, I contrast these results to those of a tariff and confirm that a higher tariff would in fact only lower the profits of the most internationally engaged firms.

The fact that most internationally engaged firms would benefit from regulatory barriers to trade is a significant revision to the political economy of trade. However, this claim is not without precedent in studies of firm interests in domestic regulation. Critics of government oversight of the economy cite the influence of large domestic incumbents in promot-

ing regulations that limit competition, resist price reductions, and restrict entry.[17] The domestic regulatory interests of firms led Stigler (1971)
to hypothesize that "every industry or occupation that has enough political power to utilize the state will seek to control entry." Nowhere in that
analysis, however, is there an expectation that such behavior could serve
the national interest.

While the model presented above emphasizes the role of productivity, firm heterogeneity could encompass other specific assets and technologies. For example, in 1977, Congress passed controls on sulfur oxide
emissions from power plants. Because of natural variation in the sulfur
content of coal, regulation of the content of emissions advantages producers of low-sulfur-content coal. However, that coal is located in western states. Eastern coal producers were able to lobby to ensure that the
regulation, rather than requiring a level of air quality, instead required
the installation of "scrubbers" in the smokestacks of every plant. This alternative regulatory mechanism eliminates the advantages to low-sulfur
western coal, leading eastern coal producers and the United Mine Workers to join environmentalists in supporting the mandatory adoption of
the scrubber technology (Crandall 1983). Moreover, firms may advocate
for regulations to improve the returns on unique technological assets. In
the UK, for example, the National Association of Waste Disposal Con-
tractors protested delays in the adoption of a new regulatory scheme.
This scheme would drive the smallest, cheapest waste managers out of
business but allow the existing companies to take advantage of investments in environmentally friendly technology.[18] These examples suggest
that firm-specific assets can encourage the use of the regulatory process
to limit competition. In light of this, some scholars argue that one should
analyze new regulations "not as the result of a dialectic between consumers and producers, but at least in part as a result of (and a contributor to) the competitive balance within the industry" (Oster 1982).

The model presented in above delineates conditions under which the
effect of competition outweighs the added costs of regulatory compliance and identifies the general equilibrium dynamics for exporters. Like
tariffs, regulatory barriers decrease foreign competition for import-
competing firms, but unlike tariffs, the effect is also to shift the market
toward productive firms. The profits of those productive firms rise with
the introduction of a fixed cost.

Table 2.1 displays these predicted trade preferences across firms of
varying size but now with a column for productivity. As in the theoret-

TABLE 2.1 **Firm productivity and regulatory preferences**

Actors	Production location	Productivity	Ideal home regulation
Home domestic	Home	Low	Lax
Home exporter	Home	Medium	Strict
Home MNC	Home and foreign	High	Strict
Foreign MNC	Home and foreign	High	Strict
Foreign exporter	Foreign	Medium	Lax
Foreign domestic	Foreign	Low	Lax

ical model, more complex firm operations, such as engaging in export, require higher productivity. Not in the simplified theoretical model but present here is the prediction that among exporters, the largest happen to be organized as multinational corporations. I do not discuss the growing theoretical literature that takes seriously the determinants of ownership or location decisions of multinationals; that literature builds on the above model to show that locating production abroad is subject to further fixed costs. In the following discussion, I informally relate these production location decisions to the decision-making of governments and show how competitive interests generate entangled mercantilism.

2.2. Profits, Public Policy, and the National Interest

Government decision-making responds to both public-policy interests and pressures from firms. Governments face two challenges in regulatory protection. As we have identified above, the first problem is that governments have an incentive to set strict regulatory policy to the benefit of large firms both at home and abroad at the expense of smaller foreign exporters. This is entangled mercantilism. The second problem is that governments face national regulatory demands that are difficult to anticipate or credibly communicate to partners. This is because the same regulatory measure can serve both competitive interests and legitimate public-policy demands.

The opacity of regulatory protection is a function of the dual effect of the policy. Every state recognizes the legitimate public interest in human health and safety, product quality, or environmental protection, even if achieving these goals means restricting competition. Moreover, governments may be unable to anticipate future demands to register, label, and test products, making international cooperation over these measures more difficult. The right of governments to adopt policies to address these goals is memorialized for WTO members in the original text of the General Agreement on Tariffs and Trade (GATT 1947, Article XX), and by the United Nations Guidelines for Consumer Protection of 1985. These same documents, specifically the chapeau of Article XX and section 3 of the UN guidelines, call for governments to choose policies that are only as trade restrictive as necessary to achieve their goals.

These international treaties would be unnecessary if governments did not have a political interest in excessively strict regulation and if the effects of these restrictions were not a problem for global commerce. However, governments vary in the degree to which they are sensitive to these restrictions abroad and vary in their own incentives to adopt these barriers. In subsequent chapters, I identify the domestic political antecedents for mercantile behavior. Here, I establish predictions at the government-industry level in a simple model of politics. Adjudicating between these competing interests requires assumptions about the structure of domestic politics. Local politicians must weigh the costs and benefits of policy to maximize the chances of retaining office, but how they do so depends on institutions and endowments. Societies vary by the size of the selectorate, the degree of institutional constraints on elites, and the prospects for governments to survive long enough to benefit from efficient policy-making.[19] In the following, I start by characterizing the political incentives that are created when a large foreign firm has a local affiliate. I then offer a simple account of government decision-making. On this account, all such politicians would favor exports and disfavor foreign regulatory barriers that limit those exports and decrease the demand for local workers.

2.2.1. Local Presence and Foreign Profits

In the model of firm interests developed above, all firms are foreign from the perspective of the regulating state. As a result, these firms do not have a role in canonical political economy models of trade policy. In those models, the government is characterized as valuing tariff revenue, domestic consumer welfare, and domestic producer surplus (via lobbying). Tariff revenue is less relevant for regulatory measures. Consumer welfare is a combination of interests—in variety, low prices, and the correction of the public-policy concern described above—with mixed implications for regulatory policy. The role of producer surplus is also mixed, including a combination of local large and small firms as well as local affiliates of foreign firms. It is the fact that this last group tends to be large and profitable that generates a commercial incentive for strict regulatory policies.

Put another way, by manipulating the composition of the foreign market, governments can ensure that the profits from trade are in the hands of local affiliates. A similar mechanism was developed by Blanchard (2007), where beggar-thy-neighbor tariffs are deterred because of the effect that such tariffs have on the profits of locally affiliated multinational producers. For regulatory barriers to trade, international ties *increase* the incentive to set strict regulations. Tariffs suppress trade volume, but regulatory barriers do not necessarily do so. Instead, regulatory barriers to trade shift the composition and ownership of that trade toward varieties concentrated in MNCs.[20]

The local presence of foreign firms is made possible by foreign direct investment (Keohane and Ooms 1972). Societies that are open to FDI allow foreign firms to produce locally, often for local sale or as part of a production process in a global supply chain. Today, 60 million workers are employed in 3,500 processing zones spanning 130 countries. Setting up these complex supply chains requires investment in regulatory and nonregulatory fixed costs, as well as the starting and operating capital for production. At the level of the firm, the ability to organize as a multinational and set up contracts with foreign affiliates is thereby as much a function of productivity as participation in international trade (Helpman 2006).

As a result, we might expect that the higher profitability of local affiliates is reason enough to raise regulatory barriers that shift profits toward these firms—regulatory policy becomes just one of the several ways that governments can promote FDI. Alongside tax incentives, legal guarantees against expropriation, or exclusive contracts, governments can set regulations in such a way that only the largest and most profitable foreign firms can operate. Local affiliates pay taxes, bolstering the local treasury; hire local workers, building an electoral advantage; and generate spillovers for local firms, who may contribute to politicians.[21]

Research on foreign direct investment offers a reason to doubt the advantages of an unconditional pro-FDI stance. The promise of tax revenue, for instance, is undercut by the incentives granted to foreign firms over international competition, particularly among low- and middle-income countries.[22] Furthermore, firms can engage in transfer pricing schemes to shift profits toward lower tax jurisdictions.[23] Evidence of a causal relationship between tax revenues and inward FDI is further confounded by the efforts that governments take to attract FDI in the first place. Still, econometric evidence suggests that inward FDI expands the tax base (Gropp and Kostial 2000). Tax competition does drive down tax levels, but not so far as to eliminate the advantages of FDI.

Besides taxation, the strongest theoretical benefit of FDI arises from the prospect of importing foreign technology and upgrading the skills of local workers, although neither is automatic. Some local affiliates are little more than warehouses for goods, while others receive substantial investments from participating in multinational production. The extent of such an investment is determined by the same motivations that drive FDI in the first place: the "make or buy" calculus that causes MNCs to internalize production within the boundaries of the firm. The advantage to paying the extra cost to acquire ownership and share profits in a local affiliate is driven by contractual problems between the self-interested managers of headquarters and local affiliates (Antràs 2003; Antràs and Staiger 2012).

Corporate profits are allocated by ownership and managerial control in a way that limits the ex ante threat of holdup. The ability to fire a manager goes a long way to resolve disagreements in contract interpretation. Antràs and Helpman (2008) describe the relationship, within the multinational corporation, between headquarters and a local manufacturer. The central determinant of the distribution of benefits of production is contractability, a measure of the extent to which production steps can be efficiently shifted from the headquarters to the manufacturer. The extent to which this is possible depends on both legal institutions and the nature of production. Theoretically, the share of profits kept in local affiliates depends on the relative share of total production contributed by each actor and the extent to which contracts can be enforced. As the local affiliate engages in fewer contractable activities, the optimal share of profits allocated to the manufacturer rises (Acemoglu, Antràs, and Helpman 2007). In theory, the extent to which profits of a foreign MNC will be shifted to its local affiliate is inversely proportional to the contractability or routine nature of the tasks contributed by that firm.

A local affiliate, and thereby the regulating government, will share in more of the profits if production is contract intensive. Insofar as the host state shares in the profits the local affiliate, the host government has an interest in shifting market share toward these productive foreign firms. This is likely to occur when the MNC is in a manufacturing-intensive sector, where a larger share of the headquarters' tasks is sent offshore. Furthermore, the share of profits allocated to the subsidiary is associated with the incentives of that subsidiary to follow through on investments into the production process. The more leeway available to the local affiliate, the more attractive that affiliate is to the host state, as profits can be locally retained and taxed.

Both intraindustry and intrafirm consequences of regulatory protection affect the choices of national regulators. As was shown in section 2.1, regulatory barriers reduce competition to the benefit of the surviving firms in the industry. As a consequence, the interests of the exporting state's government could align with those larger, more productive firms that benefit from the foreign regulation against those of small to medium-sized exporters. Section 2.2 outlines how these same barriers affect the interests of the destination state's government. Where regulations have this market-shifting effect, local affiliates of the largest exporting firms may share some of the profits. These governments could thereby raise regulatory barriers to attract investment and increase the local share of profits—all at the expense of local capital owners.

In both cases, regulatory protection has implications for competition that go beyond affecting the world price. Unlike a tariff, these barriers allow the most productive foreign firms to take market share from more marginal exporters in the foreign state and other less productive firms at home. Similar to a tariff, governments must weigh the benefits of the barrier against any costs that would be borne by local economic agents. In the following, I finalize the definition of regulatory protection by referencing policies that would maximize international welfare.

2.2.2. Government Interest in Regulatory Protection

In the following, I define entangled mercantilism as an effort to restrict competition in favor of large foreign firms at the expense of small foreign firms and consumers. This is not to say that without these incentives, governments would not choose to restrict competition for other reasons. The politically efficient level of regulation in the absence of regulatory protectionism would likely be positive and substantial. However, the fact that governments benefit from a subset of foreign producers generates a competitive interest that is globally inefficient, as those gains come at the expense of the vast majority of foreign firms and consumers.

A single government's choice of a regulatory barrier η has effects both at home and abroad. Consider two governments, a regulating home government W and a foreign government W^*. Here I assume that the regulating government's welfare consists of weighted sums of domestic economic activity $U(\eta)$, lobbying $L(\eta)$, and domestic consumption externality $H(\eta)$. The domestic consumption externality includes the expense of maintaining the regulatory barrier and the advantage that the government receives from successfully addressing some domestic problem by setting strict regulations.

Companies have two forms of influence over governments. The first is that governments may value the profits and employment of local firms. The second, following Grossman and Helpman (1994), is that companies may directly lobby. As established above, however, we would expect firms to divide based on a threshold of productivity. Firms with productivity $\phi \in [0, \hat{\phi}]$ would prefer to join a lobby in opposition to the regulatory measure. Firms with productivity above $\hat{\phi}$ would prefer regulatory protection. However, all these firms are foreign from the local governments' perspective. Only multinationals would have local affiliates, and those multinationals would all fall above the critical threshold to profit from foreign production ($\varphi_{MNC} > \hat{\phi}$). Define $\Pi_{MNC} \equiv \int_{\varphi_{MNC}}^{\infty} \pi(\varphi)g(\varphi)d\varphi$.

The government's choice of regulatory barrier, η, can thereby be determined by domestic welfare (η), lobbying (L), and public-policy demands (H) as follows:

$$W(\eta) = U(\eta) + L(\eta) + \gamma H(\eta) = U(\eta) + \beta\Pi_{MNC}(\eta) + \gamma H(\eta).$$

Here β and γ are exogenous political economy weights of the regulating government. $U(\eta)$ may be increasing or decreasing in η, depending on the home governments' distributional preferences, but both Π_{MNC} and H are increasing in the regulatory barrier. The optimal policy of the home government considers the effects on foreign consumers, foreign domestic producers, or foreign exporters. So long as foreign affiliates operate in the local market and the weight on those foreign profits β is greater than zero, the government will choose regulation in excess of what would satisfy domestic needs.[24] While I return to this formalization in chapter 7, the immediate conclusion is that the local presence of MNC affiliates creates entangled mercantilism. This generates predictions at both the industry and country levels: industries with a greater share of MNC organization and governments that have a share of the profits of those firms are more likely to adopt regulatory barriers to trade.

2.3. Explaining Regulatory Protectionism

This chapter derives the basic interests of firms and governments regarding regulatory protectionism. Larger, more productive firms benefit from fixed-cost regulations imposed by their destination markets. Multinational organization allows local affiliates of these large firms to encourage governments to adopt restrictive policies that shift profits away from their smaller competitors. This result challenges accounts of trade politics that expect large firms in general and multinational firms in particular to promote free trade and oppose regulations. Where prior research has expected a race to the bottom, with multinationals pushing governments to loosen regulations to lower the costs of doing business, it appears that we should expect governments to advance the interests of multinationals by imposing higher fixed costs via more restrictive regulations.

The insights developed in this chapter not only address the politics of regulatory protectionism but also implicitly lay out a kind of mercantilism that is rooted in the behavior of firms. Not all states will have the domestic political arrangements necessary to benefit from foreign profits. Entangled mercantilism goes hand in hand with a domestic politics that exhibits a Baptist-bootlegger coalition between public-policy demanders and the most profitable and globalized firms. Serving this coalition comes at the expense of broader consumer interests and small and medium-sized firms.[25] Identifying the intentions of such a coalition and their effects on regulatory protectionism requires a close examination both of firms in the affected market and of the politics in the regulating state. To do so, I examine two prominent cases of regulatory protection in depth.

Chapter 4 takes the case of European chemical market regulations to test the implications of the main proposition in this chapter. Examining the coalitions behind efforts to remove or bolster the European law, we find a sharp divide among US exporting firms, with the largest firms favoring stricter regulation and smaller US exporters opposing the new requirement. While smaller US chemical exporters were forced to rely on the US government to influence the European regulations, the large US multinationals could use their local affiliates to make their case. The result was a chemical safety policy opposed by environmental groups and riddled with regressive requirements.

Costly regulations can be in the interest of globalized firms and their host governments, but what of small domestic firms? Chapter 5 examines the effect of smaller, less productive domestic firms on the formation of regulatory barriers to trade. It appears that governments are in fact sensitive to the costs that are imposed on small and medium-sized firms, so long as they are local—entry conditions for small firms are carefully tuned to exclude foreign businesses.

Before establishing the mechanism by which firms influence politics, the following chapter offers evidence that governments in fact raise regulatory barriers in response to international competitiveness concerns. The chapter describes cross-national evidence of regulatory protection in the area of technical standards—labels, tests, and registration requirements. As with the US children's product regulation, governments around the world are adopting regulatory barriers to trade in sectors dominated by large firms and multinational producers. Using statistical analysis to compare cases with and without these market conditions, we see that governments are more likely to adopt a regulatory barrier to trade when conditions facilitate profit sharing with foreign market actors.

PART II
Evidence

CHAPTER THREE

Determinants of Regulatory Barriers to Trade

If, in the opinion of the Organization, the standards or regulations adopted by a Member under this sub-paragraph have an unduly restrictive effect on trade, the Organization may request the Member to revise the standards or regulations.—Havana Charter for an International Trade Organization

Most regulatory barriers to trade are unannounced and unacknowledged, but their proliferation has long strained global trade relations. Since the failure of the Havana Charter for the International Trade Organization in 1948, the global trade regime has gone a long way in reducing tariffs but has only recently developed tools to record, let alone counteract, regulatory protection. In the absence of evidence to the contrary, scholars have focused on the success story of the GATT and the broad elimination of tariffs and argued that tariff liberalization has produced a virtuous cycle of empowered exporters, multinational producers, and open commerce. In a world of multinational production, protectionism is said to make as much economic sense as "erecting a wall in the middle of a factory" (Baldwin 2016).

Meanwhile, governments and exporters struggle with regulatory barriers to trade. Complaints about regulatory matters in specific trade concerns paint a dark picture of global commercial cooperation. STCs are complaints and questions, submitted to the committee of the Technical Barriers to Trade Agreement (TBT Agreement), alleging that a WTO member is imposing a regulatory barrier to trade.[1] On this measure, new trade-affecting technical barriers are adopted by WTO members at a rate of 20 per month and are not limited to traditionally protected sectors like agriculture and textiles. As a result, regulatory barriers are not only outpacing tariffs as the principal barrier to trade but spreading to sectors, such as advanced manufacturing, that undergird the world's most advanced economies (Grieco 1990; Kono 2006; WTO 2011b).

Incipient economic evidence suggests that the measures subject to specific trade concerns are not merely a case of substitution for tariffs. Fontagné et al. (2015) use French customs data to show that while STCs produce large negative effects on the probability that a firm will export, the volume of trade rises among large firms. Gulotty et al. (2017) similarly find that Chinese exporters enjoy systematic gains in trade volume when there is a regulatory barrier in their destination market. The overall effect is to generate ambiguous effects on trade volume as well as clear benefits for the largest and most productive firms.[2] These studies, however, focus only on the effects of regulatory protection and not the cause of these measures.

This chapter takes the first steps toward substantiating the politics of entangled mercantilism. The theory developed in the previous chapter has implications for the prevalence of STCs across countries, industries, and time. In particular, I find markers of entangled markets—products that encourage globalized firms and governments that are on the receiving end of the rents of those firms—that are associated with higher rates of regulatory protection. This association arises from variation in regulatory choices within sectors and nations, holding constant time-invariant features of states and industries. Governments choose more stringent and restrictive regulations in sectors with more multinational activity. This evidence contradicts the overwhelming scholarly consensus that as firms engage in foreign investment, trade, and finance, governments will respond by lowering the barriers to trade. While this may be true for tariffs, regulatory protection exhibits the opposite pattern. Regulatory barriers are more common among developed than developing economies and are more prevalent in industries and countries that share in the profits of global production.

The analysis of STCs offers a conservative estimate of the spread of regulatory protection. STCs, like other dispute-based measures, are only recorded if a country objects to a foreign regulation. As a result, STCs may exclude measures that either are too narrow to merit a government's attention or are perceived to be too important for the regulating state to give up. That said, conditional on a country's participation in the WTO, the costs of raising a measure are low. Furthermore, excluding measures that are less harmful makes the analysis a more conservative account of regulatory protection.[3] While still subject to selection, STCs are a substantial improvement over competing ways to measure regulatory protection.

Nonetheless, the choice to raise a foreign regulation as an STC is as much a political process as the choice to impose the regulation in the first place. If the account of regulatory barriers as fixed costs is incorrect and STCs are substitutes for tariffs, it could be that measures are subject to STCs more often when multinational firms are more engaged in trade in the complaining state. If this were the case, multinationals would be merely highlighting regulatory barriers rather than causing them.[4] To address this concern, I rerun the analysis, limiting it to just STCs that are brought to the WTO by countries not part of the Organisation for Economic Co-operation and Development (OECD). Outside the OECD, smaller and less globalized firms are most likely to drive export activity. Limiting analysis to just these concerns produces an even stronger association between STCs and the markers of multinational activity.

A second concern for the analysis is the possibility that STCs are spurious to legitimate domestic demands for higher standards. Some products are more complex than others, and as consumers become more demanding in terms of safety, it would stand to reason that the first sectors to adopt higher regulation are those that also involve complex global production networks. Fears about the complexity of production have long played an important role in mobilizing consumers to push for new rules. This possibility cannot be completely ruled out in the aggregate and motivates the case studies in the following chapters. To go some of the way toward evaluating this possibility, I employ a novel measure of domestic regulatory demand: certification for ISO 9001, a quality-management system designed to help companies meet consumer expectations.[5]

The chapter is organized as follows: In section 3.1, I describe and evaluate competing measures of regulatory protection, including voluntary notification, firm surveys, and adversarial systems such as specific trade concerns. Section 3.2 operationalizes the explanatory factors described in the prior chapter, including consumer demands for protection, incentives to substitute for tariffs, and the profit-shifting argument that undergirds the theory of regulatory protection. Section 3.3 develops a statistical model of STCs and the interests of governments in the profits of large foreign firms. I show that these patterns persist when accounting for domestic sources of regulatory activity, proxied by private sector quality-management systems and the structure of domestic demand. The final section concludes with summary findings.

3.1. Measuring Regulatory Barriers to Trade

Policymakers have long sought a comprehensive approach to all forms of nontariff policies that can affect trade, creating long inventories of quotas, subsidies, and various forms of technical regulation. However, regulatory barriers have a distinct theoretical logic, imposing fixed costs in a way that other barriers do not, and are systematically identified by businesses as the primary policy burden on commerce. In this section, I draw on evidence from firm surveys to show that technical barriers to trade (TBT), the policies raised by specific trade concerns, are the most pressing policy concern for businesses and governments. Although regulatory barriers to trade are more difficult to quantify or identify than other forms of protection, they shape markets.

Developing an objective measure of regulatory protection is difficult, in part, because of the complexity of the regulatory process. Suppose a legislature passes a new technical regulation. While the text of the legislation will lay out general guidelines, lawmakers must leave substantial autonomy to administrators to set standards. The original bill, the subsequent administrative rulings, or even the informal behavior of regulators could create a technical barrier to trade. Even if one were to record every bill passed in legislatures and enumerate all administrative changes, the same rule in different circumstances could primarily limit international trade, primarily achieve a public-policy goal, or both. While it is part of the parlance of the trade law community since the creation of the Technical Barriers to Trade Agreement, WTO law does not provide a definition of *technical barrier to trade*.[6] Instead, the WTO refers broadly to technical regulations that "unnecessarily restrict" trade (WTO 2012b, 120). The category is expansive and generally represents all kinds of nonagricultural regulatory barriers to trade. The legal apparatus of the WTO has left the task of identifying regulatory barriers to outside organizations, governments, and academics.[7]

Businesses, however, are not divided over the effects of technical barriers to trade. Surveys of individual firms indicate a broad awareness of the problems raised by regulatory barriers, particularly technical standards. In 2010, the International Trade Centre began the implementa-

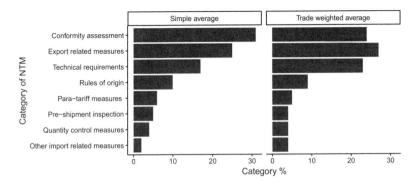

FIGURE 3.1. Category shares of burdensome measures across firms
Source: Survey measures reported in WTO 2012b.

tion of a large-scale company-level survey on a variety of nontariff measures (NTMs) in more than a dozen developing and least-developed
countries.[8] Figure 3.1 displays the kinds of NTMs experienced by firms,
according to firm reports, dividing measures into eight categories. Conformity assessment and technical requirements are clearly related to
technical barriers to trade. Preshipment inspections are also associated
with technical barriers to trade but are, for many developing countries, a
means to combat smuggling. The combined share of conformity assessment, technical requirements, and preshipment inspection make up the
majority of "burdensome" NTMs experienced by firms, whether taken
as a count or weighted by the volume of trade. The second-largest category consists of export-related measures, which are export registration
requirements, subsidies, and other policies that affect exports. These
business surveys reveal that technical barriers to trade are the most important form of nontariff measures.

The survey results, however, again do not predict what sorts of governments are enacting these measures. In addition, these surveys can
only reach firms that are active in a market. One of the principal les-
sons from the economics of international trade is that adjustment occurs
through the entry and exit decisions of firms. In order to be surveyed,
the firm must have survived the imposition of the measure.[9] Moreover,
firms that could be exporting a product are harder to identify and, even
if identified, would be hard-pressed to know about regulatory barriers
that are imposed after exporting. As a result, surveys can only provide a
partial image of the kinds of barriers facing firms.

A more systematic approach to cataloging regulatory protection is to rely on government self-reports. The WTO, and the GATT before it, encourages member states to "self-notify" new regulatory measures that may frustrate trade. In the WTO, member states are asked to submit draft legislation to standing committees where, for a period of 60 days, member states can decide whether to offer comments or complaints. Members are further asked to maintain inquiry points to receive these comments. The obligation to open the regulatory process for comments is not new for many of the WTO members; the United States and the European Union have robust notice and comment processes for regulation. Moreover, the WTO seeks to elicit notifications on even draft legislation, ostensibly to allow member states to avoid accidental trade restrictions.

Many governments do notify the WTO of regulatory changes. Since the ratification of the TBT Agreement in 1994, governments have notified the committee of more than 22,000 measures. These notifications come disproportionately from developing nations, such as Brazil, Mexico, Uganda, and South Africa. The geographic and political diversity of these notifications is matched by the diversity of the covered sectors: the state with the highest participation, Saudi Arabia, included a 7-page "Draft of Technical Regulation for Croissants" (WTO 2009) as well as 10 pages of requirements for certain diameters and tolerances for hot-rolled steel bars (WTO 2012a), both for the purpose of promoting consumer safety. These notifications are not evenly reported, and national laws mean the scope of an individual notification can vary from a specific product to whole industries. The main issue is that these notifications are voluntary. The US Consumer Product Safety Improvement Act, discussed in the introduction, was passed without notice to the WTO, as are thousands of smaller regulatory changes.

Self-reports, even if required, would be of limited value to regulatory cooperation if only for the fact that governments, and the societies they represent, disagree about regulatory intent. Societies have substantive disagreements about the appropriate risk balance as well as the likely consequences of regulation. Even among equally developed societies, governments can have strong disagreements as to the evidentiary standards for harm and the ways that states handle risk. For example, the debates between the European Union and the United States over the precautionary principle can be understood as arising from differences in social priorities (Vogel 2012). In the absence of global agreement on these issues, even states that intend to meet their obligations on self-notification are unlikely to produce exhaustive notices of their measures of regulatory protection.

In order to overcome the limitations of self-notifications and firm-level surveys, I measure regulatory protection from state submissions of concerns to the WTO Technical Barriers to Trade Agreement.[10] The TBT-STC database developed by the WTO secretariat provides information on hundreds of regulations, beginning in January of 1995. These concerns do not require self-reporting by governments; instead, they arise bilaterally. Governments use these concerns to address regulations that pose a problem for commerce without submitting a full dispute.[11] These concerns are also superior to survey techniques of firms, which are limited to a specific market or sector and are typically collected over a short period of time.

The incidence of specific trade concerns varies across both time and space. Specific trade concerns can affect individual products, classes of products, or entire sectors. The WTO secretariat identifies TBT-STC either at the level of industrial sectors, such as fruit versus vegetables, or by substantially disaggregated product categories, such as particular varieties of apples. These levels of aggregation correspond to the two-digit and four-digit levels of the harmonized schedule (HS), respectively. As a result, STCs may be narrow and targeted or very broad. When a measure applies to one or more HS2 categories, as was the case for the US Consumer Product Safety Improvement Act, a single measure can affect dozens of product varieties.

Disaggregating the incidence of the hundreds of country-year STCs to the country-HS4-year level produces 6,857 distinct country-HS4 categories that are affected at some point by a technical barrier to trade. Table 3.1 lists the 20 sectors with the highest number of country-product measures, along with the most common product mentioned in that sector. For instance, "machinery regulations" is the second most common category of regulatory measures raised by WTO members. This sector covers everything from cranes to ball bearings—but the most commonly mentioned products are air conditioners.[12] Technical barriers can affect nearly all physical goods, from consumer products such as cauliflower to industrial inputs such as aldehydes.[13]

While TBT can apply to any good, observing an STC requires that at least one government raise the concern at the WTO. At minimum, these governments must have joined the GATT/WTO system—originally an exclusive club, though today that system covers nearly the entire world,

TABLE 3.1 **Top 20 sectors of specific trade concerns**

HS2 category	HS code	Measures (#)	Most regulated product
Fats	15	422	Animal fats
Machinery	84	409	Air conditioners
Vegetables	07	266	Cabbage and cauliflower
Fruit	08	266	Apples and pears
Industrial plants	12	266	Cereal straw
Electronics	85	260	Lamps
Inorganic chemicals	28	207	Alkali or alkaline-earth metals
Meat	02	196	Offal
Beverages	22	193	Denatured ethyl alcohol
Animal products	04	192	Milk
Vegetable products	09	190	Cinnamon
Medical devices	90	188	Respirators
Preparations of plants	20	173	Fruit nuts
Vegetable products	11	172	Wheat flour
Organic chemicals	29	169	Aldehydes
Iron and steel	72	168	Angle shapes
Misc. chemicals	38	157	Monocarboxylic fatty acids
Cereals	10	152	Barley
Apparel (knit)	61	146	Garments
Apparel (not knit)	62	141	Men's suits

not just the capitalist allies of the United States (Gowa and Kim 2005). Limiting analysis to WTO members, table 3.2 displays the average market size, level of FDI, and the average most favored nation (MFN) tariff rate for country-years with and without specific trade concerns.[14]

Descriptively, specific trade concerns target larger markets, as measured in GDP, and more open markets, as measured by the number of foreign banks, FDI stock, and the average MFN tariff. Among WTO members, a one standard deviation increase in the average applied tariff rate is associated with a 25 percent decrease in the probability of a specific trade concern. At this high level of aggregation, specific trade concerns are associated with more foreign investment rather than less and higher levels of trade openness rather than less.

These results are consistent with STCs having a different driver than tariffs but are also consistent with a substitution logic. Perhaps the apparent openness of governments has merely been replaced with a new form of protectionism. To move beyond these broad associations and rule out this competing hypothesis, it is necessary to have a model of the interests that drive regulatory protection. The following develops three such models, each drawing on product- and country-level measures to explain variation in STCs.

TABLE 3.2 **Country-year characteristics with specific trade concerns**

STC	Country-years (#)	ln(GDP)	Foreign banks (#)	ln(FDI stock)	MFN tariff
Absent	2,549	23.8	9.2	8.5	9.7
Present	149	26.7	14	11.4	7.7

3.2. Measuring Interests in Regulatory Protection

Explanations for STCs fall into three broad categories. The first is consumer driven, where STCs would be incidental to governments' efforts to satisfy consumer demands for quality or safety. The second invokes tariff substitution, in which STCs are a means for developed countries to follow through on their obligations to lower tariffs without opening their markets. The third is entangled mercantilism, developed above, where governments use regulatory measures to shift profits toward local firms. Each theoretical approach suggests a different set of interests underlying regulatory behavior. In the following, I describe a cross-national proxy for each of these interests and how they vary across governments and sectors.

3.2.1. Consumer Demands for Quality: ISO 9001 Regulations

Governments insist that all regulatory measures aim to improve the health, safety, and quality of goods and services. One major effort to establish a system of voluntary regulatory standards began with the development of the Organisation Internationale de Normalisation in 1947. This organization, abbreviated "ISO" from the Greek *isos*, promulgates international standards, issues technical reports and specifications, and publishes guides. Today the ISO system is the largest voluntary organization of national standards authorities. These national standards authorities are, in turn, private organizations of industry experts, public regulatory agencies, and consumer groups. The topics of their standards range from the direction of twists in yarn to greenhouse gas emissions and, taken as a whole, are a comprehensive account of the substantive demands of global commerce.

The standards provided by the ISO aim to influence the behaviors of firms, consumers, and national regulators but are adopted on a voluntary basis, limiting their use as a direct protectionist instrument. Instead, ISO standards are certified by third-party organizations and enforced by firms and consumers. Each certification represents an investment in time and money on the part of a firm seeking to receive an ISO designation. These costs are borne by firms that aim to enhance the company image, meet consumer demands, and gain preferred supplier status (Prajogo and Sohal 2006). While many ISO designations are specific to an industry or sector, the ISO 9000 family of certifications mark organizations as compliant with broad quality-assurance procedures without regard to the industry. Voluntary adoption of ISO 9000 markings is a costly signal to consumers, employees, and downstream firms that may demand higher regulatory standards.

In addition to being voluntary, these ISO standards are international—available to both domestic and foreign firms. In general, domestic standard-setting bodies can adopt voluntary measures that can have protectionist effects, but ISO standards are given the legal presumption of consistency with GATT/WTO rules. Büthe and Mattli (2011) argue that participation in the creation of ISO standards, as well as their subsequent use, is driven by the capacity for coordination among the domestic standard-setting bodies that contribute to global standardization. More hierarchical, coordinated, and experienced domestic standard-setting systems will be more effective in influencing the design of international standards favorable to one market or another. Taking the set of available international standards as given, their uptake measures the costs associated with switching from existing procedures as well as the rewards for adoption from domestic proregulatory interests. I measure this latter motivation by tallying the number of ISO 9001 certifications at the level of the country-year. The variable *ISO* measures 1,000 of these certifications.

The breadth of ISO 9001 certifications, while precluding sectoral or product-level analysis, offers the additional advantage of addressing a prominent alternative cause of TBT: incidental protection produced by a generalized attitude on the part of the state toward risk. On this account, rather than serving consumer demands on a particular product, TBT could arise because of general rules or stances taken by the government. David Vogel (2012), for instance, argues that regulations in one area will inform the strategies taken in other policy areas: "If a government is adopting more stringent regulations toward some consumer or environmental risks caused by business, then it is also more likely to address other risks with similarly strong measures." Vogel traces these policy equilibria across time in the US and the EU, finding that regulations are interdependent and shaped by policy equilibria that can shift over time. Put simply, technical barriers to trade reflect an overall orientation of the state toward risk rather than the interests of market actors within a sector.

3.2.2. Tariff Substitution: Tariffs and Optimal Taxation

The main political economy explanation for the onset of regulatory barriers to trade is as an opaque substitute for tariffs (Kono 2006). Simon Evenett, a leading scholar and chronicler of regulatory barriers to trade, argues that much of the apparent success of the GATT/WTO system in lowering tariffs may instead be a consequence of this substitution (2013). WTO members agree to have very low applied tariff rates but then adopt high levels of opaque regulatory barriers. On this analysis, regulatory barriers to trade would be applied to the same goods that would, in the absence of an agreement, be protected by tariffs. To test this theory, I draw from political economy explanations for optimal tariffs. These theories predict that importing governments would adopt tariffs that balance domestic distortions of consumer prices against the benefits for import-competing industry. If policy substitution explains the rise in regulatory protection, the bulk of the rise would occur among those goods where domestic distortions are relatively low.

The theory of optimal tariffs extends the reasoning of Ramsey (1927) on the trade-off between taxes and consumer welfare to the question of international trade. In the domestic context, the question is, What level of tax would efficiently balance the losses associated with reductions in demand against the higher per-unit revenue? In the trade context, tariffs on the imports of inelastic goods would not substantially change the quantity demanded and so would induce lower marginal deadweight losses than a tariff on an elastic good. Grossman and Helpman (1994) derive a model in which this consideration drives tariff outcomes: the optimal tariff is inversely associated with the import-demand elasticity—the correlation between the demand for a particular quantity of imported goods and prices.[15] Nonetheless, whether governments are in practice motivated by these efficiency concerns remains an open question. In the following, I use σ to refer to the sector-by-sector measure of the elasticity of demand across countries.

3.2.3. Profit Shifting: Global Production and Local Profits

As discussed above, economic evidence and theory suggest that regulatory barriers can advantage the top firms, raising rather than lowering trade volume, at the expense of smaller producers. However, it is incorrect to infer interests from policy effects alone, particularly when the benefits accrue to foreign firms. The theory of regulatory protection developed in chapter 2 argues that when foreign firms are involved in local production, such as that established through foreign direct investment, regulating governments acquire a shared interest in their profits. The largest and most productive foreign firms that would benefit from a regulatory barrier to trade can thereby bring some of the benefits back to the regulating state. If Mattel did not have offices in California, the United States would be less enthusiastic about a regulatory choice that shifted most of the import share toward that leading company. The literature on FDI, however, makes it clear that the presence of local affiliates is not itself sufficient for foreign profits to benefit the home economy. Moreover, not all production networks involve a local affiliate—even an arm's length exchange can benefit local actors. To measure these interests, I rely on two factors that together jointly predict the presence of globalized production and the localization of profits. First, governments are more likely to share in foreign profits if the production process depends on relationship-specific investments. Second, governments are more likely in a position to share in those profits if there are high levels of technology transfer from local firms.

Production processes vary substantially in the extent that they occur in a single firm or across unaffiliated producers. The degree to which this happens can be measured by how a product is priced. For example, paper is a well-defined commodity with prices that are set by global markets. Penguin Random House does not control paper mills or own forests, and no paper producer depends on any particular publisher to earn a profit. When companies depend on one another for profits, there is an advantage to establishing control, and prices are set by bargaining between commercial partners. These differences in pricing are the basis for the product-specific measure of "contract intensity" developed by Nunn (2007) and Rauch (1999),[16] which evaluates the proportion of an industry's inputs, weighted by value, that are not sold on an exchange or reference priced.[17] Higher values of this measure indicate production is contract intensive, less commoditized, and more likely to involve affiliated or locally contracted production processes.[18]

Governments would only have an interest in shifting profits if the firms engaged in global production shift profits toward local entities. To measure these profit inflows, I evaluate the amount of income derived from foreign licensing of intellectual property. These inflows are termed royalty receipts. The World Bank reports national income from intellectual property in national measures of the balance of payments statistics, a key part of the distinction between GDP and GNP. In 2017, global receipts amounted to $366 billion, representing a significant channel for profits to flow across the global supply chain. The advantage of this measure is that it operates whether or not the relationship is within a firm or at arm's length. Higher levels of royalty receipts in the regulating state indicate that foreign partners of local producers are repatriating some share of the profits of intellectual property, which could include the profits from using that intellectual property to export into the regulating state. The higher a nation's rank in terms of being a recipient of these payments, the more likely that globally earned profits will benefit the regulating government and the more likely that efforts to reallocate profits across firms will benefit local actors. These data are skewed, ranging in magnitude from millions to billions of dollars in a single year. To account for the skew, I use the natural logarithm of the US dollar amount.

To summarize, table 3.3 displays the hypotheses about the joint effect of product characteristics and the distribution of profits across the columns. Regarding the latter, the local distribution of profits gives the regulating government a stake in the foreign market. If profits are foreign from the perspective of the regulating government, raising a regulatory measure will reallocate profits from small to large firms in the foreign market, but this reallocation will not affect the local market outcomes that matter to governments. In addition, firm-to-firm reallocations predicted by the theory depend on market structure. A fixed cost is more likely to shift profits locally if firms have some bargaining power. In perfectly competitive or commoditized products, regulatory protection is likely to serve traditional protectionist interests. If, however, production is tied into specific contracts and local firms receive substantial royalty receipts, local affiliates would profit from regulatory protection. It is the interaction between these two variables that produces high levels of regulatory protection.

TABLE 3.3 **Theoretical expectation of profit-shifting argument**

	Distribution of profits	
Production	Local	Foreign
Relationship-specific	High	Low
Commoditized	Low	Low

3.3. Predicting TBT Incidence

The general observation that STCs are more prevalent among developed and open societies is already suggestive evidence that they operate under a different logic than tariffs. However, cross-national evidence is confounded by a vast number of differences between nations. It is possible, for instance, that developed countries are accused of raising regulatory barriers because those countries are likely to listen to the complaint. Furthermore, even conditioning on consumer demands, some share of apparent regulatory barriers is motivated by consumer concerns, and some sectors are naturally more dangerous than others: for example, technical regulations on packaging croissants versus the same on lawn mowers. To address this issue, this section develops a statistical model of TBT-STC onset across sectors, countries, and years, focusing on variation within sectors and countries over time (see table 3.4).

The natural test is to compare the association among TBT-STC and each of the proxies associated with consumer-demand, tariff-substitution, and profit-shifting theories. The dependent variable is binary, taking on 1 in the presence of a TBT-STC in a sector-country-year and 0 otherwise. In the following, I estimate a logistic regression with country and industry fixed effects. By restricting analysis to just the variation within an industry and country, we can rule out the effects of a number of factors that do not vary over time. These include cultural factors that might lead societies to choose different levels of regulatory protection, slow-moving economic factors such as endowments in labor or land, geographic size and distance, and institutional factors.

Table 3.5 displays estimates of the logistic regression of specific trade concerns submitted to the TBT committee. The results suggest that both profit shifting and consumer demand play into regulatory protection. However, the coefficients in the model given in column 3 suggest that the number of ISO 9001 certifications is negatively associated with the

TABLE 3.4 **Descriptive statistics**

	Range	Median	Mean
TBT	[0, 1]	0	0.013
Contract intensity	[0.02, 0.90]	0.38	0.44
ln(royalty receipts)	[9, 25]	19.2	18.1

TABLE 3.5 **Determinants of specific trade concerns (1995–2011)**

	Dependent variable: TBT-STC				
	(1)	(2)	(3)	(4)	(5)
Contract intensity	−3.7***	−3.5***			−3.4***
	(0.5)	(0.6)			(0.6)
ln(ISOs)			−0.2***		−0.2***
			(0.03)		(0.03)
σ				−0.002*	
				(0.001)	
Cont. int.× ln(royalty receipts)	0.12***	0.18***			0.18***
	(0.03)	(0.03)			(0.03)
ln(royalty receipts)	0.05***	0.2***	0.3***	0.4***	0.2***
	(0.01)	(0.03)	(0.03)	(0.03)	(0.03)
Year	0.03***	0.04***	0.07***	−0.02***	0.07***
	(0.004)	(0.005)	(0.007)	(0.006)	(0.007)
WTO nonmembership	−4.7***	−4.7***	−5.1***	−5.1***	−5.0***
	(1.0)	(1.0)	(1.0)	(1.0)	(1.0)
Regulator fixed effects		(inc.)	(inc.)	(inc.)	(inc.)
Industry fixed effects		(inc.)	(inc.)	(inc.)	(inc.)
Observations	317,456	317,456	343,130	230,491	317,456
Log likelihood	−21,229	−15,942	−17,038	−12,362	−15,913

Note: Coefficients of logistic regression of the onset of TBT-specific trade concerns. $*p < 0.1$; $**p < 0.05$; $***p < 0.01$.

onset of STCs, the opposite of the predicted sign if STCs were driven by high demands for quality. Furthermore, the coefficient estimates displayed in column 4 shows that the elasticity of demand, σ, is negatively associated with TBT-STC, as predicted in theory, but the effect is substantively small and statistically insignificant.

The only robust pattern across the five models supports the profit-shifting theory. Local affiliates receive a share of the profits (those with high levels of royalty receipts) and impose TBT measures more often on products that are contract intense. Among governments with high levels of royalty receipts, the products that are most embedded in multinational contracts are also most likely to observe a technical barrier to trade. Specifically, in the average contract-intense sector, a one standard deviation increase in the log of royalty receipts produces a 36 percent increase in the propensity to experience a specific trade concern over a regulation. This effect is both statistically and substantively significant.

These findings do not guarantee a role for profit shifting, as these statistical results cannot establish the causal mechanism connecting market factors to government decision-making, and we must believe that the models are correctly specified to even establish an association. One threat to that inference is that the same factors predicted to support the profit-shifting theory of regulatory protection could instead be driven by the opposite. For instance, we might see similar results as in table 3.5 if large and productive multinationals encourage governments to raise concerns. By relying on data of disputed measures, it is possible these models are attributing the fire to the fire alarm. It is also possible that there is even more regulatory protection in other sectors, countries, and years that go unremarked upon.

To address this possibility, I restrict analysis to STCs raised by less developed WTO members. The models above only use information about the regulating country, the volume of royalty receipts locally transferred, the degree of contract intensity in the sector, and information about consumer demands for quality, but each STC also records a complaining government. Any WTO member may submit a regulatory barrier to trade, and although the main parties raising complaints are the EU, the US, and Mexico, many of the complaints are raised by developing countries. In table 3.6, I reestimate the first model from table 3.5's column 1, limiting the analysis to products and members where an STC

TABLE 3.6 **Determinants of non-OECD specific trade concerns (1995–2011)**

	Dependent variable: TB
Contract intensity	−6.3***
	(1.748)
ln(royalty receipts)	−0.5**
	(0.198)
Cont. int. × ln(royalty receipts)	0.3***
	(0.076)
Regulator fixed effects	(included)
Observations	23,442
Log likelihood	−1,927.082

Note: Estimating restricting sample to products mentioned in non-OECD STCs. $*p < 0.1$; $**p < 0.05$; $***p < 0.01$.

was ever raised by a non-OECD member. This substantially smaller data set nonetheless exhibits the same patterns as the full sample, with the interaction of contract intensity and royalty receipts being positively associated with the presence of an STC.

These results do not offer evidence in favor of generalized demands for quality and offer only weak evidence that governments use regulatory measures as a substitute for optimal tariffs. Instead, patterns in TBT-STCs show that regulatory protection is more likely when regulating governments could plausibly benefit from profit shifting. The relationship is probabilistic and conditional on examining within sector and country variation but overall consistent with prior research that shows higher levels of disputed regulations arising from the most integrated markets.

3.4. Discussion

The national, sectoral, and temporal distribution of regulatory protection is at odds with prevailing theories of protectionism. Tariffs and other traditional protectionist instruments are thought to be anathema to productive and globalized markets. This puzzle is resolved if regulatory barriers generate an international coalition for protectionism, one that joins the interests of local and foreign companies. While other explanations are not entirely ruled out, the quantitative results lend plausibility to the profit-shifting argument. Because the largest and most productive firms are disproportionately harmed by tariffs and high productivity insulates these companies and their local affiliates and partners, regulatory protection can promote the productive interests of large and globalized networks of firms. At the same time, less productive foreign exporters that lack a constituency in the host market are fully exposed to the costs of regulatory protection. As host governments enact stricter trade-limiting standards, licenses, and tests, the effect is to reduce competition in favor of productive and globally connected firms.

These aggregate patterns show that regulatory protection is not peripheral to the global trade regime. The United States and the European Union founded the WTO and are today the most prolific users of technical barriers to trade. However, the sectors and periods where these barriers are used are not traditionally protected industries. Instead, it is where societies are among the most globalized, with the greatest stake in the profits of foreign firms, that governments have turned to regulatory protection.

As more stringent regulations make it more difficult to participate in global markets, more firms will be excluded from them. When governments find their firms' exports frustrated by tariffs abroad, they can turn to international institutions and agreements. These institutions were developed to insulate governments from domestic protectionist pressures, giving politicians the time to strike balanced reciprocal deals and the authority to enforce their provisions on trade partners. The device that enables negotiation and ensures enforcement in the WTO legal system, however, depends on a particular kind of reciprocity to achieve balanced deals. The rules of the multilateral system are designed to limit distortions in aggregate market access or trade volume. Regulatory barriers to trade impose fixed costs that do less to limit trade volume than to affect the composition and effective ownership of trade. Governments have little recourse if the only admissible damages are measured in terms of national losses in trade volume or value. This poses a problem for measuring protectionism, monitoring compliance with trade deals, and calibrating enforcement.

Before turning to these international concerns, it is important to further substantiate the causal mechanism linking the interests of firms and governments. Why is it that certain firms are incorporated into the national interest while others are excluded? The following chapters analyze two prominent cases of regulatory barriers to trade in the EU and the US to show that MNCs both understand the advantages of regulatory protection and can play an active role in their design. However, these cases also show that governments are not merely seeking to maximize these producers' profits and that much of the impetus for regulation comes from domestic societal interests. In both cases, we see how the promise of attracting and retaining global profits influences government decision-making, alongside and complementing other regulatory aims.

CHAPTER FOUR

Regulatory Preferences in the Chemical Industry

In 2001, the European Commission took up the largest change in EU governance since the adoption of the single currency—rewriting the European chemical regulation system. This new system would centralize authority over hundreds of thousands of products and millions of consumers. The European chemical sector is globally integrated, particularly with the United States; chemicals accounts for approximately 20 percent of US-EU trade. The effort to regulate this sector produced "the most complex and intensely-lobbied piece of law the EU has produced in its 50 year history" (Rettman 2006). In this chapter, I examine the interests of industry actors within both the EU and the United States, their influence over regulatory outcomes, and the consequences for concentration in the sector. As with other regulatory barriers to trade, the new rules provided advantages to companies that were efficient and large enough to cover the fixed costs. The result was a policy initially oriented toward consumer safety but ultimately embraced by large European and American chemical producers. Regulatory protection arose from an alliance among big business, safety advocates, and environmentalists against smaller firms. Together these forces forged a new European Chemical Agency (ECHA) with a mandate to register, test, and potentially ban the production of nearly every chemical in Europe.

The European and American chemical industries meet the preconditions for the emergence of regulatory protection. First, the sectors are highly dispersed, with large firms competing with smaller companies, enabling heterogeneity in response to the regulation. In 2006, chemical companies employed nearly 870,000 workers in the United States and

1.25 million in the European Union. Second, the European chemical industry exhibits high levels of multinational activity. One-third of the American chemical industry is European-owned, and major American companies have substantial operations in Europe (Vogel 2012). These linkages generate a potential for shared interest between regulators in the European Union and a subset of the American chemical market. With these linkages, I would predict that European regulators would value the concerns of large American producers in the design and implementation of the new European chemical laws. Under these conditions, I would expect that European regulators would adopt programs that exacerbate fixed costs—policies that favor large globalized firms at the expense of smaller industries.

Identifying these cleavages over regulatory measures is made difficult by the complexity of regulatory policy. The regulatory effects of requirements to sell products in packages of a dozen or test for biohazards vary both in magnitude and in the number of plausible motivations for the policies. Compliance costs depend on factors such as the availability of substitutes and the difficulty of retooling the production process. In addition, the plausibility of the public-policy goal depends, in part, on the presence of autonomous political demands by the beneficiaries of the program. These European regulations are no exception, covering a wide variety of products and affecting nearly every manufacturing sector, with constituencies of varying strength behind the various provisions of the rule. However, by breaking apart the regulations into their component provisions, we can isolate the portions of the law that are more or less a fixed cost to identify the intraindustry cleavages over the policy.

Evidence for these cleavages is further obscured in government economic statistics for trade and investment flows. These data, as well as firm surveys and qualitative accounts of business interests, suffer from survival bias. If a regulation is an entry barrier, harmed groups will have exited the market, making it difficult to gather the experiences of the affected group. A second kind of selection bias is more technical, involving the organization of global production. In addition to exporting goods, firms can serve foreign markets by engaging in global production. If a firm decides to purchase a controlling stake of a foreign company, this is recorded as foreign direct investment and part of national accounts. However, the other option is to license the technology and produce at arm's length.[1] To remedy these selection issues, I rely on a novel form of data: patent filings, which are necessary to serve a market by exporting, licensing, or engaging in foreign direct investment.

The results of this study demonstrate the value of the regulatory-protectionism framework over either the tariff-substitution or consumer-demand theories of regulatory barriers to trade. Research into the former generally predicts that industry leaders would lead the opposition to new regulations. For example, in a case study of the French pharmaceutical industry, Helen Milner (1988a) argues that the priority of industry leaders was to reduce, rather than raise, testing requirements in France and push for a harmonized European-wide safety regime. We would expect a preference for harmonization if the regulatory barriers are primarily a variable-cost measure. In that case, top firms should favor open markets, but with fixed-cost regulations, the opposite holds. The European chemical regulations exhibit both varieties, dropping the variable costs components at the demand of large and productive firms.

Scholars of consumer-based theories of regulatory politics predict that leading companies are those most concerned with their reputation with customers and that industry leaders have a stake in their reputation or brand and may act to forestall activist pressures.[2] Support for regulation is just part of current trends to engage in corporate social and environmentally responsible practices. I establish that while there are advantages to reducing business and legal risks by acting responsibly, efforts to promote health and safety were combined with a drive toward competitive advantage. In the chemical regulatory case, activists and consumer advocates turned against the regulations as they gained support from the top producers. Just as in the case of US product safety, what starts as an effort to meet public demand can open the door to privileged interests.

This chapter proceeds as follows. Section 4.1 outlines the lobbying efforts among various firms toward the new EU chemical regulations, showing how large chemical firms broke with their smaller counterparts. To do so, I examine contributions to the public consultations the EU held in the crafting its new chemical regulations, as well as evidence from firm-level surveys conducted by the European Commission. All this data comes from incumbent firms, representing only a slice of the overall deterrent effect of a regulatory barrier. Section 4.3 uses patent data to show that in the European Patent Office, the overall number of chemicals registered stayed constant, but the number of unique registrants declined and concentration rose. Section 4.4 examines the effect of the EU chemical law on US firm patents in Europe. The regulations increased the share of patent activity filed by the largest US-affiliated firms. These findings are consistent with the lobbying activity of chemical firms and the way that the political cleavages over the policy had a practical effect.

4.1. Chemical Safety Regulation in the European Union

European Union product safety regulations began as efforts to promote trade within Europe. Tariffs between European nations were eliminated by the Treaty of Rome, but when it came to regulatory measures, the trend was in the opposite direction, particularly in the case of chemical products. Beginning with the Single European Act of 1986, the European Council was given authority to enact measures toward the completion of the common market, which meant aligning regulations across the continent. The European Council, in turn, enacted rules on everything from climate policy to road safety.

One of these directives took aim at barriers that arose from the variety of product safety rules, authorizing the European Commission to issue new community-wide regulations to promote safety.[3] These regulations allowed, for example, an emergency committee of the European Commission to ban the sale of certain soft-plastic toys used by children.[4] However, it soon became clear that even with this authorization, the commission lacked sufficient knowledge about products, particularly the chemicals used in production, to engage in effective risk assessment themselves. The global production of chemicals had increased 400 times since 1930, and almost a third of that production originates in Europe. Just as American regulators would later discover, the supply chain is too complex to monitor without cooperation from industry. Ministers of an informal environmental council concluded that any solution required expanding market surveillance to include increased industry participation.

In February 2001, the European Commission issued a white paper calling for new regulations to shift the burden of gathering information toward the chemical industry (European Commission 2001). The paper laid out four new regulation requirements for chemicals: registration, new substance evaluation (testing), chemical authorization (preclearance), and chemical restriction (bans), collectively referred to by the acronym REACH. The proposal also described a new agency to implement these rules, the European Chemical Agency. These regulations would apply to all sectors and to all chemical substances produced at a rate of more than 1 metric ton per annum, making REACH one of the most expansive regulations in history.[5]

While REACH has a number of obligations, including the requirement to obtain authorization for using certain chemicals, for most companies, the principal obligation is to test and register their products with the ECHA. Following the precautionary principle, it is up to manufacturers, importers, and downstream users to ensure that their products do not adversely affect human health or the environment.[6] Both importers and producers would be required to register chemicals produced or imported at 1 ton or more per producer or importer per year. With each registration, companies would be required to pay a fee as well as provide information, such as the chemical's identity, how it will be produced, how it will be used, guidance on its safe use, exposure information, and study summaries of physical/chemical properties and their effects on human health or the environment.

The details of these reporting requirements depend on the volume and expected toxicity of the chemical. REACH identifies four tonnage bands—1 ton or more, 10 tons or more, 100 tons or more, and 1,000 tons or more, with increasing obligations on higher bands. Once production hits 10 tons, REACH requires a chemical safety assessment including various hazard assessments and evaluation of the chemicals' potential to persist in the environment. Regulators predicted that these registration requirements would apply to hundreds of thousands of imported and manufactured products in Europe.

REACH applies to all chemicals sold in the European Union, including imported products. While the legal obligations of REACH only cover companies established in the European Union—there are technically no obligations for non-EU companies to register or participate in REACH—the effects travel back up the supply chain. Importers are required to register, and then those importers must rely on their non-EU suppliers to meet the reporting requirements. While indirect, the effect is to require non-EU manufacturers to go through the same testing and information-gathering procedures as domestic firms, with the added cost of having to then hand that sensitive data to a customer or competitor to register the product in Europe. Given this, REACH allows non-EU manufacturers the option to appoint a local EU-based agent, called an "only representative," to fulfill the obligations of their importers. As of mid-2016, only representatives make up 10,286 of the total 45,373 registrations in REACH.

4.1.1. REACH and Small Firms

One of the immediate concerns of European regulators was the effect that REACH could have on the domestic industry—particularly the 36,000 small and medium-sized enterprises (SMEs) in the European chemical sector. These SMEs represent 96 percent of the total number of enterprises and account for 28 percent of chemical production. While the original white paper produced by the EU outlining REACH did not address SMEs, the EU submitted its proposal for comments from governments, both from within the EU and from the technical barriers to trade committee at the World Trade Organization. In the 85 comments received from governments, a vast majority prioritized concerns about the treatment of SMEs.

One typical comment was provided by the Government Office for the North East, England, outlining the scale of the potential impact of REACH:

> The cost burden to the chemical industry and downstream users could be as high as 10 billion Euros. While large companies will survive these additional costs, many SMEs may not. An independent study by A D Little, concluded that the impact of the legislation on the German economy would be the loss of between 0.4% and 6.4% of GDP and between 140,000 and 2,350,000 jobs. A similar study in the UK is underway. Given the higher proportion of SMEs in the North East this legislation will lead to proportionately more closures of sites, companies and loss of jobs.[7]

These concerns were echoed by officials, ranging from those representing producers such as Switzerland and the United States to those of consumers such as China and Thailand. To address these concerns, commenters proposed introducing exemptions, special grants, financial assistance, and SME-specific help desks. By the time the proposal made its way to the council, REACH exhibited a progressive-fee structure, following EU definitions for micro, small, and medium firms. While qualifying small firms are charged €11,622 per registration of a substance produced in amounts above 1,000 tons, microsized enterprises pay €1,245.

A large firm pays €33,201, giving the micro enterprises a substantial discount for product registration.

The definitions for SME operate on the thresholds laid out in table 4.1. Firms must meet the total headcount requirements (staff and employees) and qualify under the monetary thresholds for either yearly turnover (revenue) or yearly balance sheets (assets). Furthermore, enterprises must be independent of other firms, preventing a company from nominally splitting to get under one of the thresholds. Within Europe, 92.4 percent of firms, across industries, qualify as microsized enterprises, 6.4 percent are small, and 1 percent are medium-sized. The 0.2 percent of businesses that qualify as large businesses under these criteria, however, account for a third of total employment and 41.9 percent of value added.

These criteria apply to both domestic and foreign firms that register through an only representative. The US Department of Commerce reports five aggregate size categories of US exporters to Europe in the chemical sector, displayed in table 4.2.[8] These data, derived from confidential electronic export information entered into the Automated Export System and the US Census Bureau's Business Register, cover about 89 percent of measurable merchandise export value.[9] While the categories do not match the EU SME definitions, the majority of US exporters appear to qualify for the reduced fees.[10]

TABLE 4.1 **Definitions of SME (EU recommendation 2003/61)**

SME category	Headcount	Turnover	Balance sheet
Medium	< 250	€50 million	€43 million
Small	< 50	€10 million	€10 million
Micro	< 10	€2 million	€2 million

TABLE 4.2 **US chemical manufacturing export activity (2013)**

Company size	Exporters	Manufacturing exporters	Total value ($ millions)	Manufacturing value ($ millions)
1 to 19	3,584	1,035	1,194	213
20 to 99	2,556	1,336	1,767	994
100 to 499	1,368	902	3,630	3,009
500 or more	1,219	786	42,482	27,762
N/A	2,712	690	3,134	1,949
Total	11,439	4,749	52,207	33,928

This progressive-fee structure could make the costs associated with REACH less of a competitive burden on small and medium-sized firms, but in practice, the costs associated with REACH are much closer to a fixed cost per product. ECHA registration fees only represent a portion of the overall costs of satisfying the registration requirements in REACH, and much of the costs come from hiring consultants to register the products. The 2013 REACH in Review report funded by the EU Commission found that "REACH is considered one of the most burdensome EU regulations for SMEs, despite the fact that not all of its provisions are yet applicable to a large number of companies who did not yet have to register their substances" (Prokes 2015). Using a firm survey, the commission asked companies that produce, import, or use chemicals about their experiences under REACH. In particular, firms were asked to estimate the costs of REACH, including hiring consultants and paying fines, as well as the direct costs of registration. The survey found that costs were significantly higher for large firms, amounting to an average cost of €3 million, where SMEs paid an average of €112,000. However, these costs are not properly calculated on a per-firm basis, as some firms produce many different products. Figure 4.1 displays the average costs when calculated on a per-tonnage-band and per-substance basis. The report estimates that SMEs paid an average of €86,000 per product produced over 1,000 tonnes, and large firms paid an average of €80,000; overall the costs levels are similar for both large and small firms.

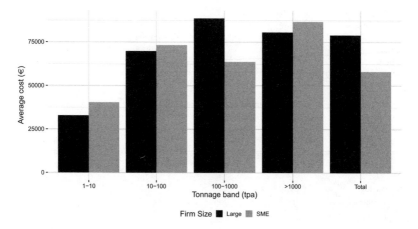

FIGURE 4.1. Per product and firm cost of REACH, calculated by Prokes (2015)

The overall effect of the tiered structure of REACH is to initially impose the same costs on small and large firms, which would have a negative impact on the majority of businesses in Europe (Vogel 2012). However, the EU offers a number of programs to help small European firms, and so it is not clear that the sticker price reflects the actual competitive effect of the program. In the commission review, most surveyed European firms (85 percent) reported that REACH had no impact on their competitive condition, but among those that did report a competitive effect, small firms were more likely than large firms to report a positive effect on their competitive position vis-à-vis firms outside the EU (46.8 percent to 31.5 percent).[11] While this effect is primarily driven by the medium-sized firms, the result is consistent with the second stated goal of REACH—to promote the competitiveness of the European chemical industry.

4.1.2. Consultations and the Costs of REACH

Given that REACH imposed fixed costs (on the order of €50,000 per product), we would expect its effects to be borne most heavily by small firms—in particular, small non-European firms that lack access to EU-specific financial and procedural aid. Lobbying activity suggests that these companies indeed have remained constant opponents of REACH, even years after its adoption. As late as 2009, the Society of the Plastics Industry (SPI), an industry group that represents companies primarily in the United States, lobbied the Office of the US Trade Representative (USTR) to take action against the measure.[12] SPI argued that REACH is only designed to enhance the "competitiveness and innovation" of the EU chemical industry rather than being necessary to promote health. To fight the measure, SPI asked the USTR to find that REACH violates not only WTO rules but also the Agreement on Technical Barriers to Trade and the Agreement on the Sanitary and Phytosanitary Measures (SBS Agreement). Going beyond trade law, the SPI further argues that the regulations violate international investment law, as "REACH's data-sharing obligations constitute an unlawful public taking without just compensation" (Pratt 2009).

Large firms, however, have taken a more nuanced approach to REACH, initially opposing it, but not on all points. The target of concern for large firms was the proposed sanction for violating the terms of the regulation. The 1,000-page draft distributed by the commission for comment called for civil and criminal penalties for noncompliance—the penalty was to be "effective, proportionate and dissuasive."[13] In particular, the fine was to not exceed 10 percent of the annual worldwide turnover of the offender, but that it would be increased if the company was a leader or instigator of violations, if the company gained "significant profit," or if the company gained increased market share as a result of the offense. For long-standing violations, the penalty was to increase an additional 10 percentage points per year of violation. These penalties, drawn from practices in antitrust law in the EU, were likely a response to research that found previous chemical regulations had "limited deterrent effect."[14] Annual worldwide turnover accounts for nonchemical sales outside of Europe, inflating the fine, and would have a disproportionate impact on violations by the largest global companies, akin to a marginal cost rather than a fixed cost.

After distributing the draft proposal, the commission began collecting contributions from stakeholders, receiving submissions from 1,135 individual firms, 469 industry associations, 18 national governments, 53 local and regional government bodies, 245 nongovernmental organizations, and 667 assorted individuals and associations. Each submission was assigned a number and the contributor's self-described country of origin. Figure 4.2 displays the country-level distribution of industry associations, showing that the majority of contributions were provided by Germany and EU-wide industry associations. The largest foreign presence is from US industry associations, ranging from the Pressure Sensitive Tape Council and the Soap and Detergent Association to the American Chemistry Council, which submitted a 98-page comment.

In absolute terms, the United States, one of the largest affected parties, falls behind Belgium in the number of associations participating in the EU process. Even more disproportionate is the number of individual firms represented within Europe versus outside. Among the 1,135 individual firms that submitted a contribution, only 23 list their country of origin as outside the scope of REACH. Figure 4.3 displays the relative share of contributions provided by associations, by country. The highlighted countries are outside of the jurisdiction of REACH and are primarily represented by associations. It appears, on its face, that there is little activity among foreign firms.

However, beneath the absence of explicitly foreign interests is the presence of multinational corporations and their affiliates. In a world of global production, relying on the self-described country of origin

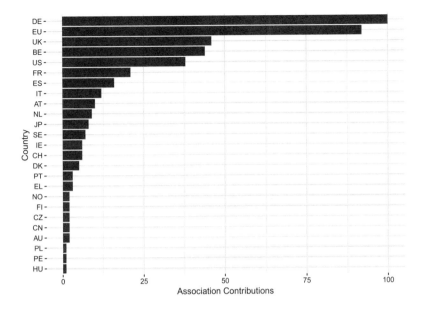

FIGURE 4.2. Industry association contributions by country (2003 Draft of REACH)

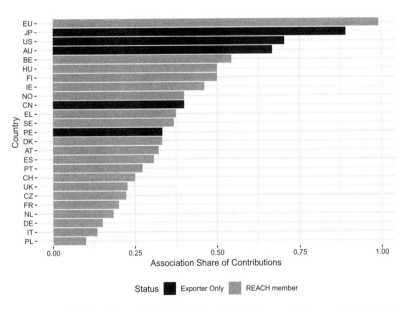

FIGURE 4.3. Relative share of individual firm to industry association contributions by country (2003 Draft of REACH)

is misleading. The 16 US-based firms that submitted a comment on REACH are just those American firms that lack European affiliates or whose international headquarters are in the United States. The largest American firms are multinationals and can submit their contributions locally. In fact, 17 of the 50 largest US-based chemical companies listed the address of their EU-based subsidiary rather than their American headquarters.[15] For example, Dow Chemical chose to use its Swiss affiliate, DuPont and Exxon Mobil their Belgian affiliates, Rohm and Haas its French affiliate, and Grace and Ford Motor their German affiliates. Among the 16 companies that listed a US location, only 2 are among the top 50 US chemical manufacturers: Honeywell International and the FMC Corporation.

The fact that any company, let alone a foreign one, was willing to lobby on their own suggests a special interest in the regulations not shared by the rest of the industry (Bombardini and Trebbi 2012). In the following section, I examine the effects of these foreign interests on the politics of REACH.

4.1.3. The Effects of Foreign Firm Representation on REACH

American chemical companies did not limit themselves to participating in the formal consultation process. Following the distribution of the REACH white paper, industry members lobbied both on their own and through their home governments, including through the US Department of State. The result was that in 2002, 2003, and 2004, US secretary of state Colin Powell sent cables to 36 US diplomatic posts in nations outside the European Union to "raise the EU chemicals policy with relevant government officials" to build an international coalition.[16] While the draft proposal had a progressive fine that could deter violation of the agreement by the largest companies, the adopted version of REACH does not include any reference to a specific penalty. Instead, the legislation has a section that only notes that "the experience of [the EUREX study] CLEEN points to the need to harmonize to some degree the sanctions imposed, taking account the need for subsidiarity."[17] This left the details up to the EU member states and, because no government chose to link fines to global sales, had the effect of limiting REACH's restrictions.

These efforts, both direct and indirect, were broadly considered successful and created a backlash among environmental groups in Europe, including those in the European political process. In addition to the changes in enforcement, environmental groups opposed the removal of provisions that would have compelled the substitution of less toxic alternatives where available and the exemption of certain polymers from registration and would have lowered the requirements for chemicals in downstream products. As one group put it, REACH is like a house with a strong foundation that has just been burglarized.[18] The European Parliamentary Party the Greens (GEU/NGL) generally favor stricter chemical regulations but found themselves opposed to REACH in its amended form. The parliamentary vote, displayed in table 4.3, split the Greens from the European United Left, two parties that generally overlap on the left-right economic dimension of politics.[19] After passage, one European parliamentarian complained that REACH is "a big Christmas present to the chemical industry."[20] REACH ended up passing with support across Europe, as displayed in figure 4.4.

While the environmental activists in Europe and the United States are quick to point to the nefarious pressure of US chemical manufacturers, many of the changes in REACH occurred after a shift in EU economic policy under the European Council presidency of Italian prime minister Silvio Berlusconi. After taking charge of the council presidency in July of 2003, REACH was transferred from the ministers of environment to the Competitiveness Council, with the goal that any EU legislation would not be a handicap to EU competitiveness and that the commission would address the needs of specific industrial sectors. Rather than a purely environmental initiative, REACH became an explicit part of Europe's overall industrial policy.

After these changes, the largest US chemical companies became

TABLE 4.3 **REACH final EU parliamentary vote (2005)**

Party	In favor	Against	Percent in favor
Independence/Democracy (IND/DEM)	0	10	0
Greens—European Free Alliance (Greens/EFA)	4	28	11
Non-Inscrits	3	20	0.12
European People's Party—European Democrats (PPE-DE)	129	77	59
Union for Europe of the Nations (UEN)	20	9	61
Alliance of Liberals and Democrats (ALDE)	54	1	79
European United Left/Nordic Green Left (GUE/NGL)	29	3	88
Party of European Socialists (PSE)	159	0	100

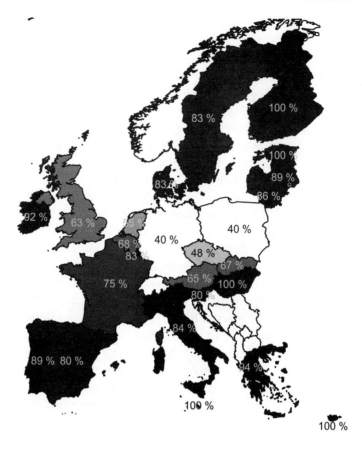

FIGURE 4.4. Percentage support for REACH across EU-member delegations

vocal supporters of the REACH legislation. Dow Chemical, which dropped its SPI affiliation in 1999, claims on its website that "since Dow has always made product safety a top priority, compliance with REACH is directly in line with [their] 2025 Sustainability Goals."[21] This is not a case of sour grapes, as Dow and these other companies have considerable opportunity to influence regulatory outcomes even after regulations are passed. BASF, the largest chemical company in the world and an SPI member, called for full REACH implementation as early as 2006.

BASF voluntarily committed to going beyond the REACH reporting requirements for all of their chemical products, joining other industrial leaders (Westervelt 2007).[22]

The end result was that BASF and Dow Chemical could voice support while the costs remained prohibitive for smaller firms in the rest of the industry. Broadly, interviews by an industry trade magazine of senior executives at 15 major multinational chemical companies revealed in 2009 that "over the next five years, companies believe[d] that regulatory compliance [would] advance from a relatively small cost of doing business to a major driver of competitive advantage" (Deise 2009).[23] Meanwhile, smaller firms, particularly in North America, were expected to suffer significant business disruptions (Scott 2008). When asked to comment on the interests of the US chemical industry with regards to REACH, an anonymous senior lobbyist for a large US chemical firm argued, "The nuanced view [of large firms toward REACH] stems from the fact that REACH often works to the advantage of large companies who have the resources to establish and run compliance programs. Smaller companies must often go outside and pay for the resources to comply. Ironically, REACH has succeeded in doing what the anti-trust laws were designed to prevent—giving a competitive advantage to large companies."[24]

This statement is corroborated by the experiences of smaller companies. According to 2012 congressional testimony offered by the president and CEO of a small chemical company based in Albany, Georgia, the effects of REACH include significant barriers to entry, preventing some companies from launching and, even upon launching, slowing down innovation. The CEO claimed that his company is "currently in the process of launching several industry changing products in the EU, and our launch will take many months longer than it would have otherwise."[25] In 2010, 86 percent of REACH registrations were submitted by large companies rather than small and medium enterprises; by 2013, that percentage was still as high as 80 percent.[26] As one BASF executive put it, "The costs are high [but] I think at the end, it is worth the money."[27]

These anecdotal statements are also supported by contemporaneous surveys of firms. In 2005, Karl-Oskar Lindgren and Thomas Persson (2008) commissioned an expert survey on REACH, aiming to determine the relevant cleavages over the new chemical regulation. The 651 respondents range from parliamentarians and academics to private business representatives and activists. That research finds that industry and environmental interests report opposite positions on REACH-related issues, with advocates for consumers, workers, and health interests arrayed between these two poles. The authors conclude that REACH reflects a general divide for and against regulation, with consumers and industry opposed to activists that support REACH.

Reexamining that survey, however, reveals significant variation within industry. Dividing the respondents into those that identify themselves as having worked for a large firm, for an industry association, or outside the chemical industry, we see significant divides over REACH. Given the proposition "When a safer chemical or technology is available at a reasonable cost, chemical producers and users should be required to adopt safer alternatives," responses varied significantly, as displayed in figure 4.5. Respondents who worked for a large chemical firm report an average of 4.5 on a 7-point scale, somewhere between neutral and weak support for a requirement—the same preference as that given by "consumer interest" advocates. Respondents that were part of an industry association at the time of REACH report overall opposition, a 3.8 on the 7-point scale.[28]

Years after the implementation of REACH, industry remains divided. Rather than a "Christmas present" to the chemical industry, REACH appears to balance competing interests within it: large multinationals benefit from its removal of size-based fines; smaller firms benefit from financial assistance and from a progressive-fee structure and financial assistance. Unrepresented in this process, and opposed from the beginning, are the smaller foreign companies. Drawing this conclusion from survey data or contributions from industry depends on company

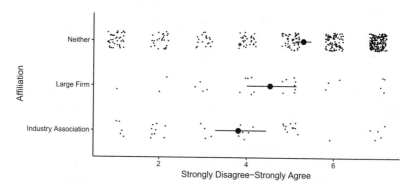

FIGURE 4.5. Survey preference for requirement to adopt safer alternatives

participation in the process. Besides the possibility of ignorance or dissembling that can interfere with survey-based measurements, the main consequence of an entry barrier is to eliminate actors from the marketplace. If the regulation drives out members of the industry, the effect changes the makeup of the industry, and for small and medium-sized firms, survival is at stake. In the next section, I address some of the limitations of the survey and self-reports by using chemical patent filings. These data show that REACH has had a significant impact on the entry of chemical companies into the European market.

4.2. REACH and European Chemical Patents

Before selling a new chemical product, firms will invariably seek a patent to allocate rights and rents to the owners of the intellectual property.[29] Obtaining a patent can help avoid losing the rights and is a precondition for licensing production. As one chemical producer put it, "If we think that we can get a patent granted on a new product, we will first apply for a patent, before disclosing anything in order not to lose any patent rights. We always have to think about patents first when registering a new or—in the REACH language—non-phase-in substance."[30] As a result, patents offer a measure of market entry for all kinds of chemical firms into the European market; foreign exporters, multinationals, and domestic producers alike have to file a patent if they hope to sell in it. At the same time, patents are expensive and time-consuming and can take up to a year to be approved—and so firms would be unlikely to file a patent in Europe unless they expected to sell in that market. Here, I describe patents as a forward-looking accounting of innovation and entry at the product and firm level, which will reflect any entry-deterrent effect of REACH.

4.2.1. Measuring Entry with Patents

Data on patents are available in a number of private and public depositories, with varying scope. One of the largest and most comprehensive is the Derwent World Patents Index, collected by Thompson Reuters. This database is organized around basic patents, collecting subsequent patents around a record of the first publication of an invention. Each patent record includes the inventor, the patent number, the assignee, and a patent classification code, which identifies the subject of the patent. I restrict all analysis to international patent classifications for chemicals: C01—inorganic chemistry, C07—organic chemistry and C08—organic macromolecular compounds. This microlevel data reveals both the concentration and the dynamics of the chemical industry at the level of the applicant. Patent records are aggregated at the level of the applicant. In 2002, for example, the European Patent Office recorded 78,377 patents from 38,667 applicants, ranging from individuals and university researchers with one patent record to large multinational corporations with hundreds of patent records per year.[31]

REACH raises the costs for each new product, which could shift patents toward the largest and most productive firms. However, patent records can reflect a change in either the number of products submitted by each applicant or the total number of applicants seeking patents. The former corresponds to the expected advantage of top applicants, with a larger share of products being introduced by the largest firms. The latter corresponds to the size of the chemical patents sector and would be most affected by a drop of applications to zero—generally by applicants with little to no regular patent activity, often individuals. For example, researchers have found that immediately following the ban on certain soft-plastic children's toys under REACH, patents for alternatives rose from one or two a year to between 15 and 20 patents per year, suggesting a higher incentive for innovation following the regulation, which could attract entrants (Tuncak 2014). However, these 15 to 20 new patents were filed primarily by the top producers—Exxon Mobil, Eastman, and Dow Chemical—rather than representing a rise in the number of total participants in the industry. Even if REACH did bring new products into the market to replace dangerous chemicals, each additional product would have to be registered, giving the top firms a market advantage.

The number of unique patent assignees dropped during the period of REACH, with fewer new patent assignees after its adoption and implementation. Figure 4.6 displays the unique patent assignments in each year in the European Patent Office, as well as the persistent participation of these assignees. The height of each bar represents the total number of unique patent assignees in each year, indicating an overall decline in patent participation following a peak in 2003, the year REACH was officially adopted. The total number of unique patent applicants appears to drop between 2003 and 2012, with a slight uptick in 2008 and 2009. The top shaded portion of each bar represents the share of patents given

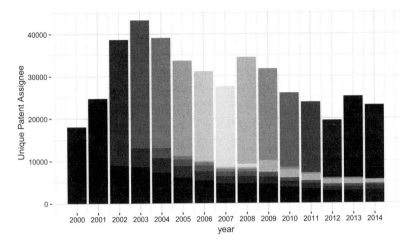

FIGURE 4.6. Entry and persistence of patent assignees, 2000–2014 (Derwent World Patents Index)

to new applicants—that is, applicants that did not appear in previous years. For example, the darkest block indicates the share of yearly patents given to assignees of patents in 2000. These assignees account for more than 10 percent of patents 14 years later. As the time period continues, we observe a divergence between short-run—one or two years of patent participation—and long-run companies, those that participate every year across the decade.

The aggregate patterns of patent activity in the European Patent Office is likely a function of both regulatory and market forces. The fact that the number of chemical patenting organizations goes down in Europe could reflect changes in the global market for chemicals, the rise of third markets such as China, or economic shocks to the industry. In order to isolate the regulatory effects, the following section examines the concentration of patent activity in a comparative context, using Japan Patent Office data from the same source, sector, and period.

4.2.2. Comparison of the EU and Japan

Japan is one of the largest chemical markets in the world, and relatively independent of the European market. Although two-way trade between the EU and Japan is over $12 billion a year and the EU accounts for 37 percent of Japanese chemical imports, it is only a small portion of

Japan's total chemical output, which exceeded $300 billion in 2016.[32] Figure 4.7A displays the Derwent World Patents Index for both the European Patent Office (EPO) and the Japan Patent Office (JPO). The dashed lines represent the chronology of REACH: the official adoption by the European Commission, the first implementation of the rules, and the final deadline for registration of most products. The overall pattern of patents contrasts to that in Japan; while EPO patents drop from 2003 to 2014, patents from the JPO remain flat.

Figure 4.7B displays the time series variation in the concentration of patents in the chemical sector by year and patent office. The figure displays the share of patents accounted for by the top 10 patent assignees in each year. The trend is declining or flat in the EPO until after the adoption of REACH and then continues on an upward trajectory through the period. During the same period, there does not appear to be a similar increase in concentration in the JPO. A similar pattern is evident among the top 25 patent assignees.

The increase in concentration among European patents is broadly consistent with registration patterns of chemical products in REACH. As of mid-2016, more than 40,000 companies have filed more than 9,000 substances, but 93 percent of substances are registered by large companies.[33] However, these data do not reveal the effects of the policy on US market concentration. If this measure is a regulatory barrier to trade, we would expect the same pattern of concentration to occur among exporters to the EU, which requires identifying patent assignees by their country of origin.

4.3. The Effect of REACH on US Affiliates

In order to identify the effects of REACH on industrial concentration in the United States, it is necessary to identify those US companies that are engaged in the European market. Neither firm-level trade flows nor foreign investments would reflect this business, as firms can engage in the European market either by producing at arm's length, with an affiliate, or by export. Instead, I again turn to the patent data, which would cover many of these relationships.

Each patent record is assigned to a company, but those companies are only identified by a name, such as BASF, W. R. Grace, or Huntsman Corporation. Given complications of assigning countries of origin

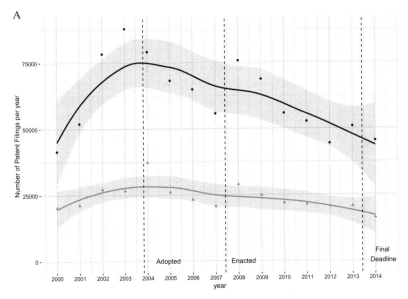

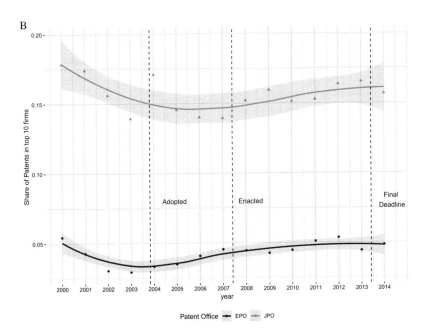

FIGURE 4.7. Analysis of Derwent World Patents Index. (A) Total patents from EU and Japan 2000–2014; (B) Patents among top 10 assignees from EU and Japan 2002–14

to global firms, I focus on US companies and, in particular, those listed as being in the top 50 in sales by the American Chemical Society. These 50 companies are large enough to be assigned a unique four-character label in the Derwent Patent Index, and given those codes, their patents can be classified as originating in the United States. The matching companies are listed in figure 4.8A, with their rank within the United States in terms of sales and their rank in terms of access to Europe. While the top 10 US companies are also heavily invested in European patents, the Occidental Chemical Corporation stands out as underrepresented in the European patent data. This lack of patent activity reflects an absence of participation in REACH: Occidental Chemicals registered 9 products during REACH's implementation, as opposed to the next largest US manufacturer, Honeywell, which registered 82 products. Another apparent outlier is Momentive Performance Materials (MPMI), which ranks below the top 38 companies in the United States but registered 99 substances in REACH. Closer examination of the records reveals that this company was formed in 2006 as a rebranding of General Electric Silicone after its sale from General Electric.

Examining the changes in patent activity over the course of the implementation of REACH, figure 4.8B shows that the total share of patents is generally stable, indicating that at least for the top 50 American firms of 2004, the effect of REACH was not to substantially drive down US patent activity relative to that of Europe.[34] Instead, the share of patents appears to be constant throughout the period. Unfortunately, this share statistic is relative to smaller American companies as well as large and small European companies. The question is whether the top producers gained an advantage over their smaller national competitors.

The increased dispersion among major chemical companies following REACH highlights the individualized advantages of regulatory protection, advantages that would be obscured in aggregated analyses of whole industries. Focusing only on patents assigned to the top 50 US chemical companies, figure 4.9 displays the share of the top 10 US companies (in terms of US sales) over the remaining 40. The top 10 companies listed 2 times as many patents as the remaining 40 US company patents prior to REACH coming into full effect in late 2007. In the years following REACH, the filings of the top 10 firms rose to 2.3 times the patent activity of the remaining 40 firms.[35] This change in concentration among American firms is consistent with the larger firms' statements of support for REACH and the continued opposition among the lower ranked firms.

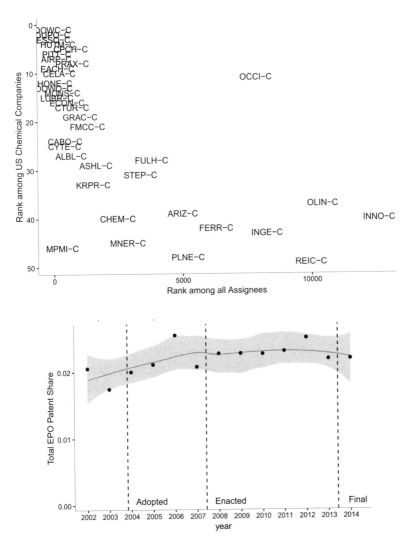

FIGURE 4.8. Rank of top 50 US chemical companies in EPO patent assignments (2004)

The patent data show that the EU REACH program concentrated economic activity among the largest firms by shifting market share away from smaller, presumably less productive firms. Unlike aggregate trade or investment flows, these data cover licensing agreements, exports, and wholly owned subsidiary sales, capturing the variety of forms of global production.

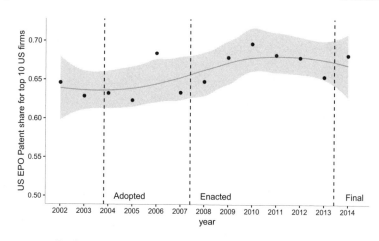

FIGURE 4.9. Rank of top 10 US chemical companies in EPO patent assignments (2004)

4.4. Discussion

The EU REACH program began with an effort to enable regulators to trace chemicals across the supply chain. The complexity of these production processes meant that regulators needed to rely on businesses to handle the reporting, testing, and labeling of their products. The theory of regulatory protection developed in chapter 2 predicts that these regulatory changes would be embraced by the largest firms, including those whose operations span national boundaries. Drawing on evidence from firm and industry group lobbying activity, statements from employees and representatives of firms, and the economic trends in the chemical industry, we see that firms were aware of and acted on their competitive interests. Large American firms opposed aspects of the regulations that raise variable costs but pushed for strict standards when those costs would not vary with company size. The outcome was to advantage large global manufacturers and disadvantage their smaller competitors.

While we see clear evidence of the interests of firms, the ability of those firms to exert political power and gain favorable policies depended on political opportunities. If not for a discovery of the dangers of phthalates in children's toys, it is unlikely that the chemical industry would have been targeted for an overhaul. If not for the European Council presidency of Italian prime minister Silvio Berlusconi, REACH would have been negotiated by the ministers of environment rather than the

Competitiveness Council. Perhaps a unification of European chemical rules was inevitable, and perhaps the exclusion of small American firms from the process was as well, but the timing and sequence of events depended on not only international structural factors but also local context and institutions.

The REACH case highlights one of the problems associated with extending the current tariff-based trade regime to regulatory politics. Despite significant barriers for producers both at home and abroad, REACH did not substantially reduce the overall volume of chemicals sold in Europe: European chemical sales rose from €428 billion in 2003 to €519 billion in 2015, and extra-EU imports rose from €54 billion to €90 billion. Instead, the composition of trade changed, concentrating a larger share of business in the hands of large, trade-oriented manufacturers. In 1995, a little more than half of chemical sales were domestic, but by 2015, that share had dropped to 15 percent.[36] Smaller firms—those that cannot cover the additional costs of the regulations—are the ones that lose out in this process.

All of this leaves us with a puzzle: if REACH is so costly to small firms, how was it that it could pass with the majority support of the center-right EPP, the neoliberal ALDE, and unanimous support from the Socialist Party? Europe has generous financial support systems for small and medium-sized enterprises, but few governments are so situated to offer ex post subsidies. Without this support, should we expect regulatory protection to only pass in instances where domestic production is small or the state is rich enough to buy off local opposition? How is it that, in general, we should expect regulations to be a global problem if they require massive state support systems to be politically feasible? In the following chapter, I take up the case of a US regulation on food, showing how small domestic companies gain influence over the shape of regulatory protection.

CHAPTER FIVE

Regulatory Preferences in the Food Industry

Under this bill [the Food Safety Modernization Act], anybody who sells more than $500,000 worth of food—that is almost every Amish farmer in America—will have to have a detailed, laid-out plan, written down, double checked, cross checked and everything else. . . . All we are doing is raising the costs and making ourselves less competitive, decreasing the number of jobs that are available in this country, and not truly ensuring an increased level of safety with our food supply.—Senator Tom Coburn[1]

The No. 1 issue [the Schwan's Food Company] raised with me was passing this bill. Do you think Schwan's is a company that doesn't care about the bottom line?—Senator Amy Klobuchar[2]

When a government raises tariffs, there is little question as to the intended effect—increasing the local price of imported goods and raising revenue at the expense of foreign exporters. When a government enacts a "behind the border" regulation, we are more confident as to the effects than the intent. We have seen how regulatory measures close the market to entrants and raise prices at the expense of small foreign exporters and that these policies can also harm local firms. We saw in the European case that domestic firms will often find themselves just as unable to meet the higher standard, pay the licensing fees, or satisfy the registration requirements as foreign firms. We might expect that the politics of regulatory protection would thereby pit local and foreign small firms against global producers.[3] In this chapter, I show that this does not occur because domestic firms have political access that foreign firms lack. Domestic firms have a voice in decision-making; foreign operations lack this channel of influence. The ability to appeal to one's government, unavailable in the international system, allows firms to avoid, or at least limit, the costs of regulatory protection.

This chapter examines the development of the US food safety regime to show how political institutions can enable smaller domestic firms to challenge and alter regulatory measures. Examining the same dynamics of regulatory protection, where large and productive multinationals seek higher standards, I find that small local firms exert real influence. Small foreign firms, however, have little to no say over these matters. It is this lack of voice, the fact that political claims do not travel across borders, that drives the regulatory outcome. While classical accounts of regulatory capture depend on the details of internal political institutions, the degree of political competition (Rogowski 1987), the presence of veto players (Tsebelis 2002), or other institutional checks (North, Wallis, and Weingast 2009), in this case, policy is set inefficiently because of an international externality.

To examine the domestic channels of influence available to small firms, I trace the political cleavages over a historically significant regulatory change in the United States food market. In 2011, the US president signed a major food safety policy: the US Food Safety Modernization Act (FSMA). The FSMA is the first substantial change in food safety regulation in the US since 1938 and one of the signature legislative achievements of the 111th Congress. The goal of the law is to enable the government to monitor an increasingly complicated global food market, and it requires the registration of all food manufacturers and farmers that serve the American market, including those located abroad. Given the importance of the US market for foreign manufacturers, these requirements have raised concerns that the policy could act as a regulatory barrier to trade. In this chapter, I show that similar concerns were also raised by small domestic manufacturers but that the law was changed to satisfy those represented interests. In addition, global manufacturers were able to get concessions on issues of interest to them; however, smaller, less globalized firms lacked the necessary political access to do the same.

While long recognized as a trade issue, the food safety case establishes the utility of the regulatory protection framework. Domestic producers in the United States face less international competition from smaller firms, decreasing the incentive to raise entry barriers. Moreover, consumers are informed and active, making it difficult to distinguish authentic concerns about safety from protectionist interests. Finally, agricultural and food production is highly diffuse and segmented, with soybean farmers in Iowa having little direct stake in policies on oranges. My aim is to show that the interests of global industry players, as with the global chemical companies described in chapter 3, act at the expense of the interests of smaller foreign exporters whose interests are unrepresented in the rulemaking process. In this case, the large domestic sector of the United States enables small domestic firms to exert real leverage over regulatory outcomes. This leverage is a function of access to domestic political institutions that are unavailable to foreign firms, especially small foreign firms.

Unlike many regulatory barriers, the US food safety regime was developed in public debates and sequenced in a way that allows within-case analysis.[4] The FSMA was only one of several contemporaneous proposals to reform the US food safety system, allowing for the comparison of legislative votes and industry support across different levels of restrictiveness. Furthermore, the administrative side of the US regulatory process depends on public comments, opening a window into the interests and influence of firms beyond the testimony and lobbying statements in the legislature. The comments collected by the enacting agencies, such as the US Food and Drug Administration, reveal the strategies of firms toward the implementation of the law. This process reveals that industry influence does not stop once the votes are counted—between the signing of the law and its final rule, the government collected thousands of statements and comments by domestic and foreign firms and their industry associations and changed their proposals in response. Moreover, because the FSMA was deemed internationally significant, the US government solicited comments from the WTO Sanitary and Phytosanitary Committee's members, allowing comparison of firm interests and insight into the priorities of US trade partners.

By opening the regulatory process, it becomes clear that regulatory protection is not just an adverse side effect of governance. In the previous chapter, larger and more productive exporters benefited from the creation of regulatory barriers in the destination market. But just showing that firms are aware that regulation can increase profits is insufficient evidence for regulatory protection. The inference from gaining a policy advantage to being a cause of that policy could suffer from a *post hoc, ergo propter hoc* fallacy.[5] In this chapter, I collect a variety of evidence to compare the interests and influence of domestic and international competitive pressures. It is no accident that regulations are burdensome for one set of small firms but not another, and in fact, industry interests form an important voice in creating regulatory barriers.

In addition to examining the overall pressure facing legislators and rulemakers, public comments offer insight into the specific regulatory priorities of firms and their associations. Using machine learning text analysis methods, I classify the content of these comments, revealing patterns in the rulemaking strategies of firms, NGOs, associations, and governments. By estimating a structural topic model on the regulatory comments, we can discern not only the issues of concern from industry but how different segments within industry talk about those issues (Roberts et al. 2013, 2014). The structural topic model reveals a general quietism on the part of American industry about the domestic exemptions in the rulemaking process. By contrast, foreign representatives, particularly foreign trade associations, raise issues with the FSMA technical requirements and do so at a rate substantially higher than individual large and global firms. However, the topics raised by trade associations are not similarly brought up by foreign governments, who might be in a position to make demands under the Agreement on the Application of Sanitary and Phytosanitary Measures (SPS Agreement).

This chapter begins by describing the state of the food market and industry in the United States. Section 5.2 introduces the legal environment for food safety in the United States at the time of the FSMA. Using variation in the scope of food safety legislation, I show that representatives of districts or states with large-scale agriculture disfavor legislation exempting small producers. The second section turns to the regulatory process, using data from the public comment system to break down the interests of domestic and foreign firms and governments on a part of the FSMA that explicitly addressed the costs for small foreign businesses. The third section estimates a structural topic model on the body of public comments, finding significant division within the food-producing industry.

5.1. The US Food Industry

The United States is a postagricultural nation. In 1900, agriculture directly employed 40 percent of the US workforce. Today that number has dropped to 1.5 percent. This does not mean that the US is not still a major agriculture producer; the output of potatoes has increased by 60 percent from 1960, and the production of corn has more than tripled in that time.[6] Since 1900, the number of farms has fallen by 63 percent, but the average farm size has risen 67 percent (Dimitri, Effland, and Conklin 2005). Still, the US agricultural industry includes millions of both small and medium-sized farms.

Today, in addition to having one of the most productive agriculture industries in the world, the United States is a major global consumer. In 2016, the United States was the top destination market for food exporters in much the western hemisphere, as well as India and the Philippines. By virtue of its proximity and natural endowments, Mexico is the primary agricultural trade partner of the United States, with total agriculture exports to the United States reaching $23 billion in 2016. The leading categories of these exports are fresh vegetables ($5.6 billion) and fresh fruit ($4.9 billion), feeding into the substantial processing industry in the United States.[7] Not all of this trade originates in Mexico. For example, the United States is the world's largest producer of pecans, primarily in the south and southwestern parts of the country, and ships these nuts to Mexico for shelling and reexport back to US consumers.

Despite its integration in global and regional production networks today, the United States, as with other developed nations has a long track record of agricultural protectionism (Davis 2004).[8] At the United States' insistence, agriculture was exempted from the rules of the GATT, allowing quantitative import restrictions, export subsidies, and various supply controls (Goldstein 1993). Agricultural issues were perennial issues in GATT disputes and have long been a sticking point for multilateral negotiations.

The United States has also had a history of regulatory barriers to trade in the food sector. While in recent years, the United States has advocated against restrictions on beef hormones and genetically modified organisms, from 1960 to 1990, the United States was more restrictive than even Europe. David Vogel explains that fear of cancerous food additives among the American public and businesses' desires to assuage these concerns drove the United States to adopt stringent regulations on food (Vogel 2012). In Vogel's view, the ebb and flow of regulatory stringency are connected to public concerns over safety, and while businesses can push for regulation, they do so more to integrate markets than to divide them. Businesses, on this account, merely seek to ensure that all markets are as regulated as the largest sector of the market—for instance matching California's preferred level of protection.

Even as consumer pressures have waned, the United States has proceeded apace with regulatory barriers on agriculture and food markets. Since the advent of the WTO, member states have raised 30 separate specific trade concerns against the United States in the committee for the SPS Agreement. These governments allege that US regulations are unnecessarily and adversely affecting trade in ways contrary to the obligations of the WTO system. In the following, I examine one of these alleged regulatory barriers, the Food Safety Modernization Act, and show that the new food safety regime was primarily caused not by a shift in consumer risk preferences or even by firms seeking to shift standards to lower barriers. Instead, the key parts of the stringent regulation were designed to exclude smaller foreign firms from the domestic market.

5.2. Food Safety Legislation in the United States

Food safety is maintained in the United States through a morass of federal, state, and local rules. At the federal level, the Food and Drug Administration (FDA), under the US Department of Health and Human Services, and the Food Safety and Inspection Service (FSIS), part of the US Department of Agriculture (USDA), split responsibilities for inspecting and managing the food supply. The FDA regulates 80 to 90 percent of the $1 trillion of imported and domestic food purchased each year, leaving the bulk of the remainder—mostly meat—to the USDA.[9] The split was created in 1940, when the FDA spun off from the USDA. The result is that the USDA's FSIS has a smaller mandate and a larger budget and staff than the FDA ($1.168 billion compared to $783 million in FY2010). Today, the FSIS is able to inspect all meat and poultry on a continuous basis, but the FDA is severely limited in its capacity (Johnson 2010). This means that frozen pepperoni pizza has ingredients that will be inspected three times while a cheese pizza produced at the same facility will probably not be inspected.

The marasmus of the FDA has a disproportional effect on import inspections. The United States imported $110 billion worth of food, feed, and beverages from more than 150 countries in 2011, accounting for 15 percent of the US diet. This ratio is higher in several sensitive sectors, with imports accounting for half of US consumption of fresh fruits. Of the 11 million imported food shipments, the FDA inspected 207,839, about 2 percent (FDA 2013). Domestically, about half of facilities experience inspections at a rate lower than once every five years; for foreign firms, this rate is many times lower. For context, the median survival of US businesses is five years, meaning that the majority of food processors will never see an FDA official.

The FDA continued to operate under the authority established in the 1940s for the remainder of the century—until global events intervened. One week after the September 11, 2001, terrorist attacks, a series of letters containing anthrax spores arrived by post to news and government facilities, including two US Senate offices. This attack killed five people and shut down mail rooms and offices across the country. In the aftermath of the attack, Congress (nearly unanimously) passed the Bioterrorism Preparedness Act of 2002.[10] The Bioterrorism Act improved the Centers for Disease Control response and training, established a national stockpile of countermeasures, and gave more authority to the FDA to protect the food supply (Redhead and Vogt 2002).[11] Under the act, all foreign and domestic facilities (excluding farms) that manufacture, process, and handle food are required to register with the FDA, and the FDA must be given advance notice (at least a few hours) of imported food shipments.[12] At passage, the FDA expected to register 420,000 food facilities worldwide.

The FDA bioterrorism registration program was hampered by lack of resources and the absence of legal authority. In 2008, tainted peanuts caused a salmonella outbreak that killed 9 people. In the subsequent investigation, the FDA found that its agents from the Georgia Department of Agriculture had been blocked from accessing 12 positive tests "lying in the files in the filing cabinet of the Peanut Corporation of America" in the year and a half leading up to the outbreak (United States 2009b). Even after an outbreak, food companies could refuse to disclose records to inspectors unless the FDA had a reasonable belief the food was adulterated or presented a risk of serious adverse health consequences or death. While the peanut-caused outbreak was only a small portion of approximately 325,000 hospitalizations and 5,000 deaths in the United States that occur each year, the fact that the FDA was stymied in the face of criminal negligence became a domestic political issue. As one senator put it, "The powers the agency was given 100 years ago were appropriate for a world in which most of our food was grown and processed domestically. That is no longer the case, and FDA's tools need to keep pace with the challenges" (United States 2009a).

Mounting political pressure allowed several legislative initiatives on food safety to reach the Senate clerk and the House hopper. Initiatives ranged from proposals to limit the overlap in authority between the FDA and the USDA to a full-scale reworking of the US food safety system. Two bills, one in each chamber, received bipartisan support in the 111th Congress: House of Representatives (H.R.) bill 2749, the Food Safety Enhancement Act, and Senate (S.) bill 510, the Food Safety Modernization Act. The House bill passed easily, 283 to 142, and was hailed by President Obama (2009) as a major step forward.

The Senate bill, S. 510, enjoyed similar levels of support initially, but the legislative process brought changes that highlight the political conflicts within the agricultural and food manufacturing industries. The bill was proposed by Senator Richard Durbin, then the majority whip, and referred to the Senate Committee on Health, Education, Labor and Pensions, chaired by Senator Edward Kennedy, accruing more than a dozen cosponsors. By the time the bill came out of committee and hit the Senate floor, however, it lost the votes of several cosponsors. The source of the controversy stems from a broader fight between advocates for small producers and a coalition of big agricultural interests and consumer groups.

5.2.1. Domestic Industry and the Tester-Hagan Amendment

In spring of 2010, Senator Jon Tester, the only organic farmer in the Senate, issued a press release announcing two amendments to S. 510 to exempt smaller producers. Under the amended rules, a producer would qualify as "small" if the facility has an average adjusted gross income of less than $500,000 for the previous three years. This amendment was then reworked by Senator Kay Hagen to additionally carve out "very small" businesses in which the majority of sales are to customers within 400 miles or within state lines. The amalgamated Tester-Hagan amendment was immediately popular among small farm advocates and received support from a number of consumer associations. At the same time, the proposal was opposed by the largest industry and consumer groups.[13]

The 2010 midterm elections brought historic losses for the Democratic Party. The Republicans took the House and six seats in the Senate. Under pressure to pass the bill in the remaining months of the 111th

Congress, the Senate bill was submitted for a cloture vote, including the amendment as a provision for "flexibility for small businesses," to be defined by the secretary of Health and Human Services. In response to this provision, four of the bill's cosponsors, senators Chambliss (R-GA), Hatch (R-UT), Isakson (R-GA), and Nelson (D-NE) voted against the motion to invoke cloture. In explaining their new opposition, the senators argued that such flexibility would undermine safety by exempting potentially dangerous businesses and the amendment would fail in its purpose of limiting economic damage. As Senator Saxby Chambliss put it, "It doesn't take many bales to reach $500,000 in gross receipts from the sale of cotton, and that doesn't count peanuts and wheat and corn and whatever else may go along with it."[14] However, Chambliss was not opposed to the amendment because the threshold was too low but rather because it was excessively permissive.

During the floor debate on S. 510, Senator Chambliss submitted a letter from 31 large producer organizations and national agricultural groups.[15] These 31 industry groups, listed in the top section of table 5.1, are primarily large umbrella organizations, such as the Produce Marketing Association, and regional food producers, such as the Idaho Potato Commission. The letter urged support for the Food Safety Modernization Act and opposition to any amendment, including the Tester-Hagan provisions. The letter argued that the safety of the nation's food supply is "the highest industry priority," which would be undermined by the exemptions for small business. Besides opposition to explicit size and proximity criteria of Tester-Hagan, the letter also opposed exemptions that would indirectly favor smaller producers by privileging certain growing practices that have high marginal costs—such as organic farming practices. Instead, the letter called for "technical assistance, training, extended transition time-frames for compliance, and financial support."[16]

A cloture vote gives the Senate 30 hours to debate the bill. In that time, the Tester-Hagan amendment was partially modified and added to the bill (S. Amendment 4715). In order to mollify the opposing industry demands for stricter standards, the amendment tightened the qualifications for exemption. Only facilities with more than half of their sales within 275 miles (or state lines) would qualify as very small businesses, rather than the original 400 miles. After the modification, the legislators received another letter, this time without the meat, dairy, and poultry associations. The remaining opponents, listed in bold and italics in table 5.1, were those companies that felt most exposed to the exemptions, and left

TABLE 5.1 **Industry opposition to Tester-Hagan amendment**

Groups opposing 400-mile exemption

American Feed Industry Assoc.	National Grain and Feed Assoc.
American Frozen Food Institute	National Meat Assoc.
American Fruit and Vegetable Processors and	National Milk Producers Federation
Growers Coalition	National Oilseed Processors Assoc.
American Meat Institute	National Pork Producers Council
Corn Refiners Assoc.	National Turkey Federation
International Dairy Foods Assoc.	Pet Food Institute
National Council of Farmer Cooperatives	Shelf-Stable Food Processors Assoc.
National Chicken Council	United Egg Producers
National Farmers Union	Western Growers Assoc.

Groups opposing 250-mile exemption

American Mushroom Institute	**National Potato Council**
California Grape and Tree Fruit League	**National Watermelon Assoc.**
Florida Tomato Exchange	**Produce Marketing Assoc.**
Fresh Produce Assoc. of the Americas	**Texas Produce Assoc.**
Georgia Fruit and Vegetable Growers Assoc.	**United Fresh Produce Assoc.**
Idaho Potato Commission	**US Apple Assoc.**
California Strawberry Commission	*Idaho Grower-Shipper Assoc.*
Florida Fruit and Vegetable Assoc.	*Washington State Potato Commission*
New York Apple Assoc.	*Northwest Horticultural Council*

alone, they turned to harsher rhetoric. They wrote, "Comments from Senator Tester and supporters are now making it abundantly clear that their cause is not to argue that small farms pose less risk, but to wage an ideological war against the vast majority of American farmers that seeks to feed 300 million Americans. We are appalled at statements by Senator Tester reported today in the Capital Press that 'Small producers are not raising a commodity, but are raising food. Industrial agriculture,' he said, 'takes the people out of the equation.'" The produce groups demanded a conference vote to eliminate the Tester exemptions and a complete reversal in policy. However, a second cloture vote passed the three-fifths requirement, losing only one vote in the process.[17] After final passage on December 20, the Senate bill was substituted into H.R. 2751, originally a bill on fuel standards, to ensure that the bill could avoid a conference vote and risk having the debate spill into the next legislative session.[18]

The House approved the substitution of the Senate bill S. 510 into a preexisting legislative vehicle on a vote of 215 to 144. During the one hour of debate allowed on the bill, some House members who had previously supported passage of the House version of the bill now voiced opposition. They were particularly displeased with the Senate, arguing that "by allowing facilities exemptions . . . the Tester amendment will set up a system full of weak links" making the new bill "a step backwards."[19] Beyond concerns over the hodgepodge of domestic standards and the potential to confuse consumers, opponents worried that the exemption would not only apply to American firms. As one member of the House argued, "We will be required to exempt similarly sized companies in developing countries from our standards."[20] As the chairman of the Committee on Energy and Commerce put it, "Republicans are saying we should reject the whole bill because of the Tester amendment. . . . Now, I would assume that some big operations don't like the fact that small ones are going to be exempt. They are only exempt from a couple of the provisions which Senator Tester and the Senate Members thought were too burdensome. And some of these small operations are limited in their income, and therefore it might be too burdensome for them."[21]

These floor statements make it clear what is at stake. Unlike the original House bill (H.R. 2749), the Senate bill's exemptions put the larger operators at risk, not only by exempting small domestic competition, but by raising the possibility that foreign firms would be exempt as well. The key debate in the legislature was over the size threshold for exemption to the food safety regulation, corresponding directly to the principal parameter of the model in chapter 2: namely, the productivity of each firm relative to their competitors.

The floor statements in the preceding paragraphs tell a story of regulatory protection that reverses the typical regulatory lines—Republicans claiming that the bill would undermine safety and Democrats arguing in favor of an exemption to support small business. However, these quotes are provided by a small set of legislators. In the following, I relate the roll call votes on the House and Senate versions of the bill to measure the conflict between big and small producers on the one hand and traditional concerns about international competition or ideology on the other.

5.2.2. The Census of Agriculture and the Distribution of Domestic Producers

In order to understand which members would have an interest in supporting one set of industry interests or another, I examine the characteristics of firms in their constituency. To do so, I rely on plant or firm size in either sales or employment as a proxy for productivity. In the following, I use the US Census of Agriculture to calculate, on a legislator-by-legislator basis, an index of relative competitiveness in agricultural production. In districts with relatively large farms, I would expect support for the unamended House version of the bill. Members representing relatively diffuse and marginal firms would prefer the Senate bill, as amended to exclude small producers.

Census data are ideal for studying the full distribution of business activity. These data represent as complete of a picture as is possible of the relative weight of large and small firms. There are, however, a few important caveats. For one, the Census of Agriculture is itself the outcome of political conflict within the agriculture industry. This affects the coverage of the census. The agricultural census covers all operations that satisfy its definition of a farm—any place that produces, sells, or normally would sell $1,000 or more agricultural products. This low number has not been updated since 1974. If it were merely adjusted for inflation, let alone consolidation in the industry, the threshold would exclude almost half of the 2012 census respondents. Efforts to raise this threshold, with its effects on smaller enterprises, have been repeatedly blocked by politicians. The result is that the 2007 census covered 2,204,792 farms, hundreds of thousands of which were operated by people who would not self-identify as farmers.[22] The advantage of this liberal coverage is that the census is an effective measure of farming as a lifestyle in addition to farming as an industry.

Aggregation of the census data indicates that the $500,000 threshold of the Tester-Hagan amendment would exclude the vast majority of farms. The 2012 edition of the USDA agriculture census records the number and aggregates sales of farms across 15 categories of farm operations, ranging from less than $1,000 to over $5 million in gross sales. According to these data, more than 93 percent of US farming operations make less than $500,000 in gross sales a year. However, the domestic farms that exceed the $500,000 threshold are responsible for more than 80 percent of gross sales, with a third of sales concentrated in firms that are in the top 0.5 percent of sales: namely, those that make over $5 million a year in gross sales.

A second challenge to using the Census of Agriculture is primarily a consequence of a mismatch between the timing of the Census of Agriculture and the US Census of Population. The former publishes results at both the state and the House district level, matching the number and coverage of House districts defined by the decennial United States Census. To examine the votes in the Senate, I use the 15 categories from the 2012 census, aggregated to the level of the state. For the House, we would ideally have the census at the level of the district, but the 2012 data are aggregated to congressional districts defined by 2010's redistricting, which was put in place for the 112th Congress, well after the food safety regulation debate was complete in the legislature. As a result, wherever the House is concerned, it is necessary to use the 2007 agriculture census, which has a coarse reporting of sales statistics at the district level.

Figure 5.1 displays the sales and number of farms across states above and below the $500,000 Tester-Hagan amendment threshold. In terms

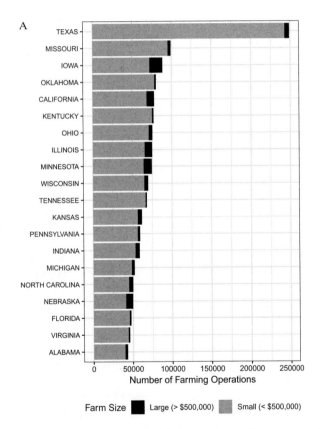

FIGURE 5.1. Farming by state in the USDA Census (2012). (A) Farm count by size; (B) Farm sales by size

of number, Texas stands out, with more than 240,000 farms with sales below the threshold. Among these small farms in Texas, 80,000 report less than \$1,000 in sales.[23] The state with the next highest number of farms, Missouri, has 95,000 small farms and ranks sixteenth in total sales. In terms of the proportion of statewide sales that are generated by small farms, states vary—from Rhode Island, where 77 percent of sales are in farms that sell below \$500,000, to Delaware, where small farms make up 7 percent of sales.[24]

These data make it clear how small firms within the United States agriculture market, while not major economic players, can nonetheless be politically influential. Having 50,000 or more independent operators offers leverage not just through lobbying or other forms of indirect

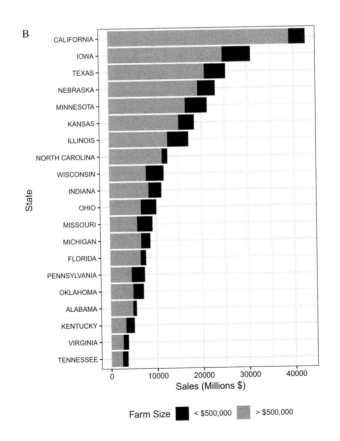

influence but as voters. This is one more reason to think that aggregate economic metrics, such as trade volume or industrial output, are a generally poor measure for commercial politics.

5.2.3. Roll Call Analysis

The roll call vote on the amended Food Safety Modernization Act passed with a bipartisan majority in the Senate.[25] This vote pitted advocates for an exemption against those that were holding out for a compromise bill or delaying action until the following legislative session. Given the floor debate and other public statements, we might expect that senators would oppose the bill because exemptions undermine confidence in the market. By contrast, if senators are instead voting against the bill and its exemptions in response to concerns by large producers, we would expect to see state characteristics predict votes. In particular, we would likely see senators that represent states with a larger share of sales exceeding the Tester-Hagan threshold to vote against the bill.

Figure 5.2 displays the share of sales held by firms that exceed $500,000 by members that voted in favor or against S. 510. Nonparametric bootstrapped 95 percent confidence intervals are displayed in the bands, revealing that on average, senators that voted against the bill represent states where the share of sales by large farms was 5.2 percentage points higher.[26] Montana, home state of Senator Tester, ranked 45 out of the 50 states in terms of share of farming sales above $500,000. This suggests that senators were voting in ways consistent with the interests of large agricultural operations.

To examine this difference more systematically, I estimate a model of the Senate roll call votes on the amended version of S. 510, controlling for the log of aggregate sales by state from the 2012 Census of Agriculture, as well as membership in the Republican Party.[27] The results of this statistical analysis are displayed in columns 1 and 2 of table 5.2. The results are inconsistent with the theory that farm sales would push members to protect the entire industry by voting down the exemptions. The regressions display no relationship between total sales of farm goods and a vote against S. 510. However, senators whose states have a larger share of firms above the $500,000 Tester-Hagan amendment threshold exhibit higher opposition to the bill. According to the estimates from the model in column 2, a state with one standard deviation higher share of sales in

TABLE 5.2 **Food Safety Modernization Act votes in 111th Congress**

	Senate votes against S. 510			House votes against H.R. 2751		
	(1)	(2)	(3)	(4)	(5)	(6)
Sales > $500k (2012 census)	3.28* (1.87)	5.81* (3.79)	5.03 (3.73)			
log(tot. sales) (2012 census)		0.02 (0.25)	−0.02 (0.29)			
log(ave. sales) (2007 census)				0.08 (0.12)	0.35* (0.18)	0.48* (0.25)
Vote against H.R. 2749				3.94*** (0.33)	4.48*** (0.45)	0.66 (0.78)
Republican		5.76*** (1.76)	1.01 (1.72)			*0.44 (1.47)
Ideology (NOMINATE)			6.53*** (1.94)			5.65*** (1.53)
State fixed effects	no	no	no	no	yes	yes
Observations	100	100	100	433	433	433

Note: Standard errors in parentheses. *$p < 0.1$; **$p < 0.05$; ***$p < 0.01$.

large farms is associated with 14 percentage points higher probability of its senator voting against the measure.

While the voting patterns on the Senate bill are suggestive, a single vote cannot determine whether larger farms are associated with more or less regulation. It may be that senators respond to the interests of large farms by opposing all regulations, not just those that exclude small businesses, or it could be, as some of the qualitative evidence suggests, that the large businesses are principally opposed to exemptions, not the regulation itself. The former dynamic would be partially accounted for by the simple indicator for party, which would capture some of the antiregulatory ideological sentiment among senators.

To further account for the possibility that ideology, rather than the state-level characteristics, drives votes in the Senate, I also estimate a model that accounts for each senator's DW-NOMINATE score. DW-NOMINATE is a low dimensional representation of all roll call votes for each member and is often interpreted as placing legislators on a single left-right scale. Column 3 of table 5.2 displays the estimates from a model that includes the first dimension of the scaled roll call votes from the 111th Congress (Lewis and Poole 2004). While the coefficient on the share of sales from the census is not statistically distinguishable from zero, the point estimate is substantively similar. One explanation for this is that the partisanship and ideology of senators are themselves an outcome of industry influence, with large farms promoting and supporting the election of partisans that favor their interests.[28]

The legislative process between the congressional chambers offers a more refined comparison. By the time the Senate bill was passed in the House of Representatives, the 111th House had already taken a roll call vote on a food safety bill without an exemption for small firms. That vote occurred in 2009, with H.R. 2749—the Food Safety Enhancement Act. Much like S. 510, the bill expanded the authority of the FDA, authorized new precautionary food safety systems, and imposed a fee-based certification process. The Senate bill, now numbered H.R. 2751, the Food Safety Modernization Act, arrived in the House with the Tester-Hagan amendment in place. In comparing the House votes, I attribute a change in the vote across the two bills to taking a position either in favor of or opposed to the Tester-Hagan exemption.

For the most part, the bills see similar levels of support, particularly among members representing districts without substantial FDA-regulated production. Figure 5.2A displays the vote of each senator by the share of farm sales exceeding $500,000. Figure 5.2B displays the total sales of FDA-regulated products[29] by each House district from the 2007 census among members that voted in favor of or against the final House bill. In the House, no member without at least some agricultural sales opposed the final bill.

The comparison of the votes across the two House bills provides further evidence for domestic intraindustry division over the exemption. In aggregate, of the 243 members that voted in favor of H.R. 2749, 9 voted against the bill with exemptions. Of the 177 members that voted against H.R. 2749, 15 voted in favor of the later version of the bill. Table 5.2 reports the predicted marginal effects from logistic regressions of votes against H.R. 2751 on member and district characteristics. Column 6 displays the coefficients from a model that controls for the prior vote on H.R. 2749, membership in the Republican Party, the first dimension of the DW-NOMINATE score, and the average sales of FDA-related products, as well as indicator variables for the state. The results indicate that representatives of districts with higher-than-average FDA-related sales are more likely to oppose the amended legislation. A Florida district with a conservative Republican representative and an average farm sales of $1 million (such as Florida's Sixteenth District) is 7.4 percentage

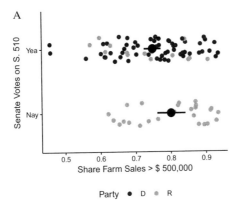

FIGURE 5.2. Votes on the Food Safety Modernization Act by chamber. (A) US Senate; (B) US House of Representatives

points more likely to vote against the bill than a member representing a Florida district with average farm sales of $100,000.

In the roll call analysis, aggregate firm size predicts legislative opposition to the exemptions in the Food Safety Modernization Act. This association is consistent with statements in the House and Senate debate, as well as the overall prediction that the FSMA would act as an entry barrier for some portion of the industry but that with exemptions, the effect on entry would be limited, leaving only the substantial costs of compliance. What the large firms wanted, and what they eventually got, was to target the exemptions to firms that sell to local consumers, limiting the competitive threat that these unregulated firms could pose to the larger producers. In this way, the legislators could satisfy the large part of the small firms—hundreds of thousands of small domestic farmers whose interest lay in ensuring an exemption. Small domestic firms with advocates such as Senator Tester could use their voices in Congress to limit the effects of regulatory protectionism. As I show in the next section, small foreign firms were not so privileged.

5.3. Food Safety Rulemaking and Foreign Firms

The legislation passed with the Tester-Hagan amendment largely intact, but the exemption only explicitly applied to small domestic farms. The legislation left exemptions for small manufacturers and foreign firms to be specified by the FDA, ideally within the normal 90 days of public comment. In fact, it would take another half decade of industry and public contestation. In the legislature, deals are hashed out by congressional staff and then delivered in a form that will satisfy a slim majority—firms can join letters and contact their members of Congress, but Congress members are under little obligation to make themselves available. By contrast, the regulatory process involves industry engagement at volume—thousands of statements, letters, and questions over the course of each iteration of the rule. In this section, I examine this rulemaking process to show the differential response of industry to the prospect of extending the Tester-Hagan amendment to cover foreign firms. Consistent with the statements by legislators and the statistical correlations in the roll call votes, the comments reveal the significant influence of large global firms at the expense of small foreign food manufacturers.

The rulemaking process in the United States requires the executive agencies that write and implement laws to interact directly with the public and private interests. After engaging in preliminary analysis, the FDA is required to submit its proposals to the public comment website, Regulations.gov. In addition, the FDA was tasked with conducting at least three public meetings, which included running a series of virtual and in-person meetings in locations around the world. In this time, the FDA was to solicit, collect, and respond to questions and comments from the public; edit the proposed regulation; and provide guidance to businesses. Because the legislation was deemed relevant to both domestic and international business, the proposed rules were also submitted through the WTO's sanitary and phytosanitary notification process, soliciting comments from foreign governments.

The FDA issued a notice of the proposed exemption for domestic businesses two years after the legislation was signed into law. The proposal offered rules covering registration and "preventive controls" for processing facilities, which extended the exemptions in the Tester-Hagan amendment to "very small businesses" that manufacture or sell food.[30] Rather than offering a single proposal, the FDA requested comment on three options for a threshold, based on gross sales caps of $250,000, $500,000, and $1,000,000. These three levels of regulation each came with an estimate of the number of facilities that would be exempt as well as the total domestic cost over seven years, reprinted in table 5.3. The FDA also produced a "breakeven illness percentage" that estimates the percentage of the existing disease burden that would have to be eliminated in order to justify the cost to industry. The table shows that the scope of the additional exemption is significantly smaller than the original Tester-Hagan amendment—the processing industry is much smaller than the agriculture industry, although many farms may be classified both as a farm and as a processing plant.[31]

After receiving hundreds of comments on its proposed rule, the FDA announced it would "tentatively conclude that the definition of very small business should exempt from the rule only a small percent of food to minimize the risk of foodborne illness and, thus, are proposing a very small business definition of $1,000,000, which would exempt less than one percent of the dollar value of food produced in the United States."[32] The $1 million threshold exceeds the Tester-Hagan amendment language for qualified facilities and effectively eliminates the requirement to sell to local markets. The exemption resolved the conflict among domestic producers but raised a new issue: how to make the law consistent with WTO rules against discrimination.

TABLE 5.3 **FDA estimates of very small business exemption**

Threshold ($)	250,000	500,000	1,000,000
Additional exempt domestic facilities (#)	34,600	45,900	63,500
Domestic cost ($)	475 million	395 million	319 million
Annual breakeven illness (%)	24	20	16

Six months after submitting its proposals for domestic food-processing facilities, the FDA initiated public comment on the application of the FSMA to foreign producers—the Foreign Supplier Verification Program (FSVP). As the Produce Marketing Association put it, "FDA will have to determine how, if at all, the Tester-Hagan Amendment applies to imported food. After all, the 275 miles between a farm or facility and certain customers includes significant foreign production near the US border, and sales directly to consumers are without limitation to distance."[33] The FDA proposed establishing the FSVP to extend the domestic regulatory process to foreign operations. The question for public comment was whether to include a Tester-Hagan type exemption for these foreign producers. Following the pattern established in the preventive controls regulation, the FDA initially proposed that "very small foreign suppliers" would be exempt if they certified they made less than $500,000 in annual food sales. In soliciting public comments, the FDA again offered the three sales caps as alternatives and also requested feedback on whether the definitions should apply only to US sales of food or to worldwide sales. The use of worldwide sales would significantly limit the application of the exemption but be similar to the definitions used in the domestic context.

The first proposal was submitted to the public comment process and was extended to receive comments for one year. In the following year, at the same time the preventive controls proposal was amended, the FDA also announced that it was revising its definition of a "very small foreign supplier" to one with a gross sales cap of $1,000,000. Across the two proposals, the FSVP provision received 336 comments from 287 distinct commentators, of which 88 commented on the threshold for very small foreign suppliers.

In the end, the final rule on the FSVP deleted the proposed provisions on "very small foreign suppliers." Instead, regulators required annual written assurances that companies would establish procedures to use approved suppliers and hire a "qualified individual" to handle the paperwork in the US.[34] Qualified firms that fall below a threshold would not need to go through regular audits or engage in a hazard analysis.[35] These qualified requirements apply under the same conditions as for the domestic food-processing facilities—a cap on total sales of $500,000, adjusted for inflation, as well as produce farms that sell less than $25,000 and suppliers of shell eggs with fewer than 3,000 laying hens.[36]

5.3.1. Domestic Divisions over Exemptions

The Foreign Supplier Verification Program received hundreds of comments from individuals, businesses, governments, and NGOs. These comments range from a few sentences entered into the Regulations.gov web portal to letters that were dozens of pages long—often point by point responses to the proposed legislation. While there is variation in each of these points, I focus on two dimensions of the policy that pertain to the exemptions for foreign suppliers: the monetary threshold to qualify for the exemption and the kind of sales that would count toward that threshold, either US or total worldwide sales. Again, of the 336 public comments in the rulemaking docket for the FSVP, 88 explicitly address the proposals for the thresholds in the program. The classification of these comments by market position reveals a clear division of preferences: larger, more productive firms and consumer advocates against smaller foreign businesses, consistent with the FSVP raising a regulatory barrier to trade.

Classification of public comments requires mapping the name signed on the comment to an economic actor.[37] These names can be usefully divided into six categories: US consumer groups/nongovernmental organizations, US producers, US importers, US government agencies, foreign industry, and foreign governments. Each comment is then coded along two dimensions: as a statement on the preferred monetary threshold, and then, if available, as a statement about whether that threshold should apply to sales of goods sold to the US or to all sales by the regulated facility. The former coding is plotted in figure 5.3 across the six categories, from the highest, most inclusive exemption to the lowest threshold for an exemption. Diamonds represent the average for each group, and shapes indicate a kernel density. Several commentators proposed eliminating the exemption or instead deploying a risk-based approach, both of which I coded as a threshold of zero dollars. In total, I found firms express support for five thresholds, following generally the FDA proposals.

Some of the heterogeneity in the preferences across these categories was driven by the changes in the proposals by the FDA, which set a benchmark from which the comments offer their position. Table 5.4 displays stated preferences over the regulatory process across two periods: The first starts in mid-2013 when the FDA proposed a $500,000 threshold to exempt foreign suppliers. The second begins in September

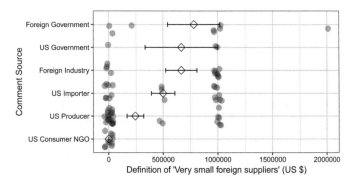

FIGURE 5.3. Preferences about Foreign Supplier Verification Program (FSVP) size limits

TABLE 5.4 **Size limit preferences across FDA proposals**

	FDA cutoff proposals		
Commenter	< $500,000	< $1,000,000	Average
US consumer advocate	0	0	0
US producer	68,333	430,357	243,103
US importers	350,000	750,000	527,777
Foreign industry	333,333	857,142	615,384
Foreign government	708,333	1,000,000	781,250
US (state) government	0	1,000,000	666,666
All	261,170	611,805	413,253

of 2014, when that threshold was raised to $1,000,000. The final rule re-
versed these exemptions for small foreign suppliers, but because the reversal involved the FDA removing the provision entirely, the final proposal did not receive comments in this docket.

The group with the most restrictive preference, across both periods, is
advocates for consumers. While other parts of the proposed regulation
received thousands of comments from individual consumers, most health
and safety advocacy over the exemption threshold in the FSVP came
from larger domestic nongovernmental organizations. These NGOs included general health and consumer advocacy groups such as the American Academy of Pediatrics and the National Consumer League, as well
as specific advocacy organizations such as the Food and Water Watch
and the Center for Foodborne Illness Research. In their comments and
public advocacy, these consumer advocates were uniformly in favor of
the Food Safety Modernization Act and generally opposed to exemp-

tions. Figure 5.3 shows that these groups were uniformly opposed to any exemption for foreign suppliers. They argued that the risk from any exemption would undermine the integrity of the FSVP, and their comments on the threshold called for deleting the exemptions from the rule.[38] These groups were not uniformly opposed to the original Tester-Hagan threshold for domestic firms, but when it came to foreign producers, they cited the additional risks associated with developing country regulatory systems. Moreover, they argued that any size threshold would have different effects in other countries, as "in some countries, a foreign supplier with $1 M in food sales could be quite large and could produce a substantial amount of food, but under the less than $1M definition, even these large foreign facilities (and their food) would be exempt."[39] Because none of these groups advocated for a threshold in any situation, these NGOs did not characterize a distinction between US sales and global sales.

The second most restrictive comments were submitted by US producers, including US agricultural interests. This includes small producers such as Naturipe Farms LLC, who argued that food safety events do not care about annual sales and, further, that any modification in requirements would lead to "creative business titling" to avoid the more stringent rules.[40] Strong opposition was also voiced by the regional and state farm bureaus. The New York Farm Bureau argued on competitiveness grounds against an exemption: "The FDA must apply and enforce any new produce safety standards on imports in a manner similar to that for domestic producers. If not applied equally, our producers will be put at a competitive disadvantage. It is crucial that this rule is enforced internationally so our growers—already at an economic disadvantage due to labor costs, environmental regulations, higher tax and other business costs—don't have another inequity added that makes them less competitive compared to imported products."[41] In addition to the loss of competitive advantage, domestic growers and producers identified several reasons to oppose lowering the burden on small foreign firms. With a high threshold, foreign suppliers could restructure their businesses, dividing into smaller companies that would each be exempt. In addition, some comments were concerned that the foreign firms could take advantage of exchange rate fluctuations to ensure that sales fell below the US-dollar-defined threshold or that the inflation calculations would be manipulated to grant more businesses exemptions than the regulators intend.

While domestic producers were generally opposed to the threshold, domestic importers were divided. Small importers were significantly more likely to favor a higher threshold—so long as it applied to them. One importer, Penny Newman Grain, argued in favor of a small business definition that would include annual receipts of $27.5 million or less. Without such an exemption, "the heavy burden of these proposed rules may drive small companies, like Penny Newman Grain, out of this business. This will reduce competition to the detriment of the dairy industry, which then will be forced [to] buy feed from the big companies who have the employees to comply with these burdensome proposed rules. It is not believed that the intent of these rules was to reduce competition, but that is the foreseeable impact that the rules may have."[42] Meanwhile, the American Herbal Products Association, an industry association representing nutritional supplements, supported setting the dollar-value thresholds at $1 million "rather than a lower number, and continuing to base them on sales of food rather than all sales."[43]

Large importers uniformly opposed exemptions for foreign suppliers. Arguing that foodborne-illness outbreaks do not discriminate based on the size of an importer or supplier, McCormick & Company, a multinational food manufacturer, pointed out that the passed legislation "does not provide any leniency based on company size. This is a contrast to the preventive controls provision of FSMA, where the Tester-Hagan amendment specifically provides less stringent food safety requirements for very small businesses."[44] Wegmans Food Markets, Inc., similarly argued that enforcing such exemptions would invite a future WTO challenge and that no produce operations, foreign or domestic, should be exempted on the basis of size. One comment by a large importer suggests that competitive interests can span across the supply chain. In justifying opposition to the exemption, the American Feed Industry Association pointed out that their members are unlikely to import from any very small foreign suppliers due to the higher risk they pose, thereby putting them at an economic disadvantage when those small foreign suppliers are exempt.[45]

5.3.2. International Divisions over Exemptions

The foreign industry comments reveal a split across firm size not only on the question of the threshold but also in the scope of the regulation. The French Food Industries Association, representing more than 10,000 small businesses, called not only for a $1 million sales threshold but for the threshold to apply to US sales and not global sales. As they put it, for a foreign enterprise with a small presence in the US, the burden of FSMA compliance would result in the foreign enterprise "exiting the US market" causing "US job loss" by imposing "an unfair burden."[46] European producers also pointed out that the whole concept of a revenue definition is discriminatory to EU companies because "a foreign supplier of food in the EU would need to produce much less in volume than companies located in other third countries in order to meet the very small business threshold."[47] By contrast, organizations of Dutch, Mexican, and Canadian produce wholesalers that represent large industrial shippers and traders oppose any revenue-based measure, preferring a threshold, if there is to be one, apply to worldwide sales, thus covering thousands of additional producers.

As the US represents the competitive interests of its small firms in the regulatory process, so do foreign governments. Following submission of the proposed rules to the SPS committee, WTO member governments offered a number of comments to raise the sales thresholds and define any threshold by the sales to the US rather than worldwide sales. China submitted a specific trade concern to the SPS committee and offered a comment that argued for a $1 million ceiling and for giving very small importers and very small foreign suppliers a transitional period of at least three years to meet FSVP requirements. Japan requested that the exemption be raised to $2 million and, in any case, that it only apply to US sales. Much as Senator Tester represents the small organic farmer, small producers in these countries are able to get their governments to push for regulatory change in the United States.

On November 27, 2015, the FDA issued the final rule, essentially following the preferences of domestic producers and large importers. Rather than a $1 million sales threshold, as proposed in the rulemaking process, the exemption was deleted, leaving the definition of qualified exemptions to the provisions written for domestic firms and a partial exemption from obligations if total average sales are below $500,000. In addition, the sales threshold would be calculated on the basis of worldwide sales, as proposed by large foreign firms but opposed by governments and foreign industry associations. In justifying this choice, the FDA argued that the final rule is necessary to "provide parity in supplier verification requirements for domestic and foreign food producers."[48] Because the provisions for foreign suppliers "are based on the underlying food safety regulations"—namely, those developed for domestic industry—the FDA concluded that the threshold for qualification should depend on the eligibility criteria "specified in those [domestic] regulations."[49] The end result is an evenly applied law that has an uneven effect on smaller foreign producers.

One advantage to deferring to the domestic criteria arose from institutional rules. This move gave the FDA authority to cease collecting comments and issue the final rule. The adopted threshold was from outside the Foreign Supplier Verification Program, and so "concerns regarding the appropriateness of these eligibility criteria are beyond the scope of this rulemaking."[50] Not only does this rule satisfy the interests of domestic and large international producers; there were legal reasons to shut down the comment process. In 2013, a US district judge ruled that the FDA violated federal law in its excessive delay in implementing the FSMA.[51] Consumer groups sued to force the FDA to issue its regulations, and the judge agreed. Initially, the FDA had until June 30, 2015, to publish all regulations, but in light of the government shutdown, the FDA was allowed to issue its rule on imported food and foreign suppliers by October 2015 (Sundhar 2014). While still failing to meet the court-ordered deadline, punting the definition to the parts of the regulation already published allowed the FDA to satisfy its legal—and political—obligations.

To identify these cleavages, each comment in the FSMA docket was individually read and coded, but the 336 comments on exemptions for foreign suppliers are only a small subset of the thousands of total comments on the FSMA. In the following section, I draw on techniques from machine learning and computer automation to analyze all the comments submitted to the FDA during the regulatory process. I show that there are significant differences in the substantive concerns of these groups and the ways that they approached trying to convince the FDA.

5.4. Structural Topic Model of Public Comments

Topic models are a collection of statistical techniques developed to examine the underlying structure of a collection of documents. Topic models of US public comments have uncovered the discursive strategies and concerns of individuals and industry in the implementation of electronic monitoring in the trucking system. With structural topic models, the analyst can incorporate document-level covariates into the analysis, allowing topics and the words used in topics to vary from other observed data (Roberts et al. 2013). In this section, I describe the collection and processing of public comments on the FSMA into documents. I then specify and estimate a structural topic model, which predicts the content of those public comments using characteristics of the commentators, including country of origin and affiliation.

5.4.1. Obtaining Public Comments

The FDA published 29 rulemaking dockets on the new food safety regulations, including guidance for industry, proposed rules, and final rules. Each of these dockets applies to a broad aspect of the rule, such as the fee structure, the notification requirements, or rules on the transportation of food. By passing the docket number to the Regulations.gov application programming interface (API), the title and text of each comment for each docket can be retrieved automatically.[52] Each public comment can be submitted either through the government portal or through an attached file. After processing the attachments into text, there are 2,493 comments with a median length of 249 words, the shortest being the request "Leave my supplements alone" and the longest a 134-page contribution from the Grocery Manufacturers Association.

In addition to the text, each comment contains metadata, including a title that indicates the submitting organization, company or individual. Titles are labeled with a country of origin as well as whether they represent a foreign government, a trade association, an individual firm, a testing lab, or a nongovernmental organization. The frequency of comments and the average word count from each of these coded groups are displayed in table 5.5.[53] After processing, 1,207 unique individuals or organizations are present in the collected comments.

TABLE 5.5 **Comment statistics from Regulations.gov**

	Firms	Gov.	Labs	NGO	Trade assoc.	Individuals
Number of comments	457	354	43	245	1,176	287
Average word count of each comment	5,566	2,938	2,336	5,658	4,176	867

5.4.2. Structural Topic Model

Quantitative approaches to text data analysis begin with pieces of text, called documents, within a collection of texts, called a corpus. The union of unique words, or *terms*, used across the corpus forms a vocabulary. Using this vocabulary, it is possible to construct a vector of word counts for each document, with each entry in that vector mapping to a unique term. This framework ignores word order and is referred to as the *bag of words* representation. The analytical question is, Which of K topics generates each document? In this case, characteristics of these documents are thought to affect the relative frequency of topics raised by a public comment (topic *prevalence*) as well as the words associated with a given topic (topic *content*).

The structural model developed by Roberts et al. (2013) makes specific distributional assumptions about the data-generating process for word counts, topic prevalence, and topic content. The parameters of these models include coefficients that govern the effect of document characteristics on topic prevalence. For this application, I estimate 15 topics according to equation (5.1). The model includes author and document characteristics—here eight categories of US and foreign governments, firms, individuals and trade associations, as well as a fourth-order spline of the date of the submission:

(5.1)   TopicPrevalence ~ AuthorIndicator + s(Date,4).

The 15 topics are displayed and labeled in figure 5.4A. Topics range across the sorts of concerns brought about food safety, such as illness; product-specific concerns, such as dietary supplements or producer requirements; and statements about the affected industry, such as small farms, the transportation sector topic, or the warehousing rules. Among these topics, four pertain to concerns over competition and trade openness: "small facility," "small farm," "import suppliers," and "produce requirements." If small domestic producers are voicing opposition to the effects of onerous regulatory requirements on behalf of small foreign firms, then it is possible that the government would have less interest in mercantilist policies. By contrast, if small domestic producers ignore the import requirements, this would be evidence that the sorts of exemptions developed in the legislative process were effective at undercutting domestic opposition.

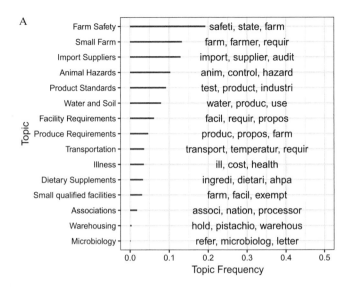

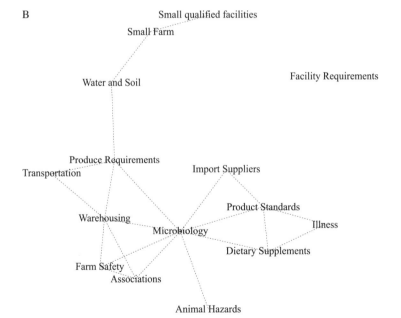

FIGURE 5.4. Topic network of FDA public comments. (A) Topics from STM model of FDA public comments; (B) Topic network

The topics suggest that the issues for small producers are disconnected from import rules. Figure 5.4B displays the positive correlations among topics in public comments in a graph, where edges represent a correlation among topics higher than 0.01. The graph indicates that the topics that address small farms and small facilities, the primary target of exemptions under the FSMA, are associated with one another, but not with the discussion of importers or the "product requirements" topic. In the public comments on the FSMA, it appears that the problems associated with imports are discussed separately from the issues pertaining to size, consistent with a wedge between the interests of small domestic actors and those engaged in trade.

To further identify the substantive meaning of these topics, figures 5.5A and 5.5B display sentences drawn at random from three documents in the most frequent topics.[54] The "farm safety" topic, the most common one in this analysis, is also one of the broadest, primarily representing statements by large groups of state-level agriculture boards and commissions. These commissions represent large collections of domestic firms, including large agribusiness and smaller farming concerns. The second panel provides the sentences from the "small farms," topic, which reflect concern among both small farmers and individual consumers that advocate local and small-scale production for cultural, environmental, or sustainability purposes. These sentences are indicative of the nature of this topic—it is a topic that is generated by individuals following a template.

One such template was distributed by the National Sustainable Agriculture Coalition:

Sample Farmer Comment

Re: Preventive Controls Rule: FDA-2011-N-0920, Produce Standards Rule: FDA-2011-N-0921

> I am a __ [farmer, entrepreneur, processor, parent . . .]. [Customize your comment with your story: What is the name and location of your farm? What do you grow? How long have you been in operation? Where do you sell your products and how do you already ensure their safety?]
>
> I am writing because I am concerned about the impact that FDAs proposed FSMA rules will have on [my farm / business operation, the practices I use on my farm, other farmers in my community, the farms that I buy food from, etc. . . .]. I ask you to ensure that new regulations do not put safe farms

A

NFBF is Nebraska's largest
farm and ranch organization
and is in the unique position
of representing all sectors of
Nebraska agriculture.

- -

FDA previously, we believe
that fostering a cooperative
atmosphere creates the
opportunity for paving the way
to the most abundant, safe and
affordable food source in the
world.

- -

We applaud your team for
the work they have done in
listening to the concerns of
processors, growers, consumers
and state regulators.

B

I am a concerned parent
writing because I am concerned
about the impact that FDA...s
proposed FSMA rules will have
on the farms that I buy food
from and the environment.

- -

I am concerned about the
impact that FDA...s proposed
FSMA rules will have on the
small local family farms
that we have been working
diligently to bolster in our
region.

- -

I am concerned about the
impact that FDA...s proposed
FSMA rules will have on
American's ability to purchase
local, organic food, and the
impact the rules will have on
the environment.

FIGURE 5.5. Topics from STM model of FDA public comments. (A) Thoughts on farm
safety; (B) Thoughts on small farms

out of business, harm farmers' soil, water, and wildlife conservation efforts, or shut down the growth of local and regional healthy food systems!

Because of all of the specific issues described below, I urge FDA to publish a second round of draft rules for public comment before finalizing the produce safety and preventive controls regulations.

This particular template uses some language that is atypical of normal political speech, such as reference to "regional healthy food systems," but it is the beginning line of the text that indicates the document as based on a form letter: "I am writing because I am concerned about the impact." Figure 5.6A displays estimates from the 15-topic model that show that American individuals are 30 percentage points more likely to be using the "small farms" topic than state or national government official submissions. The least likely group, besides governments, to discuss these small firms are industry associations. Industry associations tend to advocate for the Tester-Hagan amendment, but they are also less likely to follow the formulation of a form letter.

Given that small foreign firms are much more likely to comment through an association rather than on their own, we should expect, in general, that foreign associations would voice opposition to strict regulatory measures. Individual foreign firms that manage to comment in the US public comment process are likely paying that additional cost in order to voice opinions at odds with the rest of the industry. Figure 5.6B displays coefficient estimates for the difference in topic prevalence for "small facility," "small farm," "import suppliers," and "produce requirements" topics between firms and associations in US and foreign comments. In the first three topics, foreign firms and associations are no more likely to include these topics in their comments. However, we do see differences in foreign firms and associations' treatments of the "produce requirement" topic. There foreign associations, which presumably represent small firms in addition to major exporters, are substantially more likely than individual firms to raise this issue, whereas US firms and associations are equally likely to discuss the technical producer requirements.

As expected given the intraindustry divisions over regulations, foreign trade associations differ from foreign firms in their advocacy on produce requirements. Figure 5.7 displays the coefficients from the "produce requirements" topic for the indicator for foreign and US-based

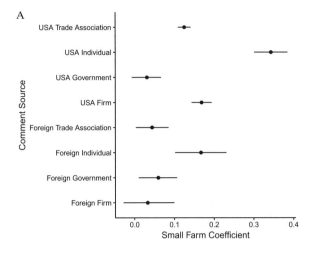

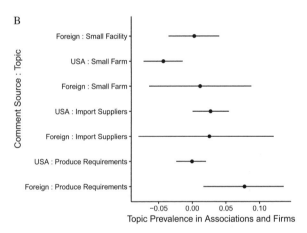

FIGURE 5.6. Coefficient estimates from STM model of firms and associations. (A) Topic model coefficients for "small farm" topic; (B) Association topic relative to firm topic prevalence

firms, associations, and governments. These produce requirements are high stake for small producers, as even small delays in inspection can ruin shipments. The question is, however, whether governments will take up these same concerns, and the estimates suggest that they do not. The same pattern arises for the other technical requirements topic, "facility

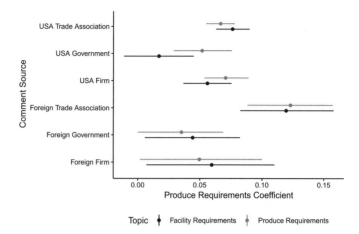

FIGURE 5.7. Coefficient estimates for "facilities" and "produce" topics

requirements," which indicates substantial trade association interest, as displayed in figure 5.7. In fact, foreign governments appear closer to the individual firms than the industry associations. One explanation for this pattern is that industry associations, here representing small firms, are less influential as US trade partners than large firms, a result consistent with work on lobbying and political access (Bombardini 2008).

5.4.3. Domestic Concerns about Imports

One of the channels of influence for small foreign firms in the US regulatory process is advocacy on the part of their customers. If small producers have little say in their own governments, there may still be advocates for less stringent standards among customers, particularly for intermediate and input goods producers. In fact, among the 15 topics identified by the structural topic model, the third most common topic concerned the audit controls on foreign suppliers. Figure 5.8 displays the average proportion of each submission on the "import supplier" topic by comment source. This indicates that this topic was more prevalent among foreign commentators and US trade associations than US individuals or firms. Given that trade associations cover a wider variety of firms, this could reflect the fact that industry associations include domestic importers who are not productive enough to establish foreign affiliates and may rely on unaffiliated foreign exporters for their products. If this is the case, then perhaps small foreign firms have some influence over regulatory stringency and are not completely excluded from the political process.

However, the content of these industry association contributions suggests that small foreign firms are of little interest to the US industry associations. For example, the American Frozen Food Institute (AFFI) represents both large multinationals and smaller importers that depend on foreign suppliers. The AFFI raised concerns that the foreign audits could be impractical and costly and wrote of the possible trade effects of the bill. Moreover, the AFFI called for limiting oversight to "one step back" in the supply chain, which the AFFI argues would maximize the importer's leverage over compliance. However, this seems to be primarily for the benefit of the importer, not their foreign partners. The comments further called for ensuring that any verification program apply to all suppliers, that it exclude intracompany shipments, and with regards to the expedited import program (the Voluntary Qualified Import Program), that the FDA adopt "a flat, set fee for each VQIP importer without scaling based on the volume of importers or the size of the importer."[55] This preference for a fixed, flat fee mirrors the opposition on the part of large US firms to a size-based penalty to violations of the European chemical regulation.

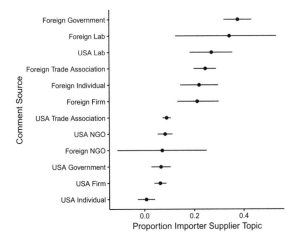

FIGURE 5.8. Coefficient estimates for "import supplier" topic among domestic commentators

5.5. Discussion

Regulatory barriers to trade are, at root, domestic regulations as well. These domestic regulations generate winners and losers within the regulating market, harming small firms and benefiting larger, more productive companies. However, small firms in the domestic market are less often the target of these regulations. This is because these small firms have political access to the regulating government that is unavailable to foreign firms. The Food Safety Modernization Act shows how that access is handled by proregulatory forces, in essence offering exemptions that peel off large portions of the local opposition, here exemplified by the Tester-Hagan amendment. Despite the efforts of foreign lobbyists in the rulemaking process, no such exemptions were extended. Instead, the government took the position advanced by the largest producers and consumer interest groups.

The broader insight is that like regulatory capture, regulatory protectionism is a cause for slower economic growth, increases in economic inequality, and high consumer prices, but that these effects even more pronounced in international relations (Lindsey and Teles 2017). Small local firms can lobby before and during the legislative process and can even provide feedback on rulemaking after legislation is passed; in each stage of the rulemaking, smaller domestic firms are able to leverage their political representation to limit the negative domestic consequences of a regulatory barrier. Small foreign firms, by contrast, are the least likely to have a voice in this process. The result is that local market actors are shielded from the consequences of stricter regulations.

The cases of food safety in the US and chemical regulation in the EU have substantive differences in the industry affected, the kinds of concerns facing consumers, and the extent of small firms' involvement in the regulatory process, but both reveal the relationship between global production and regulatory protection. In both cases, the government was initially motivated by a challenge brought by the globalization of production—the inability to trace products across the nodes of the global supply chain. The complex nature of the food and chemical markets has quickly outpaced the governments' oversight capacities, and in trying to bolster those capacities, the EU and the US turned to imposing more of the information-gathering requirements on industry. The result was a requirement for firms to register with a central authority, including, in effect, foreign firms. Because registrations are defined by product or firm and do not scale with production volume, the effect is to privilege those firms that sell at scale.

The result is that regulators in the United States and the European Union chose fewer exemptions and more demanding standards with the support of the largest and most globalized firms. Following the public unveiling of the European chemical regulations and the US food safety rules, dozens of countries raised alarm, worried about the consequences for small and medium-sized exporters.[56] The US and the EU serve half of global consumption, and these were two of the largest regulatory changes in modern history, but as we saw in chapter 3, regulatory protection is increasingly the principal problem for global cooperation.[57]

Recognizing these problems, the director general of the WTO has predicted that "the proper management of NTMs is among the greatest challenges we face in international cooperation" (Lamy 2012). The factors explored so far—the absence of representation by small foreign firms and the competitive interests of multinationals—only explain why management is necessary, not why it is difficult. The following chapters show why governments cannot easily extend institutions that have worked in tariff cooperation to limit regulatory protection.

PART III

Institutional Design

CHAPTER SIX

The Design of Reciprocal Trade Agreements

The global trade regime is underwritten by two normative principles: nondiscrimination among the membership and the norm of reciprocity. The former is what makes the multilateral trade system multilateral, inscribed in Article I of the General Agreement on Tariffs and Trade. The latter requires governments to raise or lower barriers to trade in concert, exchanging equivalently valuable market access.[1] The norm of reciprocity governs both the negotiation and the subsequent enforcement of tariff negotiations in trade agreements. However, sustaining reciprocity requires a judgment as to the value of a policy—value that assumes the kind of variable cost created by tariffs. In this chapter, I examine how the GATT's norms have broken down when facing regulatory barriers to trade.

Reciprocity is a near universal norm of cooperative behavior and an almost trivial demand of fairness. In trade relations, it takes on a more specific meaning: the mutual exchange of policy commitments to allow foreign products and services to be sold domestically. Today economists evaluate the extent of this commitment in terms of aggregate market access, the relative prices of a nation's exports and imports. Raising a tariff barrier raises the price of imports relative to exports, degrading foreign market access. Mutual and reciprocal tariff reductions would keep the relative prices constant. The United States, by extending the practice it had developed in the Reciprocal Trade Agreements Act (RTAA) of 1934, managed to make the measurement of tariff reductions in market access terms the global norm.[2] In theory, ensuring equal market access allows governments to avoid the possibility that a partner would unilaterally defect from their cooperative policy obligations.[3]

While reciprocity in market access has well-understood advantages for cooperation over tariffs, it is not clear the same would be true for regulatory barriers to trade. First, regulatory barriers to trade are less legible to both domestic and international audiences, complicating their detection (Kono 2009). However, even if regulatory intentions were perfectly observable, their effect on market outcomes is less straightforward than tariffs. Tariffs raise marginal costs, reducing trade volume. Regulatory barriers raise fixed costs, which reduces the number of profitable product varieties even as the price on each individual variety is unchanged.[4] Second, GATT rules are designed to generally permit nondiscriminatory regulatory measures, even if such measures can shift market share toward favored firms. As I show below, the GATT rules were designed to address the challenges of prior centuries of commercial policy.

This chapter offers evidence that the GATT rules, particularly the commitment to reciprocity in market access, have maintained trade volume for the better half of a century, but now fail to elicit concessions on tariffs. As governments seek to narrow the channel, the largest producers can enter a market at the expense of their smaller competitors. The consequence for international cooperation is stark—if reciprocity as a negotiating norm depends on measurements of market access, the negotiations will underserve small and medium-sized exporters, valued constituents of the exporting state. The consequence could be that tariff negotiations are undercut, as lowering tariffs can exacerbate rather than correct for the effects of regulatory protection.

Below, I provide econometric evidence that reciprocity fails in the presence of regulatory protection during the GATT Uruguay Round. In evaluating tariff changes from 1995 and 2000, following the Uruguay Round, I will show that US tariff concessions in sectors with regulatory barriers to trade are met with higher, not lower, tariffs on average. Contrary to the expectation that modern production practices remove barriers to cooperation, I find that the breakdown in reciprocity is highest in exactly those sectors where products are relationship specific, those where firms are most likely to be affiliated with foreign multinationals.

This chapter proceeds as follows. Section 6.1 identifies the role of reciprocity in the GATT/WTO system. Section 6.2 provides evidence for the use of reciprocity in the context of modern trade negotiations. Section 6.3 uses econometric evidence to show that the reciprocity norm breaks down in the presence of regulatory protection, producing what I term *negative reciprocity*. Section 6.4 concludes the chapter.

6.1. Measuring Reciprocity in Law or Effect

Reciprocity was the operating principle of eighteenth- and early nineteenth-century commercial agreements, but it was not initially measured in terms of market access. Instead, reciprocity referred to equivalent legal concessions, such as commitments to jointly remove all bounties on ships or to treat foreign products as favorably as local products in all ways (Setser 1937). These agreements adopted a form of *mirror reciprocity*. The shift to graduated, measured reciprocity in market access reflects the limits to mirror reciprocity and the importance of accounting for the effects of policy in commercial relations. The use of market access reciprocity required developing new negotiating strategies that could account for the effects of agreements. In this section, I describe the measurement of reciprocity as equivalence in market access rather than equivalence in formal obligations for early nineteenth-century commercial relations among the Atlantic powers.

Mirror reciprocity was a key principle of US commercial policy from 1774 to 1829. During this period, the US strategy was to insist that trade partners entirely abandon the use of discriminatory duties on shipping in exchange for the same from the United States. As John Quincy Adams, then US secretary of state put it, "[The] first principle, therefore, of all negotiation upon such interests is reciprocity; and wherever a collision of interests exists, it is apparent that they can be conciliated only by reciprocal concession" (April 27, 1821; Monroe 1822, 167). In this period of American development, this insistence on one rate would harm less-productive partners' shipping interests and profit American exporters. However, this also made it difficult for the United States to find viable trade partners. In negotiating with Bourbon France, Adams himself was forced to resort to an embarrassing and Rococo strategy to maintain a single mirrored tariff rate for both nations: French products would be measured in smaller units so as to accrue lower effective tariff rates, while American products would be measured in large quantities, increasing the effective rate of French protection; shipping practices had yet to adopt a single standard of measure. A bushel of cotton from one port would be packed differently, and weigh differently, than that from another port. This meant that a ton of American products—cotton, potash, and rice—would be measured as 882 pounds, 2,240 pounds, and 1,792 pounds, respectively. In effect, by altering the weights of products that count as a ton, the negotiators could settle on one mirrored rate. The effect was to resolve these market access barriers, which managed to reduce discriminatory tariffs by more than two-thirds, and the agreement was eventually even extended to a full elimination of discriminatory tariffs.

Since the 1820s, mirror-market-access-based reciprocity has waned as the principal norm for governments in trade negotiations. Graduated reciprocal negotiations became the mainstay of British negotiations through the nineteenth century. The United States gave up its demand for mirror reciprocity in the McKinley Tariff Act of 1890. That act authorized the US president to impose duties on sugar, molasses, coffee, tea, and hides coming from countries that levied duties on US goods to an extent, in his judgment "reciprocally unequal and unreasonable" (Ashley 1910, 293). Using this method, the United States could raise the tariff on these formerly duty-free products to induce countries (mostly in Latin America) to enter into negotiations. The effort was broadly successful, as governments ranging from Brazil to Germany entered negotiations to keep their products on the "free list," but was abandoned nonetheless with the Wilson Tariff of 1894.

While most governments adopted reciprocity in market access, the 1934 Reciprocal Trade Agreements Act of the United States most closely resembles the future multilateral trade regime. The act authorized the US president to find foreign countries whose duties or import restrictions were unduly restrictive of US exports and offer "market opportunities" for foreign products in the US to encourage the removal of those barriers. During these and subsequent tariff negotiations, tariff agreements generally assumed that participants would only agree to reduce their level of protection in return for a reciprocal "concession" from their trading partners, what economist Paul Krugman calls "reciprocal mercantilism" (1997, 114). In theory, the GATT/WTO system follows these same principles: an equal change in import volume ensures that neither country is worse off after an agreement.

In practice, however, negotiations varied substantially between using mirror reciprocity and market-access-based reciprocity. Table 6.1 lists each GATT/WTO round, the official membership, and a characterization of the negotiation procedure.

TABLE 6.1 **Negotiations during WTO rounds**

Round	Members (participants)	Form of reciprocity
Geneva, 1947	23 (23)	Product-by-product
Annecy, 1949	23 (13)	Product-by-product
Torquay, 1950	32 (38)	Product-by-product
Geneva, 1956	36 (26)	Product-by-product
Dillon, 1960–61	41 (26)	Product-by-product
Kennedy, 1963–67	76 (62)	Product-by-product and formula
Tokyo, 1973–79	86 (102)	Product-by-product and formula
Uruguay, 1986–94	128 (127)	Product-by-product and sectoral

Source: Data calculated from Davis and Wilf (2017) and WTO (2007).

Starting with the 1947 Geneva Round, trade negotiations proceeded on a product-by-product basis, allowing governments to focus negotiations among "principal suppliers" and maintain reciprocity in market access. With the increased number of GATT negotiators, the product-by-product negotiations became "cumbersome and unwieldy." The shift back from a "request-offer" system to mirror reciprocity took the form of a formula-based approach, where governments would agree to reduce all their tariffs by a particular percentage of the prior bound rate (Low and Santana 2009). In the Kennedy Round, the GATT negotiators switched to a formula-based approach but even then proceeded to negotiate exceptions that rebalanced the rounds. The result was that even as the GATT negotiators agreed in principle to a 50 percent tariff cut across all products, the result was only to reduce tariffs by an average of about 35 percent.[5] Subsequent negotiations varied the degree to which they adopted linear cuts, but product-by-product reciprocal negotiations remained in use throughout the history of the agreement.

The last successful round of the GATT experimented with mirrored tariffs by sector. These could be a common "zero-for-zero" commitment, or a common harmonized rate. The United States, Canada, the European Communities, and Japan announced mutual agreement on the complete elimination of tariffs and nontariff measures on pharmaceuticals, construction equipment, medical equipment, steel, and beer.[6] In other sectors, the United States succeeded in negotiating tariff and nontariff barriers on a product-by-product basis (Croome 1996, 188). As I describe in the next chapter, the Uruguay Round did not create a schedule of product-by-product commitments on regulatory barriers, instead opting for a rules-based approach.

In the following section, I examine whether market-access-based, product-by-product reciprocity works as expected in the presence of regulatory protection. Empirically identifying the effect of reciprocity in actual negotiations, however, is made difficult by the endogeneity of trade concessions. Limão (2006) identified a particular historical event in which the United States made tariff reductions in exchange for unilateral tariff reforms made prior to the negotiations. Extending this analysis, I find that adherence to the norm of reciprocity broke down in sectors with nontariff barriers to trade.

6.2. Regulatory Barriers in Reciprocal Trade Negotiations

The GATT rules require that members maintain a general level of reciprocal and mutually advantageous concessions.[7] This principle, laid out in Article XXVIII:2, was interpreted to justify tariff-by-tariff concessions in terms of the effect on the treatment to trade—that is, market access—and was enforced by the threat of withdrawal of concessions. This would ensure a balance of interests, overcoming domestic protectionist pressures (Gilligan 1997).

Much of the theoretical literature on the effects of regulatory barriers to trade claims that such measures would undercut negotiations. The availability of an unconstrained policy instrument would deter nations from making the concessions in the first place. Ideally, the GATT contracting parties could communicate their product-by-product requests with the expectation that they would have to grant tariff reductions in return. If these tariffs were substituted with nontariff barriers, then there would be no reason to reciprocate.

All of this is to say that negotiations that proceed on a reciprocal basis would be fruitless if they were not somehow enforceable. The framers of the GATT were well aware that tariffs were not the only means for governments to frustrate trade. Governments had already discovered countless domestic and international commercial alternatives to tariff protection, many of which were more difficult to evaluate than traditional tariffs and import quotas (Kono 2006). To resolve this issue, the GATT/WTO system introduced a mechanism for reciprocal negotiations for increases—the dispute-settlement mechanism. By allowing states to bring suit at the organization, the GATT enables what Bagwell and Staiger (2002b) refer to as "reciprocity up." Violations of GATT tariff concessions are discouraged by the authorization of retaliation up to an equal volume of trade by the complaining state. The ability to ensure reciprocity in the enforcement stage is a prerequisite for governments to participate in the reduction stage.

The success of the GATT dispute-settlement mechanism depends on having rules that can distinguish between policies that do and do not count as violating the agreement. Not all violations are obvious, and thus the threat to remove concessions to deter regulatory protectionism suffers from a clear measurement problem. How is one to know whether a regulatory barrier is a legitimate public policy or a substitution for tariffs? The GATT rules appear to resolve this balance in two ways: first, by requiring that any domestic measure be applied in a nondiscriminatory way and, second, by allowing frustrated exporting governments to make claims that regulations are otherwise distortionary. The former, known as the national-treatment doctrine in the GATT, restricts protectionism in cases where domestic producers would be negatively affected but does not eliminate the use of nondiscriminatory regulatory barriers to trade. The latter, the "nonviolation" doctrine, allows governments to claim that any foreign activity, even that otherwise permissible under WTO law, frustrates their reasonable expectations for market access. If a government violates its commitments by raising a nontariff barrier, their partners can appeal to the nonviolation clause in the GATT and recover their losses up to the amount promised in the negotiation. Staiger and Sykes (2011) point out that while this provision would theoretically fill the gaps in GATT rules, in practice, governments have feared that the breadth of this provision would undermine the agreement.

While most GATT/WTO negotiations operate under a formal norm of reciprocity, there is debate over the degree to which reciprocity actually is satisfied in negotiations. Trade data from early rounds reveals that increases in import flows were not compensated in terms of exports. Figure 6.1 compares the change in imports and exports with the United States before and after each bilateral trade agreement using statistics gathered in the League of Nations Directions of International Trade publications.[8] Overall, the United States experienced a $120 million excess of exports over imports after these trade agreements were signed, amounting to approximately 18 percent of total exports prior to negotiations. Moreover, in a similar analysis of reciprocity in the GATT, Finger,

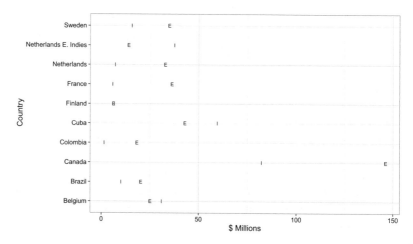

FIGURE 6.1. Reciprocity in the bilateral period: change in US trade volume after RTAA treaty, imports (I) and exports (E)

Reincke, and Castro (2002), find no evidence for market-access-based reciprocity in trade outcomes from the Uruguay Round. In that study, 23 of 33 countries had an imbalance at least half as large as their concessions given (Finger, Reincke, and Castro 2002). This evidence suggests either that reciprocity was merely hortatory, a cover for fundamentally unequal negotiations, or that concessions were somehow unable to account for the interests of US trade partners.

It would be incorrect to draw strong conclusions from trade flows alone. Reciprocity aims to keep constant relative market access, not necessarily equalize changes in imports and exports. Moreover, any concession in a bilateral agreement was predicated on obtaining concessions from trade partners—both imports and exports are thereby endogenous functions of negotiations.

In the following section, I reexamine the Uruguay Round negotiation, deploying an identification strategy to address the endogeneity of reciprocal negotiations and the presence of economic policies not constrained by reciprocity in market access—regulatory protectionism. Once this endogeneity is addressed, I find that the limits of reciprocity are not in their utility for tariff negotiations but rather in how market-access-based methods struggle to discipline the use of regulatory barriers to trade.

6.3. Negative Reciprocity in the Uruguay Round

Aggregate evidence that outcomes are not balanced is insufficient to establish the extent to which market-access-based reciprocity governs modern trade negotiations. In this section, I discuss a tariff-line-level analysis to examine the conditions under which reciprocity generates mutual exchanges of market access. I find evidence in favor of market-access-based reciprocity norms and, where those norms break down, that the absence of successful exchanges of market access can be accounted for by the presence of regulatory protection. The norms of trade negotiation were developed in the early nineteenth century to account for the consequences of tariffs for trade volume; they break down in the face of regulatory barriers to trade. Instead of reciprocity across all products, I find negative reciprocity, a relative withdrawal of concessions, when regulatory barriers to trade are present.

Accounting for the various confounding factors that can generate differences in trade flow outcomes after a negotiation requires substantially more data than that available in cross-country trade flows or the rudimentary data from the early nineteenth century. Building on prior work by Limão (2006), I turn to the Uruguay Round negotiations, which offer a detailed, disaggregated picture of reciprocity by the US with its trading partners. The Uruguay Round offers standardized tariffs, listed in harmonized tariff schedules, as well as a wide variety of products and partners to allow coverage of a variety of political and economic confounding factors (Limão 2006). During the Uruguay Round, the GATT negotiations that formed the WTO, the US negotiated down tariffs by an average of 2.8 percent and negotiated on thousands of tariff lines. Despite this complexity, these negotiations still formally operated on the principle of reciprocity, where trade negotiations balance the trade-weighted reductions in tariff protection.

To evaluate partner market access changes, more than 5,000 US tariff lines are matched with an aggregate tariff change by the foreign suppliers of that product. Because of the variety of capacities and sizes of markets, this aggregation has to take into account both the foreign changes in tariffs as well as the share of trade in those tariff lines prior to the change. Lower tariffs would shift trade proportional to the underlying capacity of the producers in that market. In the Uruguay Round, governments used their existing trade patterns to draw inferences about the beneficiaries of a tariff concession. This inference was formalized in the 1934 RTAA as the *principal supplier rule*, which limits negotiations to the main producers of a given import (Goldstein and Gulotty 2014b; Gowa and Hicks 2018).

Given that the unit of analysis is the US product-level tariff, Limão aggregates proposed changes to tariffs by measuring changes in market access in each country, k, by $\Delta ma_t^k = \Sigma_j (-\Delta\tau_{jt}^k) w_{jt}^k$, where $\Delta\tau_{jt}^k$ is the percentage of tariff reduction by country k in each imported good j weighted by trade share w. For example, if Germany lowers its tariffs on soybeans, the effect of that change will be weighed by the consumption of American soybeans by Germany.[9] This weighted tariff change is then summed over all products that Germany imports. Each American import is then connected to the change in market access of the principal suppliers of each of those imports. Germany's tariff reduction on soybeans would enter the US calculations for a tariff on German export, such as automobiles, along with the market access changes of all other principal suppliers of automobiles.

Limão (2006) controls for nontariff measures as a potential confounding factor. However, the Uruguay Round occurred before the completion of the SPS and TBT agreements so regulatory barriers to trade were not yet explicitly measured in the multilateral trade system. Instead, Limão relies on the TRAINS NTM measure data described in chapter 3. These data cover a variety of nontariff barriers to trade and are not only limited to fixed-cost regulatory measures. Unfortunately, TRAINS suffers from inconsistent data collection across years and are not comparable to the later STC data used in chapter 3. Nonetheless, I rely on this measure to maintain fidelity to Limão (2006).

Regressing US tariffs, here the difference in the natural log of ad valorem tariff, on this aggregated measure with an interaction with the NTM measure, we can estimate the relationship between foreign tariff concessions and US tariff concessions. This model includes controls for the relative natural log of the GDP of the foreign governments supplying each product (bargaining power), as well as the presence of preferential trade areas (PTA) and an indicator variable for whether the observation covers multiple tariff lines at lower levels of aggregation (I[Multi HS8]). The net effect of a tariff concession in a product with a nontariff barrier is estimated to be statistically indistinguishable from zero, suggesting the Uruguay Round did little to move tariffs when NTMs were present. To put it another way, a reduction in tariffs by foreign partners saw no concession from the US when the US was using an NTM on any country.

6.3.1. Instrumenting Reciprocity with Prior Concessions

The statistical results from the basic regression reflect an underidentified model. Reciprocal trade negotiations, by definition, require that changes in US tariffs to be made in response to changes in tariffs by partner countries. Determining the direction of causation between US tariffs and foreign tariffs requires taking into account the fact that in most cases, they are codeterminative. To address the endogeneity problem, Limão uses the unilateral liberalization in each product by US trade partners (1986–92) as the instrument for the total liberalization in that product (1986–95). This assumes that the choice of unilateral liberalization occurred without regard to the possibility that the US would reciprocate eventually and that no third factor drove both unilateral liberalization and the US response.[10]

The negotiated tariffs were implemented between 1995 and 2000. The second-stage instrumental variable estimate of the marginal effect of foreign tariff concessions for products with a US nontariff barrier is displayed in column 1 of table 6.2 in the appendix of this chapter. The result, originally reported in Limão (2006), is that for those products with NTMs, not only did the US not reciprocate but foreign governments experienced a higher tariff when they had made a concession.[11] That is, US tariff changes among those products with NTMs are negatively correlated with the changes in market access by the principal suppliers of those products. This means that not only did the US reduce tariffs more on those products with NTMs, but among those products with NTMs, those with the fewest foreign concessions experienced the largest reductions. This is consistent with neither the practice of market-access-based reciprocity nor any other form of negotiating strategy.

Limão explains the lack of reciprocity as an unwillingness of US partners to demand reciprocal reductions when those reductions will be watered down by an American NTM. The tariffs concessions on NTM measures reflect the endogenous choice to substitute for tariff concessions.[12] In fact, there is a statistically significant correlation between US NTMs and US tariff concessions during the Uruguay Round. US tariff concessions were larger on average among those products with existing NTMs than those without, even though foreign concessions, both unilateral and overall concessions, were lower. To explain the disconnect be-tween foreign concessions and US tariff changes, the following section tests the possibility that regulatory protection is responsible for under-mining negotiations.

6.3.2. Narrowing the Channel and Reciprocity

The failure to account for NTMs appears to undercut reciprocal tariff negotiations in the Uruguay Round. This shows that the consequences of entangled mercantilism are not limited to regulatory cooperation. It ap-pears that US partners were unwilling to overlook the use of NTMs, not offering concessions when NTMs were present. For governments that have a stake in multinational production, this may be a trade-off worth making.[13] Other states, seeing their smaller firms disadvantaged, would face losses by agreeing to a tariff concession that does not account for the fact that their firms are forced to exit the market.

Normally, we would expect that an NTM that substitutes for a tar-iff would be handled by the nonviolation nullification of benefits claims available to governments under Article XXIII of the GATT. Recall that under that article, governments are owed restitution following any ad-verse change to market access from a previous concession, whether or not that change is attributable to foreign economic policies. However, if those losses are in both traditional forms of protection—a reduction of market access as well as a shift of market share away from smaller firms—the latter would not be recoverable under the existing norms of GATT dispute settlement. Access for small firms is not recognized as a benefit under the current rules. The result is that if governments see an NTM on a product, and the US has an incentive to adopt NTMs to engage in this profit-shifting effect, the foreign governments may in fact raise tariffs, or at least not cut them, in expectation of US tariff liberalization.

The profit-shifting incentive to adopt NTMs—that is, the aim of mov-ing a larger share of business toward productive foreign multination-als—is highest when there is a larger share of multinationals in a sec-tor. Following the analysis in chapter 3, I again use a product's contract intensity to capture these dynamics. Contract-intense production gener-ates externalities that are resolved by establishing vertically integrated supply chains that allocate profits across countries. Insofar as these prof-its enter the US, increasing the share of business held by multinationals is in the US national interest. The intraindustry reallocative effects of the agreement, much like the differences in shipping productivity, need to be included in the overall accounting of trade negotiations.

To determine whether the results regarding NTMs are driven by these international contracting incentives, I extend the analysis to include the measure of contract intensity. The results, displayed in column 2 of table 6.2, replace the NTM indicator with the measure of contract intensity. The results are estimates of reciprocity for concessions among foreign suppliers in contract-intense goods that are of a comparable magnitude to those products that are subject to NTMs. Contract-intense products do not experience reciprocal concessions, in much the same way that the original model found for products experiencing US NTMs. These results suggest that it is not the presence or absence of NTMs but rather the contract intensity of the product that best predicts the failure of reciprocal reductions during the Uruguay Round.

The puzzling result that sectors with NTMs experienced negative responses to concessions, or negative reciprocity, is only partially resolved by showing that these products are also contract intensive. Theories of international cooperation in a global production environment identify intrafirm bargaining problems that may similarly challenge international negotiators (Staiger 2012).[14] Moreover, the negotiations described here occurred before the conclusion of two important new agreements on regulatory barriers to trade, the TBT and SPS agreements. Interestingly, these agreements go beyond attempting to identify specific regulatory levels and instead appeal to international standards.

6.4. Discussion

This chapter has shown the importance of accounting for the effects of trade policies in negotiating treaties over those policies. Early US insistence on mirror reciprocity failed to enable negotiations. The equivalent elimination of tariffs would only hand the market to the largest and most productive nations. It was only when the US and other major powers adopted graduated reciprocity in market access that negotiations between unequal parties were possible. Today these are the norms embedded in the multilateral trade regime, enabling progress on tariffs in the twentieth century.

That progress has ground to a halt. The statistical analysis above indicates that the warning signs were present in the Uruguay Round, with governments refusing to deal with products that faced nontariff or regulatory barriers to trade. This breakdown in the market-access-based system underlying the WTO is not, however, a sign that the broad principle of reciprocity is flawed but rather that the measure of that reciprocity, trade volume, may not be accounting for the concerns of states. Examination of the product-by-product tariff changes in the Uruguay Round reveals substantial variation in the success of negotiations and that the source of the problem is in those products most embedded in global production networks.

The evidence developed in this chapter also helps resolve an outstanding puzzle in the welfare and market access implications of regulatory measures.[15] A survey of econometric studies of technical barriers to trade finds that regulatory barriers do not have a consistent effect on trade flows (Swann 2010). Using disaggregated trade data, Crivelli and Gröschl (2012) find that governments are more likely to file complaints at the WTO against foreign sanitary and phytosanitary measures that increase the volume of exports. The willingness on the part of governments to voice concerns about measures that increase exports implies that trade volume does not track interests, which is explained by the fact that governments are not acting against the market access implications of regulatory barriers but instead are objecting to distortions in the composition of trade. As more products are produced within global supply chains, we might expect that further trade-volume-based negotiations will see the same fate at the Eden Treaty, hopefully with less disruptive consequences.

6.5. Technical Appendix: Replication and Extension of Limão (2006)

The following regression examines US ad-valorem-bound rates, logged, and the difference from before and after the Uruguay Round. The independent variables include an NTM indicator ("NTM"), contract intensity from Nunn (2007; "contract intense"), and bargaining power of the suppliers of each product ("bargaining power"). Bargaining power is calculated by averaging the difference of GDP for each supplying country weighted by the extent to which that country produces that product:

$$\Sigma_k S_{iT}^k \Delta(\ln \text{GDP}_t^{\text{US}} - \ln \text{GDP}_t^k),$$

TABLE 6.2 **Instrumental variable estimates from Limão (2006)**

	Dependent variable: US liberalization: $\Delta\tau$	
	(1)	(2)
Tariff concession	0.02***	0.73***
	(0.01)	(0.16)
NTM × concession	−0.06***	
	(0.01)	
NTM (TRAINS)	−4.03***	
	(0.57)	
Contract × concession		−1.52***
		(0.34)
Contract intense		−77.36***
		(17.57)
PTA	1.20***	1.06***
	(0.15)	(0.21)
I(subcat.)	−0.84***	−1.26***
	(0.21)	(0.32)
Bargaining power	0.01***	0.03***
	(0.002)	(0.01)
Constant	−2.54***	34.16***
	(0.36)	(8.67)
Observations	5,079	5,079

Note: *$p < 0.1$; **$p < 0.05$; ***$p < 0.01$.

where k is the country, and S_{iT}^k is the share of good i supplied by that country. Finally, trade costs are the average transport cost factors for HS eight-digit products over all exporters of the product to the US in 1994 (Limão 2006). There are additional controls for the presence of multiple HS eight-digit products in a sector and an indicator for whether the product was exported to the United States by a PTA partner ("PTA export"). See table 6.2.

CHAPTER SEVEN

Designing Optimal Standards Agreements

$\mathbf{P}$ostwar tariff agreements codify product-by-product tariff rates on pre-agreed product categories. To arrive at these rates, governments often engage in drawn-out and complex negotiations where their own tariffs are traded away for concessions abroad. This reciprocity is how otherwise mercantilist states managed to create and sustain a relatively open economic order, at least among GATT/WTO members. However, governments struggle to adopt these procedures for regulatory barriers to trade. One important reason for this is that regulatory barriers to trade have dual uses; they can shift profits, but they can also protect citizens' health, safety, and welfare (Marette and Beghin 2010). Whether a trade-affecting regulation is necessary is difficult to anticipate or measure objectively. Worse, governments may have incentives to exaggerate their regulatory needs to hide their mercantilist policies. Equivalent exchange of predefined tax rates appears simple by comparison.

Governments have developed a series of tools to address regulatory protection, including two multilateral agreements on health, quality, and safety standards: the Sanitary and Phytosanitary and the Technical Barriers to Trade agreements. These regulatory agreements lack the specificity of product-by-product obligations typical of tariff negotiations and do not specify regulatory standards or codify permissible and impermissible aims. Instead, these agreements use an apparently more modest battery of transparency provisions and references to international standards and scientific evidence. While much of the theoretical literature on international organizations focuses on the technical and capacity problems addressed by transparency provisions, it is rather the references to international standards that help sustain cooperation. These tools offer an alternative to product-by-product reciprocity as an efficient solution to the problem of regulatory protection.

While regulations are technically complex and their effects difficult to predict, this is not what makes regulatory protection such a difficult problem for international cooperation. Rather, the problem facing governments, as is the case in many areas of international relations, is the difficulty of discerning intentions. The normal GATT/WTO solution to this kind of uncertainty is to adopt a form of flexibility. The GATT/WTO rules specify escape mechanisms, formalized side payments, and periodic renegotiation rights to ensure the right mix of incentives and constraints (Grieco 1990). Ex ante forms of flexibility include a series of listed exceptions in GATT Article XX; ex post flexibilities include the dispute-settlement process, where states may choose to compensate their partners for violating their commitments.[1] Formally, these flexibility provisions reduce the costs associated with periods of punishment, enabling deeper tariff commitments for otherwise reluctant governments.[2]

The SPS and TBT agreements introduced a new form of flexible cooperation. These agreements do not specify regulatory procedures, set standards for risk assessment, or even offer a schedule to form the basis of negotiating standards. A common refrain, repeated on the WTO official website, is that "the WTO itself does not and will not develop such standards." Instead, governments are authorized to choose a preferred "level of protection," with a gentle legal encouragement to use internationally recognized standards.[3] While both agreements defer policy details to the member states and international standard-setting organizations, the text of the SPS Agreement goes further: the only justification for restricting trade more than would occur under an international standard is the consideration of "scientific arguments resulting from an assessment of the potential health risks."[4] In both the SPS and TBT agreements, trade discrimination is not a prerequisite for violation of the agreement (Hudec 2003, 187).

The appeal to scientific evidence appears to introduce objectivity into international governance, moving toward what Robert Hudec terms "Post-Discriminatory Law." However, in practice, the legal apparatus of the GATT/WTO has interpreted the law as limiting the intrusiveness of the agreement, holding that "science did not necessarily mean mainstream or majority scientific opinion."[5] For instance, in order to justify its ban on beef products with certain hormones, the European Union needed only to "provide a report by some competent, respectable scientist (who may well be expressing a minority or idiosyncratic point of view) that is coherently reasoned and that supports the existence of the risk against which the Member is regulating" (Howse 2016, 59–60). It is surprising, then, that the SPS and TBT agreements have become the basis for dozens of challenges of foreign, trade-restrictive regulations, suggesting that even without a consensus requirement, governments expect the agreements have teeth.

The provisions on international standards and scientific evidence in the SPS and TBT agreements are broadly consistent with a class of principal-agent problems identified by Amador and Bagwell (2012, 2013) as optimal delegation. *Optimal delegation* occurs in the design of contracts that motivate a biased but informed agent to act in a principal's interest. Politics is rife with examples of division between authority and information: congressional committees, representative governments, and bureaucracies.[6] In the international relations context, scholars have used the principal-agent model to characterize relations between citizens and international institutions. This framework forms a chain of delegation, from citizens to their elected officials, to international negotiators, to the formation of an international organization (Vaubel 2006). In this framework, the collectivity has an objective to maximize the aggregate welfare of the membership of the agreement, while the individual has privately informed interests that diverge from the remainder of the group. In this case, the agent is the individual regulating state, and the principal represents the amalgamation of the interests of the international agreement. The problem is to find the set of options or decisions that should be left to the individual, conditional on the nature of the information (the state); the extent of the bias of the agent; and the value to the principal of cooperative behavior. Optimal delegation describes the shape and extent of flexibility granted to regulators as consistent with the agreement.

I develop the results from the optimal-delegation framework where regulators are motivated by regulatory protection. This focus on regulators' interests rather than firm profits allows me to forgo some of the details of the Melitz framework developed in chapter 2. In that model, firms were modeled in general equilibrium, showing that the effect of regulatory protection traveled through aggregate prices. Here I develop a simplified environment, Cournot competition with endogenous entry, following prior research on fixed costs regulations (Suwa-Eisenmann and Verdier 2002; Fischer and Serra 2000; Costinot 2008). These papers model an international duopoly to show that fixed-cost regulations can deter entry of foreign firms. Costinot (2008) compares the effects of international institutional arrangements, such as the national-treatment rules of the GATT/WTO system and the mutual recognition rules of the European Union, in addressing regulatory protection.[7] Unlike those models that focus on duopoly, I allow an endogenous number of domestic entrants that vary in their marginal productivity. As with the model developed in chapter 2, these firm-level differences within a market can drive regulatory protection.

This chapter proceeds as follows. First, I briefly develop a model of standard setting that captures the trade-off between regulatory autonomy and disguised protectionism in a competitive market. I then show that this model satisfies conditions for optimal delegation to take the form of a cap—a kind of ex ante flexibility. Given this framework, I describe the practice of regulatory cooperation in the GATT and WTO standards agreements, comparing the design of multilateral standards agreements. The fourth section concludes the chapter.

7.1. Regulatory Protection under Cournot Competition

Suppose a paternalistic government is attempting to correct a consumption externality from imported goods. Consumers often have imperfect information about the quality of an imported product, as was the case of lead in toys and salmonella in peanuts, a problem that is exacerbated with modern long supply chains. When the government becomes aware of the issue, it can impose a fixed-cost regulatory barrier to limit consumption of the good. At the same time, as argued earlier, this action can serve the interests of some part of the industry. In this section, I characterize basic economic preferences and behavior subject to the inefficiencies created by these regulatory barriers. As with the model in chapter 2, prices, quantities, and the number of producers are each determined by the extent of a fixed-cost regulatory measure.

Consider two imperfectly competitive exporting economies, home (·) and foreign (†), with complete and mutual dependence on imports for consumption. For simplicity, assume that these two economies are symmetric, allowing us to focus on one relationship, foreign producers and home consumers. These consumers demand a single good, imported from one low-cost producer and an endogenously determined number of high-cost firms located in the foreign economy. Formally, consumer economic welfare will be a linear function of total quantity consumed:

$$U(Q) = \alpha Q - \frac{Q^2}{2}.$$

While all products are the same, firms are differentiated in terms of their marginal costs. In this case, firms may either have high (H) or low (L) marginal costs of production $c_H, c_L : c_H > c_L \geq 0$. The $N^\dagger + 1$ foreign firms sell at a price determined by linear demand $P = \alpha - Q$, where $Q = N^\dagger q_H + q_L$ is the quantity of goods sold by high- and low-cost firms and α is the size of the market.

In order to export their products, foreign firms must pay a fixed cost $F \geq 0$. These are the regulatory barriers to trade that arise from both natural and policy-determined consequences of licenses, labels, and packaging requirements. Imposing this regulatory burden is costly for the state and is applied to all goods consumed in the home market. These costs are linear and, when combined with the marginal costs, determine firm profits $\pi_j(P, q_j) = Pq_j - c_j q_j - F, j \in \{H, L\}$.

Firms decide their production levels strategically. In a Cournot-Nash Equilibrium, a high-cost firm $i \in N^\dagger$ conjectures that the other firms will produce $(N^\dagger - 1)^* q_{H-i}$ and q_L. Each firm also correctly conjectures the level of endogenous entry, $N^\dagger = N^{\dagger *}$. Profit maximization generates equilibrium prices and quantities for high- and low-cost producers as a function of the equilibrium level of entry $N^{\dagger *}$.[8] As $N^{\dagger *}$ rises, the quantity produced rises, lowering prices.[9]

The equilibrium number of entrants is determined via entry, which will occur until the profits of the entrants are zero ($\pi_H = 0$).[10] The equilibrium number of high-cost exporters can be written in parameters:[11]

$$N^{\dagger *} = \left\lfloor \frac{\alpha + c_L - 2c_H}{\sqrt{F}} - 2 \right\rfloor.$$

Given this endogenous number of entrants, we can write the profits of the low-cost firm as a function of the fixed costs and the marginal advantage of the low-cost firm:

$$(7.1) \qquad \pi_L(F) = \left[c_H - c_L + \frac{\alpha + c_L - 2c_H}{\left[\dfrac{\alpha + c_L - 2c_H}{\sqrt{F}} \right]} \right]^2 - F.$$

There are three immediate results from this framework, consistent with the model in chapter 2. First, the profits of the low-cost firm are increasing in the regulatory barrier F, albeit in a stepwise manner. Figure 7.1 displays this stepwise function alongside the equilibrium entry decision. The black lines indicate the number of entrants in equilibrium. The discontinuous gray lines represent the increasing profits induced by the exits of marginal-cost firms. The profits increase in this manner until the point that no high-cost firms remain in the market.

Second, the profitability of the low-cost firm is increasing in the marginal-cost advantage over high-cost firms. If the policy were a tariff (a marginal cost) rather than a regulatory barrier (a fixed cost), then the policy would have no effect on the profits of the low-cost firm. Although the higher marginal cost brought by the tariff restricts entry, the low-cost producer's benefit is perfectly offset by having to pay the tariff on each good sold. Instead, the surviving high-cost firms experience a gain in profits from the higher tariff, as they do not sell as many products and can capture the remaining market share.

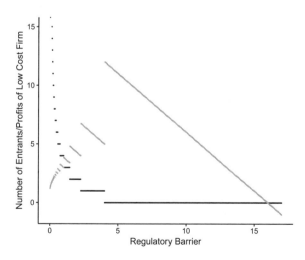

FIGURE 7.1. Entry and profits under varying regulatory barriers

Third, while the quantity of sales drops with the regulatory barrier, as more firms exit, the price rises. In equilibrium, $Q = \alpha - c_H - \sqrt{F}$ and $P = c_H + \sqrt{F}$. This complicates the measurement of regulatory barriers to trade and the enforcement of traditional market access rules, as both depend on trade volume. In any case, consumers are worse off, having to pay higher prices for fewer products. However, understanding the distributional effects of regulatory barriers within an industry, or the consequence for trade volume, depends on the structure of the market.

The problem with regulatory protection, as described in chapter 2, is that these policies can be used for competitiveness or public-policy goals. The latter are difficult to contract over in advance, arising from changes in consumer taste and awareness, social expectations for safety and health, and activist pressures. For the purposes of this model, I assume that the good in issue can impose a pure externality that increases in the quantity sold, subject to a privately observed random political economy weight γ. Let G indicate the cumulative distribution function of γ with support on $\Gamma = [0, 1)$.

The two governments, home and foreign, value both consumer interests and public-policy goals, as well as producer interests. While each government regulates the other, here we restrict attention to a foreign exporter sector and home's regulations and consumption. The foreign government's welfare (V) depends on the size of the export sector and, in particular, the number of firms that are able to operate $N^{\dagger*}$. In equilibrium, the higher the number of firms, the higher the quantities of exports, which can have revenue or employment implications. Furthermore, the government may directly benefit from lower inequality among producers. These interests in the extensive margin motivate the foreign government to expand opportunities for entry:

$$V^{\dagger}(F) = N^{\dagger}(F).$$

The home government's choice of a regulatory barrier balances concerns for profits that do not include the number of high-cost firms that are able to enter the market. Because these foreign high-cost producers are small and unprofitable, it is unlikely that they would have any influence in the home state. A low-cost producer is larger, more profitable, and in models with foreign production, more likely to organize as a multinational corporation.[12] These capacities are associated with lobbying activity and influence, even beyond the borders of their home state (Bombardini and Trebbi 2012; Jensen, Quinn, and Weymouth 2015; Weymouth 2012). As a result, the home government shares a partial interest in the profits of the low-cost firm (π_L).

Equation (7.1) shows that the home government can use a regulatory barrier to promote the profits of the low-cost firm so long as there is at least some cost advantage relative to the high-cost producers. So long as there is at least some threat of entry, regulatory barriers that raise fixed costs increase the profits of the low-cost firm. This is because a productive (low-marginal-cost) firm can benefit from the competitive consequences of the regulatory barrier. Prior work on the effects of fixed costs by Rogerson (1984) obtains a compatible result using a model in which limited pricing by a leading firm deters entry. To a point, raising a regulatory barrier that harms all firms equally advantages the leader by allowing a higher limit price—and hence higher profits.[13]

Taking these effects into account, the home government's welfare W consists of a weighted sum of consumer welfare ($U(Q^*)$), the profits of the low-cost foreign firm (π_L), a domestic consumption externality, including the expense of maintaining the regulatory barrier, with weights β and γ on profits and the externality, respectively. Given the economic environment above, note that the equilibrium quantity Q^* is a decreasing function of the regulatory cost F; we can write government utility either as a function of Q or as a function of the regulation F. Assume that the consumption externality is a simple linear function of regulatory stringency: $\gamma F - c_E * F$, where $c_E > 0$ is the cost of maintaining the regulation:

$$W(F|\gamma) = U(F) + \beta\pi_L(F) + \gamma F - c_E * F.$$

Given this government utility function, the following section describes the inefficient behavior of governments in competition with one another.

7.1.1. Regulatory Protection

In the absence of any agreement, self-interested governments enact policies that are globally inefficient, regulating in such a way that harms their partner. These "Nash" quantities ($F^N(\gamma)$, $F^{\dagger N}(\gamma^*)$) of each good arise from the unilateral choice of each government to maximize domestic welfare W and, for each country, only depend on the realization of the domestic regulatory demand. Specifically,

$$F^N(\gamma) = \left[\frac{\beta(c_H - c_L) - \dfrac{c_H}{2}}{c_E + 1/2 - \gamma} \right]^2.$$

As the government becomes more sensitive to either the externality (γ) or producer interests (β), the government would prefer to adopt a higher regulatory barrier. As the difference between the high-cost and low-cost producer declines, the preferred regulatory barrier approaches zero.

Each government observes political economy weights γ and γ^*, which are randomly and independently drawn from G. The internationally efficient regulations maximize $W(F, \gamma) + V^\dagger(F)$, generating $F^E(\gamma)$. Because the regulations of one country negatively affect her partner, the efficient level of trade is higher than under the "Nash" regulatory policy. Efficiency can be improved if a government is constrained in its regulatory choices. The problem is that governments might be tempted to enact restrictive policies to take advantage of their flexibility. The following section describes the optimal shape of that flexibility under these constraints.

7.1.2. Optimal-Delegation Framework

A standards agreement sets the range of behavior that counts as cooperation by identifying a menu of permissible regulations, negotiated prior to when private political pressures are realized. Given a range of permissible options, the government merely picks its preferred regulatory option within that range. An optimal agreement maximizes, jointly, the welfare of all of the governments in the agreement, subject to incentive compatibility constraints. To use the results from Amador and Bagwell (2013), I show that the regulatory protection problem can be formulated to isolate the political economy shock γ from the negative externality imposed on the trade partner $V(F)$. These results apply in a setting with "money burning," a provision in the agreement that requires some amount of wasteful activity that hurts all members of the agreement. However, in the conditions described here, no money burning is used in an optimal agreement.

Formally, a standards agreement is a pair $(\mathbf{F}(\gamma), \mathbf{t}(\gamma))$, the regulation and the extent of money burning. The joint membership of the standards agreement, the principal, calculates welfare as a continuous function of the regulation and the regulatory demand. Let $\Omega(F, \gamma) \equiv \gamma\mathbf{F} + B(\mathbf{F}(\gamma)) +$

$V(\mathbf{F}(\gamma))$ be the combined utility of the two trade partners, where $B(\mathbf{F}(\gamma))$ is the welfare of the home government, net of the consumption externality. The problem for the principal is therefore to solve

$$\max_{\mathbf{F}(\gamma),\,\mathbf{t}(\gamma)} \left\{ \int_{\gamma\in\Gamma} \big(\Omega(\gamma,\mathbf{F}(\gamma)) - \mathbf{t}(\gamma)\big)\,dG(\gamma) \right\}$$

such that the incentive compatibility constraint holds

$$\gamma\mathbf{F}(\gamma) + B(\mathbf{F}(\gamma)) - \mathbf{t}(\gamma) \geq \gamma\mathbf{F}(\gamma) + B(\mathbf{F}(\gamma)) - \mathbf{t}(\gamma);\,\forall\gamma,\gamma\in\Gamma$$

and the costs of obtaining scientific evidence are nonnegative:

$$\mathbf{t}(\gamma) \geq 0 \quad \forall\gamma\in\Gamma.$$

One set of solutions to this maximization problem takes the form of an interval. Given that $F_r\in \text{argmax}_F\{\gamma F + B(F)\}$ is the preferred flexible choice, an interval allocation is an allocation $(\mathbf{F},\mathbf{t})$ with upper bound b if $b\in\Gamma; \mathbf{t}(\gamma)=0\ \forall\gamma\in\Gamma$ and

$$\mathbf{F}(\gamma) = \begin{cases} F_r(\gamma), & \text{if } \gamma\in[\underline{\gamma},b) \\ F_r(b), & \text{if } \gamma\in(b,\bar{\gamma}] \end{cases}.$$

From this definition and lemma 1 in Amador and Bagwell (2013), an interval allocation with bound γ_H is optimal among interval allocations if and only if

(i) $\int_{\gamma_H}^{\bar{\gamma}} \Omega_F(\gamma, F_r(\bar{\gamma}))g(\gamma)d\gamma = 0;$

(ii) $\Omega_F(\underline{\gamma}, F_r(\underline{\gamma})) \leq 0.$

Here $\Omega_F(\gamma, F_r(\gamma))$ is the derivative of the principal's welfare when the agent receives a political shock γ and selects her best flexible response, indicating the direction of the bias of the agent who observes a particular regulatory demand γ. Condition (i) describes the "cap" on regulatory behavior, here indicated by γ_H. This cap is optimal if setting the policy at the cap generates unbiased policy on average. Otherwise, the principal would do better by raising or lowering the boundary to ensure either more regulation to favor the home government or less regulation to favor the foreign government. When condition (ii) is satisfied, the optimal interval allocation does not include a lower bound—the government's flexible choice is less extreme than what the principal would demand.

Under the assumption that the regulatory demand is independent of the protectionist interest, the conditions on the existence of an optimal interval allocation $(\mathbf{F}, \mathbf{t})$ simplify to three conditions on parameters. The first condition depends on the relative policy risk aversion of the home and foreign governments. In particular, the foreign government's welfare must be no more than twice as convex as the home government's welfare function, and their joint interest must be to avoid policy risk.[14] To satisfy this requirement, it must be that the home government is not able to set the regulatory barrier too low, as the subsequent entry would make the foreign welfare, and the weight on foreign welfare, exponentially larger than the interests of producers or consumers at home. This condition is both technical and substantive. Technically, because the optimal-delegation model is concerned with the joint welfare of both countries, foreign producer interests have the potential to outweigh any regulatory needs. Substantively, if the foreign producer interests are not incorporated into the agreement, there is no reason to incorporate regulatory barriers into a standards agreement.

The second condition is that the regulatory demand shocks must be sufficiently common.[15] If actual regulatory demands are unlikely to occur, governments are better off not offering any flexibility in agreements. It is the presence of occasional severe regulatory demands, such as the discovery of lead in children's toys or the outbreak of salmonella in peanuts, which motivates flexibility.

Finally, there must be some interior cap that balances the negative effect of the regulation on foreign welfare against the likelihood of the regulatory demand. This is the $\gamma_H \in (\underline{\gamma}, \overline{\gamma})$, which solves

(7.2) $$V'(F_r(\gamma_H)) + E[\gamma \mid \gamma \geq \gamma_H] - \gamma_H = 0,$$

where V' is the derivative of the foreign government's welfare function, evaluated at the cap. Determining whether this condition applies requires understanding the way that incentives work not only in the regulating government but in the foreign state. Where an antitrust regulator makes judgments about market structure, this final condition also requires taking a position on the interests of the government. The following uses these conditions to derive the level of the optimal cap on regulatory activity.

7.1.3. Optimal Cap on Regulatory Behavior

Because the economic environment is imperfectly competitive, the foreign partner may have a convex valuation of the home country's policy. From the foreign government's perspective, the uncertainty associated with regulatory activity is beneficial—the possibility that the home government will experience low levels of regulatory demand, opening up their market, is more valuable to the foreign government than the certainty of a particular regulatory environment. However, offering a constrained interval of flexibility is valuable if the government has a sufficiently high weight on producer surplus; we can still apply the proposition described above.[16] If the principal's utility overall is sufficiently "risk" averse, then there may exist some interval, capped by γ_H, that balances between the benefits of shifting the cap (γ_H) upward against the losses to the foreign state. The necessary and sufficient conditions on the cap on regulatory behavior are then that the average political economy demands above the cap are equal to the losses in the foreign state at the cap.

To find the functional form of that cap, assume that the regulatory demands facing the home government are uniformly distributed. Given this functional form to the uncertain regulatory needs, we can apply equation (7.2). The optimal cap is therefore set at the γ_H, which solves the following:

$$\frac{[(c_H - c_L) - (\alpha - c_H)]}{2[\beta(c_H - c_L) - \frac{c_H}{2}]^3}\left(\left(c_E + \frac{1}{2}\right) - \gamma_H\right)^3 + \frac{1}{2} - \frac{\gamma_H}{2} = 0.$$

These conditions are together necessary and sufficient for an optimal agreement to take the form of an upper bounded interval. That is, the agreement offers some maximal level of regulation or protection but allows governments to apply regulations below the maximal level. This has the advantage that governments can use flexibility to apply moderate levels of regulatory restrictions when political pressures are low while retaining the ability to clamp down if a crisis arises. Figure 7.2 plots the choice of F over ranges of γ, with the thicker line indicating government behavior under the optimal agreement. Governments with higher levels of regulatory demand "pool" at the maximal regulation.

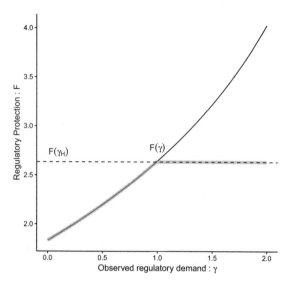

FIGURE 7.2. Simulation of regulatory protection as a function of regulatory demand: optimal ex ante flexible agreement with regulatory cap

Note: $\alpha = 30, c_H = 5, c_L = 4, \beta = 20, c_E = 3.5$

The optimal level of the regulatory flexibility for governments is sensitive to both economic forces and government interests. The gap between the interest of the home and foreign government has a nonlinear effect on the height of the optimal cap—if the weight on producer interests is insufficiently large, then the principal would prefer a higher cap. However, a higher regulatory cost (c_E) lowers the optimal cap, as flexibility is less valuable. For agreement memberships with insufficient effects on foreign welfare $V'(F) \to 0$, an agreement would optimally set the cap so high as to afford governments' full flexibility over their regulatory choices.

Under the conditions described above, optimal delegation takes the form of an interval. This means that the ideal contract between governments assigns flexibility of regulatory choice short of a cap. The conditions on the likelihood of the shock and the preferences of the governments determine the optimality of that interval as well as the height of the optimal cap. In the following section, I distinguish this kind of flexibility from other concepts of flexibility in the design of international institutions.

7.2. Ex Ante and Ex Post Flexibility

Interval delegation, policy choice short of a fixed ceiling or floor, is a form of institutional flexibility. Flexibility is a key design element in the rational design of international institutions. However, that literature emphasizes the costs to rigidity in terms of the incentive compatibility constraints. To loosen these constraints, governments insert ex post flexibility, which enables governments to take actions that deviate from their prior obligations. The emphasis in this literature is that without such flexibility, deviations would meet severe punishments—placing pressure on governments not to make substantial agreements in the first place. Interval delegation, on the other hand, allocates policy options—here a range of policy options from which the government makes their choice—ex ante flexibility.

Governments are expected to achieve ex post flexibility with escape clause provisions. For example, Rosendorff and Milner (2001) develop a repeated game in which governments aim to cooperate over tariffs in the presence of privately observed political economy shocks. Compared to a "Grim Trigger" equilibrium in which tariffs do not vary with the observed political economy shock, the introduction of a public, costly mechanism to temporarily defect—an escape clause—improves the situation, enabling governments to match the political economy shock with a period of defection. So long as the cost of using the escape clause is not worse than permanent defection, there is no incentive for a government facing moderate pressure to outright defect. Furthermore, because the using the escape clause is "self-enforcing" in the sense that the cost is immediately and publicly observed, a government facing little to no political pressure would not opt to use the escape clause.[17] Decreasing the cost to temporarily defect (increasing ex post flexibility) facilitates deeper cooperation under uncertainty.

When will governments incorporate escape clauses or renegotiation? In the context of tariff cooperation, Koremenos (2001) develops a model with hidden actions, where governments are unable to determine the effects of a policy. There, the degree of risk aversion is positively associated with escape and negatively associated with certainty about the partners' cooperative behavior. Johns (2014) develops a model with privately observed shocks on the political economy weight for import-competing firms. Conditional on maximizing the cooperative benefits of a treaty, we should expect flexibility provisions when agreements have particularly low tariff bindings.

Escape clauses that enable ex post flexibility often also require the escaping government to pay some cost to achieve its optimal policy. As a consequence, the defecting government never actually achieves its ideal option. The advantage to ex ante flexibility is that governments in many conditions need not pay to achieve their preferred policy—the goal is to allow governments to match the domestic political pressures with actions. As a result, we might expect that ex ante flexibility would allow governments to satisfy temporary political concerns more than a strict tariff commitment. On the other hand, ex ante flexibility does not necessarily mean the deepest regulatory commitments: the expected regulatory level under a flexible agreement is higher than under an inflexible binding (Bagwell 2009). This is because when agreements are inflexible and governments behave optimally, a fixed obligation generates a lower average level of protection to reduce the international externality. When agreements are flexible, cooperation is shallower, but governments benefit from being able to shift policy to meet domestic political demands. It turns out that the form of flexibility matters for the operation of the agreement and what kinds of problems agreements are designed to resolve.

When might the two forms of flexibility, ex ante and ex post, be used in a multilateral standards agreement? From the conditions for the optimality of a regulatory cap, we would expect ex ante flexibility when high levels of regulatory need are likely to occur (or at least not decreasingly likely). In addition, because flexibility with a cap is only of interest to governments with sufficiently similar welfare functions (jointly concave), flexibility is more likely when there is sufficient interest in producer profits (high β). However, in order for that cap to be interior to the range of γ, it must be that the regulation is not excessively costly to the home government (medium c_E). If, on the other hand, governments rely on ex post flexibility—escape clauses and other temporary exceptions to the limits set by the agreement—then we would expect these to occur more often in more ambitious agreements.

To empirically adjudicate between ex ante and ex post flexibility provisions, I examine the historical development of international standards and the use of scientific evidence in the TBT and SPS agreements. I find that scientific evidence is not necessarily a marker of an efficient or even scientifically legitimate policy. Rather than certifying cooperative intent, commissioning a study or publicly announcing a scientific rationale for a public-policy measure can serve to raise the costs of regulatory protection. Requiring the payment of these costs to regulate beyond the international standard can offer governments ex post flexibility—a costly escape that improves the extent of cooperation. Scientific evidence requirements allow governments to credibly signal political pressures for regulatory protection. In the optimal-delegation framework, this would be akin to money burning, which would not occur in equilibrium under an optimal interval-delegation agreement.

7.3. Historical Evidence for Institutional Flexibility

Regulatory protection has been a concern for governments since well before the creation of the GATT, falling under the general rubric of internal discrimination. In this section, I examine the historical record of agreements to limit that regulatory protection, tracing the extent to which the presence of flexibility in design features is chosen in response to the levels of regulatory demand in the population and the heterogeneity of trade partners. The use of international standards and scientific evidence marks a significant shift in the history of trade negotiations, which until that point had focused on inflexible prohibitions against de jure discrimination.

Consideration of internal discrimination is apparent even at the advent of long-distance commercial relations. During the Commercial Revolution of the Middle Ages, privately organized guilds were the principal guarantors of the quality and safety of goods, and these guilds could enforce limits on trade under the pretense of these quality standards (Richardson 2001). In response to this private protection, importers petitioned governments to limit discrimination. In one letter from a French cloth merchant to the King of England, the merchant requested permission to "import into the realm cloth of the same measure as that sold in the fairs of Champagne, Franche-Comte, and Burgundy, arguing that [these goods] were duly controlled by the eswardeurs of the town, so that no cloths that did not fulfill the requirements could be exported." He added that "if permission were not given to them, they would be unable to import any cloth at all because the necessary changes to be made to the tenters and other manufacturing processes could only be done at great expense and loss."[18] The proposal from the cloth merchant amounted to *mutual recognition*, where the French judge's rulings would be held up in English markets.

Even with these efforts, economic cooperation in the Middle Ages was limited to a patchwork of local laws and regulations rather than formal agreements. In terms of the model, this may be because monitoring or regulating commerce was costly for the state (high c_E). Richardson (2008) argues that while towns can and did inspect some manufactured merchandise, bureaucrats lacked the knowledge, skills, and resources needed to detect hidden defects. As a result, there was less benefit to creating institutions that allowed local policy choice in regulating safety or quality. With limited ability to regulate the market, consumers were primarily left to their own devices.

With the rise of international trade in the eighteenth century, governments began to adopt formal agreements to reduce barriers to commercial activities. These agreements often included "national-treatment" provisions that guaranteed that foreign citizens would pay duties no higher than natives in the same circumstances.[19] While initially focused on port fees, these provisions became the basis for offering broad, formal assurances that domestic public policies would not undermine tariff concessions. Any country that agrees to national treatment uses the treatment of their own citizens as a floor of guaranteed treatment for foreign agents.

In modern agreements, national treatment requires governments to ensure that foreign products receive at least as favorable treatment as "like" domestic products. This effectively constrains internal taxation or regulations to policies that do not discriminate between domestic and foreign sources of supply. If governments cannot distinguish foreign or domestic goods in the application of their policy, a restrictionist policy would be required to also apply to domestic firms whose interests could serve as a counterweight to restrictionist policies. One such obligation is inscribed in Article III:4 of the GATT: "The products of the territory of any contracting party imported into the territory of any other contracting party shall be accorded treatment no less favourable than that accorded to like products of national origin in respect of all laws, regulations and requirements affecting their internal sale, offering for sale, purchase, transportation, distribution or use."

Article III supports the tariff concessions by maintaining market access expectations—limiting the substitution of regulatory protection for tariffs. For example, suppose a country makes a concession, lowering tariffs on paint products, in exchange for some valuable market access in a partner state. In the absence of a national-treatment provision, the government could attempt to use a health warning label to limit imports of foreign paint, surreptitiously increasing the sales of favored paint manufacturers. A national-treatment provision requires that the labels on foreign products are the same as those found on domestic products. The government is thereby required to either not adopt the health measure or adopt it evenly for the entire market.

The "like" product provision helps enforce obligations in the GATT/WTO system but is substantially limited for many trade relationships. With comparative-advantage-driven trade, we would expect cases where a country fully specializes out of producing a product and engages only in import. Because the legal analysis of a national-treatment provision asks whether a regulation differentially advantages some "like" domestic product over a foreign product, the absence of a domestic benchmark might give governments a free hand. Consider a restriction that states that paints sold in a market could not contain toxic lead. If there are no domestic paint manufacturers, it is difficult to establish that the regulation is not evenly applied to all goods in the market and thereby does not establish a discriminatory effect (Horn 2006). To correct for the limitation in the "like" product analysis, the GATT introduces mechanisms designed to limit de facto discriminatory measures. Article III:1 of the GATT requires that laws and regulations affecting commercial exchange "should not be applied to imported or domestic products so as to afford protection to domestic production." Invoking this provision depends on showing that some harm has come to market access, as determined by trade volume.

However, if regulatory barriers take the form of a fixed cost, as is the case for many standards, licenses, and labeling requirements, the main effect of a regulatory barrier on a product may be to induce exit among foreign firms rather than to protect domestic production of that product. In the previous sections, governments use measures that apply to all products evenly, but the effect is to suppress entry in favor of political motivations. As a result of these limitations, the rigid application of the national-treatment rule may do little to address the challenges posed by regulatory cooperation.

These limitations to the operation of national-treatment and other

original GATT rules may be partially addressed by the judicial apparatus of the agreement. The dispute-settlement procedure provides rulings
on complaints by the members over violations of the agreement and can
go some of the way toward clarifying or emphasizing aspects of it. However, prior to the 1994 Marrakesh Declaration, any government could
block an adverse ruling by the GATT dispute-settlement system. This
meant that there was little capacity for courts to lower the costs of using rigid national-treatment rules in the enforcement stage. With the creation of the WTO in 1994, the agreement gained the capacity to limit
such costs. For example, considering the example of paint above, if a foreign manufacturer of paint switches to a lead-intensive manufacturing
process, a rigidly applied national-treatment provision might not allow
governments to respond to the change, as the manufacturing process
was not explicitly included in the tariff schedule. In this way, a dispute-
settlement process can rule that the national-treatment provisions need
not apply and that the lead in the manufacturing process distinguishes
the goods from a regulatory standpoint.[20] The availability of a dispute-
settlement process can fill in incomplete agreements. However, relying
on individual rulings is inefficient and the appellate body has been hesi-
tant to fill out the obligations of the agreement to new products.[21]

Wishing to avoid the uncertainty and costs of complicated judicial
proceedings in parallel to bolstering the judicial mechanism, the GATT/
WTO members sought reassurances of their rights to promote public-
policy objectives while limiting the effects of measures that escaped
the national-treatment rules (Sykes 1995). These regulatory issues were
taken up in three agreements, the Tokyo Round agreement on technical
barriers to trade (the "Standards Code") and the two Uruguay Round
agreements: the TBT Agreement and the SPS Agreement. These agreements vary in their use of ex ante and ex post flexibility, concordant with
the characteristics of the growing membership and their respective policy domains.

7.3.1. Ex Post Flexibility in the Tokyo Round

The 1973 Tokyo Round saw the first successful efforts to develop additional rules on regulatory protection, and the first introduction of international standards and scientific evidence into the GATT system. The
round began as an effort to address the trade consequences of domestic

policymaking, spurred by the increase in the membership of the GATT from its original 23 members to 102, including a large number of less developed economies, and the perception that the largest economies were using nontariff barriers to protect their markets. The agenda expanded to include items of interest to the new membership, including the regularization of safeguards for workers and firms and the expansion of the GATT into new sectors, in particular agricultural and tropical products. The wide scope of topics to be addressed raised the expectation that regulatory protection might be one of them.

In order to navigate these expanded issues, the Tokyo Round membership adopted a strategy—introduced in the 1967 Kennedy Round—the use of "plurilateral" negotiations. Plurilateral negotiations meant that new issues would be negotiated among an interested subset of the membership and the obligations would be limited to just those that chose to participate. Based on this model, the Tokyo Declaration set out to find a coalition willing to join an agreement on regulatory issues. As the round progressed, it became apparent that negotiating each issue in isolation limited the range of trade-offs at the bargaining table. Thus when it came time to extend the deals beyond the main negotiating countries, few countries were willing to join on.

As a consequence of the limited buy-in, the Tokyo Round Standards Code did little to change the obligations under the national-treatment provision except in the narrow field of technical regulation. The Standards Code covered technical regulations, defined as "a specification contained in a document which lays down characteristics of a product such as levels of quality, performance, safety or dimensions," excluding measures relating to production and processing standards common for agricultural products. The codes did offer a number of new obligations; the 33 signatories were asked to refer to international standards in the development of their regulations and, if there was a dispute, to provide "detailed scientific judgments" on the formulation of the regulation. In addition, regulations were to be transparent, offering the opportunity for trade partners to comply or complain. While these provisions went well beyond tariff schedules, these obligations did not come with substantive or well-defined enforcement procedures.

Given the lack of new substantive obligations beyond national treatment, how can we understand the institutional design changes made in the Tokyo Round? The rise in membership during the Tokyo Round expanded the potential space of regulatory demands. The institutional approach taken during the round addressed this expansion in two ways. First, making the Standards Code optional allowed governments to opt in to the agreement. This opt-in provision did not necessarily mean as much in the GATT system, which had rules that allowed any member to block a panel report. However, governments were offered flexibility short of blocking a dispute. Governments were encouraged to provide scientific evidence for the necessity of a trade-restrictive measure.[22] Thus without changing the severity or cost of punishments, this provision introduced a mechanism that may have provided ex post flexibility on the part of the signatories. As a result, the Standards Code has had some success in formalizing limits to regulatory protection.

The effectiveness of ex post flexibility in the Standards Code depends on governments being unwilling to pay the cost associated with providing scientific evidence for their preferred measures. However, because of the limits on the judiciary in the GATT, the Standards Code was the basis of only a few disputes that resulted in a public report. Furthermore, this mechanism predicts that governments would avoid imposing measures that would require this sort of evidence in the first place. Despite these substantial limits, there were several cases that invoked the Standard Code obligations, primarily involving Japanese technical regulations.

One prominent example of the effectiveness of ex post flexibility arose in a dispute about a safety standard. The standard, set by a Japanese industry group, was alleged by the US and several Alpine countries to be a violation of Japan's obligations in the Standards Code. The regulation was challenged on the grounds that it was unique to Japan rather than the existing international standard. To receive the Japanese Consumer Product Safety marking, skis had to be a certain thickness rather than following the international standard, which emphasized the effectiveness of the bindings. This regulation made it into the American press and filtered into popular culture as a blatant effort to protect local industry. In the best-selling novel/polemic *Rising Sun*, Michael Crichton characterized the regulation as typical of Japanese protectionism: "[The Japanese] say 'business is war,' and they mean it. . . . The obstructions are endless. . . . Foreign skis were once banned because Japanese snow was said to be wetter than European and American snow. That's the way they treat other countries, so it's not surprising they worry about getting a taste of their own medicine" (Crichton 1992, 144).

In reality, this incident was a success of the Tokyo Standards Code. After formulation of the standard by the industry group in 1986, the US and others raised concerns, but rather than officially defend the proposal using scientific evidence that Japanese snow is wetter, the Consumer Product Safety Association withdrew the standard before a formal dispute was raised, and ski sales were not affected (Rapoport 1992).[23] The use of scientific evidence, akin to requiring socially inefficient money burning, was avoided, along with the inefficient policy.

There were cases where the threat of adjudication was insufficient to deter even openly discriminatory regulation. In a case that reached consultations, the US raised concerns about the discriminatory effect of the Japanese practice of "lot" inspections. The US alleged that Japan allowed domestic producers to get approved to sell a "type" of product while foreign shipments had to be analyzed on a shipment-by-shipment basis. Following consolations, Japan changed the law rather than offer any scientific evidence that such inspections were more effective than the alternative "type" inspection technique (Edelman 1987). Again, this is a partial success of the agreement, suggesting that the costs of defending the measure were sufficiently prohibitive to change behavior. The success was only partial in this case because Japan was also subject to a number of coercive efforts by the United States that did not depend on the findings or rules of the Standards Code.

7.3.2. Ex Ante Flexibility in the SPS and TBT Agreements

The provisions of the Standards Code were strengthened by the automatic adoption of dispute-settlement proceedings and redesigned during the Uruguay Round negotiations. After the 1994 formation of the WTO, all WTO members would also be members of new standards agreements. These WTO agreements, including the agreement on technical barriers to trade and on sanitary and phytosanitary measures, were covered by the umbrella of the WTO dispute resolution system, in which all 123 members of the agreement could freely participate under the new "right to a panel." These changes increased the prospect of formal legal sanctions upon violating the agreement, which would suggest a decrease in ex post flexibility. However, in addition to strengthening the ex post sanction, the TBT and SPS agreements clarified and consolidated the design principles of the Tokyo Standards Code, introducing provisions that expanded the ex ante flexibility of it.

For example, the TBT Agreement clarified the right of governments to pick their preferred regulatory standard. Reiterating the national-treatment obligation from the GATT, the TBT Agreement requires members to ensure that technical regulations are "not prepared, adopted or applied with a view to or with the effect of creating unnecessary obstacles to international trade." The interpretation of necessity requires that regulatory measures are no more trade restrictive than other available regulatory policies that reach the same public-policy objective. However, those public-policy objectives are left unspecified, allowing governments to determine their own levels of acceptable risk. This regulatory autonomy limits the need for foreign governments in general and the WTO dispute-settlement system in particular to try to infer intent or come to some kind of consensus about the appropriate level of protection across the heterogeneous membership of the organization. Instead, governments are free to pick a public-policy goal that demands robust regulatory measures without regard to the trade consequences.

Rather than determining the intent of governments, the TBT and SPS agreements depend on two features that help align incentives: provisions for the harmonization of regulatory barriers to international standards and, failing that, a restated requirement to produce scientific evidence. Specifically, the agreements say that WTO member states "shall" use international standards as the basis for their technical regulation. The SPS Agreement enforces this requirement by providing a legal incentive—those measures that conform to international standards "shall be deemed to be necessary to protect human, animal or plant life or health, and presumed to be consistent" with the obligations under the GATT/WTO. This presumption rules out challenges to regulatory protectionist measures that reach, or are less than, the level of restriction induced by the adoption of international standards and removes the burden on governments to provide evidence of the efficiency of their chosen levels of regulation.

The SPS Agreement also increases the ex post flexibility to adopt regulations more restrictive than an international standard. Again, the cost of adopting a standard beyond the international standard is that the government must develop and publicly report a scientific justification for the regulation. This cost was proposed by the United States toward the beginning of the Uruguay Round in the form of a requirement that measures be based on "sound and verifiable scientific evidence."[24] That proposal was watered down, and subsequent GATT/WTO jurisprudence defines "scientific justification" as an examination and evaluation of available scientific information, a determination based on scientific inquiry as to the use of the regulatory barrier. Rather than sound and verifiable evidence, any evidence deemed scientific would be sufficient to justify a regulatory measure.

These definitions were soon part of a dispute between the US and Japan (*Japan-Varietals*). In 1997, the Japanese Ministry of Agriculture, Forestry, and Fisheries implemented an SPS procedure that sought to prevent the introduction of an invasive moth carried by certain fruits. Japan's Plant Protection Law banned the importation of untreated apricots, cherries, plums, pears, quinces, peaches, apples, and walnuts. The issue was over the evidence necessary to show that the treatment was effective. The Japanese rule required that any proposed treatment for the pest must be proven not only to kill the invasive species but to kill it on each variety of agricultural product. Each variety of apples, cherries, and peaches would require a separate test. The United States argued that this stringency was not justified by the scientific evidence and that Japan made no effort to obtain such evidence. After the panel ruling and appeal, the WTO appellate body found that the existence of a scientific justification for regulatory measures depends on there being a "rational" relationship between the SPS measure and the available scientific information.[25] Japan was found lacking such a rationale and lifted its requirement on December 31, 1999.

The institutional history of multilateral agreements on standards suggests that governments have appealed to international standards as a sort of cap for their regulatory activity and that scientific evidence requirements provide some reassurance to governments concerned about the limitations of international standards. After the Uruguay Round, these limits on governments appear to have had positive effects. The need to provide scientific evidence, for example, led to progress in a number of cases involving Japanese protectionist measures. At the same time, the number of announced and potentially trade-restrictive measures has not declined in the face of these requirements. While, in the final analysis, it is difficult to determine the counterfactual level of regulatory protection, the design of the SPS and TBT agreements at least offers a strategy that addresses some of the shortcomings of typical trade agreements.

7.4. Discussion

The use of international standards and scientific evidence in the SPS and TBT agreements mark an alternative means of cooperating on commercial policy than that offered by the standard tit-for-tat exchange of market access. By building on advances introduced in the Tokyo Round, the GATT/WTO system has developed a novel form of flexibility: the use of international standards. These agreements set the international standard as the upper boundary on the trade restrictiveness of regulatory policies. This flexibility allows governments national autonomy in raising regulations while still offering bounds on the harm that those regulations can impose on outside parties, particularly small firms.

It may be that some international commercial agreements have already seen success in enabling smaller firms to enter markets. Baccini, Pinto, and Weymouth (2017) find that "market-friendly" provisions in preferential trade agreements that remove behind-the-border barriers reallocate sales from the largest to the smallest affiliates of American multinationals. The preceding analysis suggests, however, that these same agreements can risk being insufficiently attentive to national regulatory needs to survive in the long run. Flexible commitments would balance the concerns of smaller firms against those of meeting difficult-to-anticipate demands for regulatory oversight.

Nonetheless, flexibility is no panacea either. The utility of ex ante flexibility depends on the issue area. The mechanism enables governments to satisfy their realized regulatory needs short of a boundary while avoiding extreme policies. Doing so depends on the political effects of satisfying societal interests and producer interests in both countries. In the context of regulatory protection, whether governments would benefit depends on the likelihood of unanticipated public-policy demands and the political benefits to advantaging large firms both at home and abroad. In other issue areas, these parameters would require different institutional solutions. The particularities of the framework developed here can be read as a justification for diversity in institutional forms across substantive applications. In summary, regulatory cooperation will not arrive from one institutional norm or practice. There are substantive differences between the optimal designs of agreements on technical regulations, health, consumer safety, and environmental protection.

Part of the challenge of this institutional diversity is that it suggests that theories of the design of international agreements cannot be meaningfully divorced from the substantive issues addressed by the agreement.[26] Where prior work has attempted to analyze international institutional design from observed practices, within issue areas, there is insufficient variation to make credible inferences about how these organizations work. My approach instead relies on what would be theoretically optimal, with the idea that this baseline sheds light on the workings of these institutions.

CHAPTER EIGHT

Conclusion

Markets and Borders

Regulatory protectionism is endemic to contemporary commercial relations. This is in part because governments are tasked with protecting the health, safety, and environment of their citizens. Achieving this requires the development of new tools to monitor and regulate complex international trade networks. However, in a world of globalized markets, registration requirements, and testing requirements, mandatory standards can be designed in ways that shift profits away from smaller foreign producers toward larger ones. When markets are entangled, the national interest may extend across borders. The result is that regulations are excessively strict, designed in ways that shift trade profits through large multinational corporations like Mattel, DuPont, and McCormick & Company to advance local affiliates. In sum, efforts to promote public-policy aims can also advance a certain form of mercantile interests—but one that is less about shutting off the market than narrowing the channels of global commerce to a few favored firms.

This book documents conditions under which governments would use regulatory protection to achieve mercantilist aims. Cross-national evidence suggests that regulatory protection is most pronounced among governments in highly globalized industries, particularly when profits are shared with local affiliates. That finding, laid out in chapter 3, suggests that further market integration will do little to deter the rise of regulatory protection. Entangled mercantilism is not, however, universal: just as not all governments can affect global prices with their tariffs, not all governments face international market conditions that give them a stake in foreign profits. The costs of entangled mercantilism, however, are widespread and growing as more firms must overcome regulatory hurdles to trade or be forced out of the market.

While regulatory protectionism is enabled by global production, its contours and extent depend on domestic political arrangements. Just because it is theoretically in the national interest to engage in profit shifting, in practice, a government's willingness to do so depends on the degree of domestic opposition. That is, while unaffiliated foreign firms lack access to the levers of power and are excluded from any calculation of the national interest, smaller local firms often are negatively affected as well. The case studies in chapters 4 and 5 show that in practice, the patterns of regulatory protection are contingent on the outcomes of complex and heated political debates. The regulatory innovations in the European Chemical Agency, the Food Safety Modernization Act, and the Consumer Product Safety Improvement Act began as efforts to resolve legitimate public-policy needs. In the chemical safety case, the debate began with the environment and shifted to competitiveness concerns. Small European producers were initially opposed to the regulation but later mollified with financial incentives and less onerous registration fees. In the case of food safety, small-scale farmers and specialty producers opposed new food safety rules and managed to extract exemptions in the legislative and rulemaking process. In each case, an alliance between large producers and consumer advocates sought to limit exemptions from reporting requirements, advocating for strict regulations, but were largely satisfied when those exemptions primarily targeted domestic firms.

As small firms have been closed out of markets, their governments have turned to the global trade regime for redress. The GATT/WTO system has had marked success with past mercantilism, offering states a rules-based forum for their disputes. Unfortunately, that global trade system is ill-equipped to handle the form of profit shifting produced by regulatory barriers to trade. While the GATT/WTO rules ensure equitable market access as measured in trade volume, these rules have little to say about the equitable distribution of trade across firms. This problem is exacerbated by the fact that any rules must contend with the legitimate purposes that regulatory measures can serve. The Uruguay Round agreements built a system that holds real promise, using references to scientific evidence and international standards to disincentivize hidden protection. Making hidden protection transparent, however, is only part of the issue. Effective governance will require reworking the rules of the global trade system to account for the ownership of trade between multinationals and foreign firms. The danger is that without a mandate for innovation on the part of the member states in Geneva, regulatory protection will continue to not only concentrate global markets but also undercut cooperation on traditional forms of protectionism.

8.1. Implications for Scholarship

This book aims to contribute to both the theoretical scholarship in international relations and the empirical study of commercial cooperation. Regarding the former, this book grounds mercantilist behavior in the joint interests of firms and states. The way that chapter 2 roots regulatory choices in the competitive interests of firms follows theories of international politics that emphasize interdependence as well as liberal theories that root commercial policy in domestic arrangements (Lake 2009; Moravcsik 1997). The problem of regulatory protection is driven by not only the distributional fights within nations but also the influence of market power across international borders. Globalized firms have competitive profit motives that lead them to benefit from changes in policy abroad, but their effect depends on governments devaluing the interests of small foreign firms and sharing in those profits. Only in those conditions would regulations serve mercantilist interests.

This book explores entangled mercantilism as an explanation of regulatory protection. Existing explanations of regulatory barriers to trade generally fall into three categories: barriers as accidents, barriers as substitutes, and regulatory capture. The first argues that regulations are an unfortunate side effect of otherwise legitimate public-policy demands (Vogel 2012). The problem of regulatory protection is thereby just the problem of coordinating on a standard, which may have distributive consequences for the party forced to make the largest adjustments (Grieco 1990). The patterns of regulatory activity in chapter 3, however, persist after econometrically controlling for the presence of domestic demands for regulation.

The second major explanation for regulatory barriers to trade is as a substitute for tariff barriers (Kono 2006). Regulatory barriers have the advantage of being opaque, lowering the likelihood of punishment from either domestic audiences or foreign partners. While this is an important motivation for regulatory protections, they exhibit very different patterns than tariff measures. Tariffs protect import-competing industries while harming internationally engaged firms, but as demonstrated in chapters 4 and 5, major international firms are often supportive of more restrictive regulatory measures. While small firms are decimated, larger firms often see an increase in trade volume (Fontagné et al. 2015). As with the politics of tariff protection, as theorized by Milner (1988a) and Blanchard (2007), globalized firms encourage governments to value foreign market players, but now these foreign entanglements promote mercantilist behavior.

The third major set of explanations for regulatory protection draw on domestic theories of regulatory capture. Incumbent firms have long been suspected of using political access to close off their competitors at the expense of national welfare. Governments are indeed not the simple national-income-maximizing machines theorized in chapter 2, often weighing some domestic interests over others. However, they must at least contend with the domestic losers from market restrictions. In the design and implementation of regulatory barriers, we see how smaller domestic firms are accommodated. Early in the process of regulating European chemicals, major American companies opposed introducing the regulation. It was only when the measures were reworked with lower variable costs, eliminating progressive-fee structures and the prospects of outright bans on lucrative product lines, that these large multinationals began to support the regulation. As regulations move out of the sight of the public and into the details, large producers find willing audiences in regulators who are accountable for national competitiveness. At the same time, regulators are often sensitive to smaller domestic firms, incorporating exemptions, subsidies, and other corrective measures that are not extended to foreign producers. Regulatory protection is an international phenomenon, but its practice is shaped and enabled by domestic conditions.

The history of tariff policymaking suggests that one way to escape a mutually destructive mercantilist cycle is through trade treaties and organizations. Chapter 6 shows how the global trade regime was designed to handle tariffs and tariff substitutes. For those measures, governments can rely on a form of reciprocity that measures the mutual exchange of commitments in aggregate trade volume. A 5 percent tariff reduction that generates $10 million of market access for imports can be exchanged for a 10 percent reduction that generates the same market access for exports. Reciprocity in market access, however, is of little use if the problem is not overall trade volume but rather the exclusion of smaller firms. This is a conclusion that depends on a particular attentiveness to the economic character of the policy and the market those policies govern. Tariffs impose variable costs; regulations can impose fixed costs. Markets can be more or less imperfectly competitive. Future research into commercial policy must be attentive to the interaction between policies and the conditions of competition that mediate the economic incentives of governments, consumers and firms. While the general problem of competition is never going to be eliminated, its expression of regulatory protection can be curtailed. The model of firm interests suggests that monopolistic rents are particular to fixed costs measures. Insofar as regulators can design progressive-fee structures and help ameliorate the costs of reconfiguring and relabeling goods, the problems of regulatory protection can be dampened.

Finally, this book suggests a positive approach to institutional design for governments facing value trade-offs. No government will be satisfied delegating their choices over fundamental questions such as the appropriate tolerance for health risks or other safety concerns to a supranational body. Chapter 7 describes how nations that aim to maintain national regulatory autonomy but limit the costs of regulatory protection for smaller businesses can adopt flexible bindings. The World Trade Organization's legal provisions, such as the reference to scientific evidence and international standards, can be understood not as an appeal to some sort of universal or objective stance on national regulatory choices but rather as incentive-aligning devices. The World Trade Organization's stance that it is not a standard-setting body is not a concession to the reality of politics but rather a feature of an optimal agreement when future regulatory needs are difficult to predict or contract over.

8.2. Regulatory Protectionism and Inequality

The firm-driven politics described in this book have direct implications for the workings and design of the global trade regime but also speak to a pressing concern of contemporary politics—rising and persistent economic inequality. While incomes and wealth have generally been unequal, recent decades have exhibited a striking rise in income inequality. While the cause of this inequality is far from certain, the character of the rise is suggestive of firm-level advantages: the rise of inequality is less in exacerbating the differences between CEOs and janitors and more in expanding the disparity among more and less competitive firms.

Recall that trade is concentrated in the hands of a few large exporters.[1] Not only are these firms large and productive; they are able to pay a wage premium over other firms. This dynamic generates intraindustry income inequality. Song et al. (2015) use a comprehensive matched employer-employee database in the United States to show that the rise in income inequality is driven by these intraindustry, cross-firm differences. Moreover, while the wages of the average worker at the average firm have remained static, differences across firms for the same position have risen drastically: more than two-thirds of the variance in earnings inequality between 1981 and 2013 was driven by differences across firms. The result is more wealth concentrated in the hands of a few firms. Regulatory protection can exacerbate this concentration.

The fact that regulatory protection raises costs for smaller exporters—driving them out of the market, reducing competition, and raising aggregate prices—does not imply that public-policy goals always come hand in hand with mercantilism. We have seen that tracking chemicals through the supply chain and ensuring the integrity of a food supply can be done in a way that limits the effects on smaller producers. The spread of multinational corporations reinforces interests that have long been at play in international commercial relations. Borders are still relevant: chemical producers from Australia to Vietnam and farmers from Jamaica to Pakistan have little influence over the regulatory choices of the European Union or the United States. Foreign producers lack a voice in the process.

What is at stake in resolving conflicts over regulatory protection is not just avoiding trade disputes but also ensuring effective and equitable participation in a global economy. The predominant framing of this question asks whether globalization has "gone too far," pushing up against national demands for autonomy and the desire to shield domestic markets and social orders from the destructive power of international competition (Rodrik 1997). But this framing misses an important factor behind contemporary commercial relations: the fact that governments have incentives to shift profits that can neatly coincide with their interest in regulatory autonomy. Instead of a natural effect of globalization, some of the rise in antitrade nationalist and populist politics may have to do with the concentration of the profits of globalization in the hands of a few elite producers.[2] Uncorrected, entangled mercantilism may undercut its own preconditions by undermining political support for global commerce, particularly in an environment where the public is already skeptical of the benefits of trade.[3]

Thankfully, international commercial cooperation has never meant eliminating mercantilist interests. In the future, perhaps some coalition of small firms will manage to convince their governments to develop new global institutions that can address regulatory protection in these industries. Success depends on recognizing the incentive on the part of governments to maximize their global profit share. This book shows that rather than undercutting national regulatory autonomy, globalized firms, in their competition for market power, benefit from stricter standards, higher levels of protection for consumers, and higher prices. Decades of liberalization of tariffs has created global producers who are in a position to sell at scale, providing governments one more reason to choose more stringent regulations. The problem is not economic but political, as governments often choose their own over their neighbors.

Technical Appendix

This appendix walks through the economic model described in chapter 2, extending the analysis to an open-economy model.

A.1. Melitz's Closed Economy under Pareto Distribution

Derivation of CES Consumer Demand and Expenditure

Consumer Maximization. Suppose the preferences of a representative consumer are governed by a constant elasticity of substitution $\sigma > 1$. This elasticity determines the "love of variety" over all the individual varieties of goods $\omega \in \Omega$. The following CES function aggregates the quantity consumed of each variety $q(\omega) > 0$, $\omega \in \Omega$, and $\rho = (\sigma - 1)/\sigma$:

$$U = [\textstyle\int_{\omega \in \Omega} q(\omega)^\rho d\omega]^{1/\rho}.$$

Consumers can purchase goods of variety ω at price $p(\omega)$ and maximize their consumption subject to a budget constraint, which sets total expenditures to be no more than nominal income $R \geq 0$:

$$\textstyle\int_{\omega \in \Omega} p(\omega)q(\omega)d\omega \leq R.$$

Demand is determined by solving the consumer's maximization decision, subject to an aggregate budget constraint. The following Lagrangian $\mathcal{L}$ defines the consumer's maximization problem:

$$\mathcal{L} = [\textstyle\int_{\omega \in \Omega} q(\omega)^\rho d\omega]^{1/\rho} - \lambda[\textstyle\int_{\omega \in \Omega} p(\omega)q(\omega)d\omega - R].$$

The consumer's first-order condition is as follows:

$$\frac{\partial \mathcal{L}}{\partial q(\omega)} = U^{1/\sigma} q(\omega)^{(-1)/\sigma} - \lambda p(\omega) = 0$$

$$\Leftrightarrow q(\omega) = U\lambda^{-\sigma} p(\omega)^{-\sigma}$$

$$\Leftrightarrow p(\omega)q(\omega) = U\lambda^{-\sigma} p(\omega)^{1-\sigma}.$$

Integrating, we can get the total nominal income R,

$$R = \int_{\omega \in \Omega} p(\omega)q(\omega)d\omega = U\lambda^{-\sigma} \int_{\omega \in \Omega} p(\omega)^{1-\sigma} d\omega,$$

$$\Leftrightarrow U\lambda^{-\sigma} = RP^{\sigma-1},$$

where P is an aggregate price index:

$$P \equiv [\int_{\omega \in \Omega} p(\omega)^{1-\sigma} d\omega]^{1/(1-\sigma)}.$$

Combining terms, we find that demand for each variety $q(\omega)$ and the amount of money spent on each variety $r(\omega) \geq 0$ is a fraction of overall demand:

(2.1) $$q(\omega) = \frac{R}{P}\left(\frac{p(\omega)}{P}\right)^{-\sigma}$$

(2.2) $$r(\omega) = p(\omega) * q(\omega) = R\left(\frac{p(\omega)}{P}\right)^{1-\sigma}$$

Derivation of Equation (2.3)

Producer Maximization. Prices are set for each variety by maximizing profit (π), subject to the demand function $q(\omega) = ((p(\omega))/P)^{-\sigma}(R/P)$ and taking all other firms production decisions as given:

$$\pi(\omega) = p(\omega)q(\omega) - f - \frac{q(\omega)}{\varphi}$$

$$\pi(\omega) = p(\omega)^{1-\sigma} P^{\sigma-1} R - f - \frac{p(\omega)^{-\sigma} P^{\sigma-1} R}{\varphi}$$

$$\frac{\partial \pi(\omega)}{p(\omega)} = P^{\sigma-1}R[(1-\sigma)p(\omega)^{-\sigma} + \sigma\varphi^{-1}p(\omega)^{-\sigma-1}] = 0$$

(2.3) $$p(\omega) = \frac{\sigma}{\sigma-1}\frac{1}{\varphi} = \frac{1}{\rho\varphi}.$$

From equation (2.3) and the fact that each firm produces exactly one variety, we can identify firms directly by their productivity. Plugging in these prices from the first-order condition (2.3) into the demand equations (2.1) and (2.2), the revenue of each firm and the profits of each firm can be written as a function of endogenous price indexes and each firm's productivity:

$$q(\varphi) = RP^{\sigma-1}(\rho\varphi)^{\sigma}$$

$$r(\varphi) = R(P\rho\varphi)^{\sigma-1}$$

$$\pi(\varphi) = \frac{r(\varphi)}{\sigma} - f.$$

A.2. Equilibrium Market Forces

Having restated prices and profits as a function of productivity and exogenous demand parameters, we can now turn to ask how market forces shape the distribution of participants by affecting the entry and exit decisions of entrepreneurs and firms. We then identify conditions where the firms enter and exit at equal rates. In such an equilibrium, the economy is fully characterized by the mass of entrants and the average productivity.

Entrepreneurs are forward-looking and make rational decisions about entry and exit. Following the formalization in Melitz (2003), upon paying a sunk entry cost, $f_e > 0$, some number of entrepreneurs ($M_e \geq 0$) start a firm. Each draws a productivity φ from a known distribution $g(\varphi)$ that has positive support over $[\varphi_{min}, \infty)$ and with a cumulative distribution function $G(\varphi)$.[1] Firms may exit immediately after learning their productivity if it is too low to be productive.

In addition to this endogenous selection process, each firm faces a constant risk of forced exit, independent of productivity, at a probability $\delta > 0$. This constant churn allows for the analysis of the composition of entrants.

The formal decision process for each entrepreneur depends on the expected value of the discounted stream of future profits v relative to the fixed costs of entry:

(A.1) $v(\varphi) = \max\{0, \sum_{t=0}^{\infty}(1-\delta)^t \pi(\varphi)\} = \max\{0, \frac{1}{\delta}\pi(\varphi)\}.$

The lowest productivity level that allows a firm to survive is $\varphi^* \equiv \inf\{\varphi : v(\varphi) > 0\}$. All firms with productivity below that cutoff will exit. The $M \geq 0$ remaining firms survive.

Given this productivity threshold (φ^*), the endogenous distribution of productivity in surviving firms is $\mu(\varphi)$:

$$\mu(\varphi) = \begin{cases} \dfrac{g(\varphi)}{1 - G(\varphi^*)} & \text{if } \varphi \geq \varphi^* \\ 0 & \text{if } \varphi < \varphi^* \end{cases}.$$

The striking result from this framework is that the single endogenous productivity cutoff is sufficient to characterize the weighted average of all firm productivities:

(A.2) $\varphi(\varphi^*) = \left[\dfrac{1}{1 - G(\varphi^*)} \int_{\varphi^*}^{\infty} \varphi^{\sigma-1} g(\varphi) d\varphi \right]^{1/(\sigma-1)}.$

The fact that the average firm productivities are only a function of the cutoff productivity levels simplifies the analysis substantially, allowing the performance of the whole economy to be measured on one scale despite the heterogeneity in firm-level productivity.

Given this aggregate performance, we are left to characterize the price index, which is a function of productivity and the number of varieties. The number of varieties is set so that the number of entrants whose draw of productivity is high enough to enter is exactly equal to the number of firms forced to exit in every period. Formally, this *stationary* equilibrium sets $(1 - G(\varphi^*))M_e = \delta M$.

Rather than characterize the dynamics explicitly, the equilibrium is fully characterized by the mass of entrants (M_e) and the cutoff productivity (φ^*), which determine the average productivity. These two parameters can be determined in the model by standard economic assumptions:

φ^* is determined by a zero-cutoff-profit condition and a free entry condition, and M_e is determined by market clearing.

Derivation of Average Productivity: Lemma A.1

Lemma A.1. Let $\tilde{\varphi}(\varphi^*)$ be the average productivity as defined above. If φ is distributed Pareto with support over $[\varphi_{min}, \infty)$ and dispersion parameter $k + 1 > \sigma$, then $\tilde{\varphi}(\varphi^*)$ is a fixed proportion of the cutoff productivity φ^*.

Proof: Let the cumulative distribution function G be Pareto with a dispersion parameter k:

$$G(\varphi) = 1 - \left(\frac{\varphi_{min}}{\varphi} \right)^k$$

$$g(\varphi) = k(\varphi_{min})^k \varphi^{-(k+1)}.$$

Plugging in these distributions into equation (A.2), we see the following:

$$\varphi(\varphi^*) = \left[\left(\frac{\varphi^*}{\varphi_{min}} \right)^k \int_{\varphi^*}^{\infty} \varphi^{\sigma-1} k(\varphi_{min})^k \varphi^{-(k+1)} d\varphi \right]^{1/(\sigma-1)}$$

$$\Leftrightarrow \varphi(\varphi^*) = \left[k\varphi^{*k} \frac{\varphi^{*\sigma-k-1}}{1+k-\sigma} \right]^{1/(\sigma-1)}$$

$$\Leftrightarrow \varphi(\varphi^*) = \left[\frac{k}{1+k-\sigma} \right]^{1/(\sigma-1)} \varphi^*.$$

Derivation of the Equilibrium Productivities: φ^*

To determine the equilibrium cutoff, we use two conditions, the zero-cutoff-profit condition and the free entry condition, defined as follows:

Definition. The *zero-cutoff-profit* (ZCP) condition finds the level of productivity for which the profits of the firm are zero. At the cutoff, firms should be indifferent between producing and exiting the market.

(A.3) $$\pi(\varphi^*) = \frac{r(\varphi^*)}{\sigma} - f = 0.$$

Definition. The *free entry* (FE) condition requires that entry should occur until the present value of average profits is set to the fixed cost of entry. Given the expected profits induced by the cutoff level of productivity, entrepreneurs should be indifferent between entering and paying the fixed cost and staying out of the market.

(A.4) $$\int_0^\infty v(\varphi)g(\varphi)d\varphi - f_e = 0.$$

Rewriting the ZCP (equation [A.3]) with lemma A.1, combined with the fact that $r(\varphi_1)/r(\varphi_2) = (\varphi_1/\varphi_2)^{\sigma-1}$, we can characterize the ZCP as a function of exogenous parameters. Specifically, lemma A.1 shows that average productivity only depends on the cutoff productivity. This allows us to write average profits ($\bar\pi$) as the profits of the average firm:

$$\bar\pi = \pi(\varphi(\varphi^*))$$

$$\bar\pi = \pi(\varphi) = \frac{\pi(\varphi)}{\sigma} - f$$

$$\bar\pi = f\left(\left(\frac{\varphi(\varphi^*)}{\varphi^*}\right)^{\sigma-1} - 1\right)$$

(A.5) $$\bar\pi = f\left(\frac{\sigma-1}{1+k-\sigma}\right).$$

Using equation (A.1), we can rewrite the FE condition (equation [A.4]) as a function of the endogenous cutoff profits:

$$\int_0^\infty v(\varphi)g(\varphi)d\varphi = [1-G(\varphi^*)]\frac{1}{\delta}\int_{\varphi^*}^\infty \pi(\varphi)\mu(\varphi)d\varphi = [1-G(\varphi^*)]\frac{1}{\delta}\bar\pi$$

$$\bar\pi = \frac{\delta f_e}{1-G(\varphi^*)}$$

(A.6) $$\bar\pi = \frac{\delta f_e}{(\varphi_{min}/\varphi^*)^k}.$$

Finally, using the parameterized forms of ZCP (equation [A.5]) and FE (equation [A.6]), we determine a unique endogenous cutoff as a function of exogenous parameters:

$$f\left(\left(\frac{\varphi(\varphi^*)}{\varphi^*}\right)^{\sigma-1}-1\right)=\frac{\delta f_e}{1-G(\varphi^*)}$$

$$f\left(\frac{\sigma-1}{1+k-\sigma}\right)=\delta f_e\left(\frac{\varphi_{min}}{\varphi^*}\right)^{-k}$$

(2.5)
$$\varphi^*=\left[\frac{f}{\delta f_e}\left(\frac{\sigma-1}{1+k-\sigma}\right)\right]^{1/k}\varphi_{min}.$$

Market Clearing

Market clearing requires that aggregate expenditure is equal to aggregate revenue: $L = R$. Noting that aggregate revenue is just M times the average revenue, we can rewrite the aggregate revenue, R, as a function of average revenue. From the formula for firm profits (7.1), we can rewrite average revenue as a function of average profits and the fixed cost:

(A.7)
$$L = R = M\bar{r} = M(\sigma(\bar{\pi}+f)).$$

From the definition of the stationary equilibrium concept, we can use equation (A.7) to characterize the mass of entering entrepreneurs:

(A.8)
$$M_e = \frac{\delta}{1-G(\varphi^*)}M = \frac{\delta}{1-G(\varphi^*)}\frac{L}{\sigma(\bar{\pi}+f)}.$$

Equations (2.5) and (A.8) fully characterize the closed-economy stationary equilibrium.

A.3. Proof of Proposition 2.1.1

Proposition A.1. Given CES utility, a Pareto productivity distribution with dispersion parameter $k > \sigma - 1$ and lemma A.1, there exists a level of productivity $\hat{\varphi}$ such that all firms with higher productivity benefit from an increase in the fixed cost of production.

Proof: Using the formulation of profits (7.1), the ZCP (equation [A.3]), and the endogenous cutoff (2.5), we can write profits as a function of exogenous parameters:

$$\pi(\varphi) = \frac{r(\varphi)}{\sigma} - f$$

(A.9) $$\pi(\varphi) = \left(\frac{\varphi}{\varphi^*}\right)^{\sigma-1} f - f.$$

From equation (A.9), we can consider the effect of a change in the fixed cost of production:

$$\frac{\partial \pi(\varphi)}{\partial f} = \left(1 + f\varphi^*(f)^{-1}(1-\sigma)\frac{\partial \varphi^*(f)}{\partial f}\right)\left(\frac{\varphi}{\varphi^*(f)}\right)^{\sigma-1} - 1.$$

Given the Pareto distribution and equation (2.6), this equation can be simplified:

$$\frac{\partial \pi(\varphi)}{\partial f} = \frac{1+k-\sigma}{k}\left(\frac{\varphi}{\varphi^*}\right)^{\sigma-1} - 1.$$

Finally, $(\partial\pi(\varphi))/\partial f > 0$ if the firm's productivity draw is higher than some productivity threshold $\hat{\varphi}$:

$$\varphi > \left(\frac{k}{1+k-\sigma}\right)^{1/(\sigma-1)} \varphi^* \equiv \hat{\varphi}.$$

Because $k > 1 + k - \sigma > 0$, $\hat{\varphi}$ is *higher* than the cutoff profit level: $\hat{\varphi} > \varphi^*$. The firms with profit levels $\varphi \in [\varphi^*, \hat{\varphi}]$ will remain in the market but receive lower profits under a higher fixed cost.

A.4. Melitz's Open Economy

Opening the economy to trade allows firms to profit from exporting on top of serving the domestic economy. Assuming that there are two identical economies, we can write profits as a linear function of revenue at home $(r_d(\varphi))$ and revenue from abroad $(r_x(\varphi))$. To sell abroad, assume there is a fixed cost $f_x \geq 0$ and a tariff $\tau \geq 1$. Following Melitz (2003), we can write the combined revenue of the firm, $r(\varphi)$, depending on the firm's export status:

$$r(\varphi) = \begin{cases} r_d(\varphi) = R(P\rho\varphi)^{\sigma-1} & \text{if the firm does not export} \\ r_d(\varphi) + r_x(\varphi) = (1+\tau^{1-\sigma})r_d(\varphi) & \text{if the firm does export} \end{cases}.$$

Similarly, each exporting firm's profits can be divided into profits earned from domestic sales and export sales:

$$\pi_d(\varphi) = \frac{r_d(\varphi)}{\sigma} - f$$

$$\pi_x(\varphi) = \frac{r_x(\varphi)}{\sigma} - f_x.$$

Again, the cutoff level of productivity is set by the ZCP and FE. There are two cutoffs: a cutoff for entry (φ_d^*) and a cutoff for export (φ_x^*). The ZCP condition sets the cutoff to the level that sets the profits of the firm at the point of participation to zero, but this will be a function of separate cutoffs for domestic sales and export activity:

$$\bar{\pi} = \pi_d(\varphi_d) + p_x\pi_x(\varphi_x)$$

$$= \frac{r_d(\varphi_d)}{\sigma} - f + p_x\left(\frac{r_x(\varphi_x)}{\sigma} - f_x\right)$$

$$= f\left(\left(\frac{\varphi_d}{\varphi_d^*}\right)^{\sigma-1} - 1\right) + p_x f_x\left(\left(\frac{\varphi_x}{\varphi_x^*}\right)^{\sigma-1} - 1\right),$$

where p_x is the probability of export, conditional on having produced

$$p_x = \frac{1-G(\varphi_x^*)}{1-G(\varphi_d^*)} = \left(\frac{\varphi_d^*}{\varphi_x^*}\right)^k.$$

Using the ratios of the zero-profit conditions, it is possible to show that the cutoff for export can be written as a function of the cutoff for domestic production, the fixed costs, and the tariff, which allows us to write the probability of export as just a function of fixed costs and tariffs:

$$\left(\frac{\varphi_x^*}{\varphi_d^*}\right)^{\sigma-1} = \tau^{\sigma-1}\frac{f_x}{f}$$

$$\frac{\varphi_x^*}{\varphi_d^*} = \tau\left(\frac{f_x}{f}\right)^{1/(\sigma-1)}$$

$$p_x = \tau^{-k}\left(\frac{f_x}{f}\right)^{-k/(\sigma-1)}.$$

Finally, the average productivity of exporters is

$$\varphi_x = \left[\frac{1}{1-G(\varphi_x^*)}\int_{\varphi_x^*}^{\infty}\varphi^{\sigma-1}g(\varphi)d\varphi\right]^{1/(\sigma-1)}$$

$$\varphi_x = \left[\left(\frac{\varphi_x^*}{\varphi_{min}}\right)^k\int_{\varphi_x^*}^{\infty}\varphi^{\sigma-1}k(\varphi_{min})^k\varphi^{-(k+1)}d\varphi\right]^{1/(\sigma-1)}$$

$$\varphi_x = \left[k(\varphi_x^*)^k\int_{\varphi_x^*}^{\infty}\varphi^{\sigma-2-k}d\varphi\right]^{1/(\sigma-1)}$$

$$\varphi_x(\varphi_x^*) = \left[\frac{k}{1+k-\sigma}\right]^{1/(\sigma-1)}\varphi_x^*.$$

Putting it all together, we can rewrite the ZCP as follows:

$$\bar{\pi} = \left(f + \tau^{-k}\left(\frac{f_x}{f}\right)^{-k/(\sigma-1)}f_x\right)\left(\frac{k}{1+k-\sigma}-1\right).$$

Combining the ZCP condition with the FE condition, we can nail down the productivity threshold for the open economy:

$$\left(f + \tau^{-k}\left(\frac{f_x}{f}\right)^{-k/(\sigma-1)}f_x\right)\left(\frac{k}{1+k-\sigma}-1\right) = \delta f_e\left(\frac{\varphi_{min}}{\varphi_d^*}\right)^{-k}$$

$$\varphi_d^* = \left(\left(1 + \tau^{-k}\left(\frac{f}{f_x}\right)^{\frac{1+k-\sigma}{\sigma-1}}\right)\frac{f}{\delta f_e}\left(\frac{\sigma-1}{1+k-\sigma}\right)\right)^{1/k}\varphi_{min}.$$

A.5. Open-Economy Comparative Statics

Melitz's (2003) appendix E.1 shows that, in contrast to the closed-economy case, increasing the fixed cost to export *decreases* the domestic productivity cutoff:

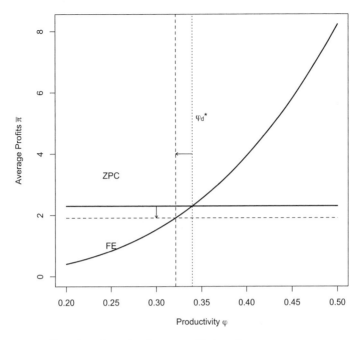

FIGURE A.1. Effect of regulatory barriers on equilibrium φ_d^*

$$\frac{\partial \varphi_d^*}{\partial f_x} = \frac{-1}{k}\left(\left(1+\tau^{-k}\left(\frac{f}{f_x}\right)^{\frac{1+k-\sigma}{\sigma-1}}\right)\frac{f}{\delta f_e}\left(\frac{\sigma-1}{1+k-\sigma}\right)\right)^{(1-k)/k}\varphi_{\min}\tau^{-k}\frac{1}{\delta f_e}\left(\frac{f}{f_x}\right)^{k/(\sigma-1)} < 0.$$

Figure A.1 plots a discrete change in f_x for equilibrium domestic entry conditions. On the x-axis is a range of productivity draws and on the y-axis is the subsequent average profits as determined by the free entry condition and the zero-profit condition. The intersection of the FE condition and the ZPC condition determines the equilibrium domestic cutoff productivity. A rise in f_x for both countries leads to a fall in the ZPC line, which in turn lowers the threshold for domestic entry. This is because raising f_x decreases foreign competition in the home market, allowing weak domestic firms to stay in the market.

Using this formulation of the endogenous cutoff and the symmetry of the two economies, we can write profits as a function of exogenous parameters:

$$\pi(\varphi) = \pi_d(\varphi) + \pi_x(\varphi)$$

$$= \frac{r_d(\varphi)}{\sigma} + \tau^{1-\sigma} \frac{r_d(\varphi)}{\sigma} - f - f_x$$

$$= (1 + \tau^{1-\sigma}) f \left(\frac{\varphi}{\varphi_d^*} \right)^{\sigma-\sigma} - f - f_x.$$

Given the endogenous cutoff, it is possible to take direct comparative statics with regard to the fixed costs of export:

$$\frac{\partial \pi(\varphi)}{\partial f_x} = (1 - \sigma)(1 + \tau^{1-\sigma}) f(\varphi)^{\sigma-1} \varphi_d^{*-\sigma} \frac{\partial \varphi_d^*}{\partial f_x} - 1.$$

Note that in this case, $\partial \varphi_d^* / \partial f_x < 0$. Again, $\partial \pi(\varphi) / \partial f_x > 0$ if the firm's productivity draw is sufficiently high:

(A.10) $$\varphi > \left((1 - \sigma)(1 + \tau^{\sigma-1}) f \varphi_d^{*-\sigma} \frac{\partial \varphi_d^*}{\partial f_x} \right)^{(-1)/(\sigma-1)}.$$

This suggests that the top producers in an economy are able to directly benefit from an increase in the fixed cost to export to a destination market. Interestingly, this change in profits arises because increasing the fixed cost of exporting *lowers* the threshold for domestic entry. These new domestic entrants are inefficient relative to those that were driven out from exporting, improving the profitability of the firms at the top of the productivity scale.[2]

Finally, considering a change in the tariff, we can see that the change in profits does not depend on productivity. Moreover, as is well-known in these models, an increase in any tariff $\tau > 1$ will lower *all* exporting firm profits so long as there are at least some firms for whom exporting is more costly than producing domestically. So long as at least some firms do not export, tariffs harm the profits of all exporting firms (Melitz and Redding 2015).

Proof: From the equation for profits, we can take the partial derivative with respect to the tariff τ:

$$\pi(\varphi) = (1 + \tau^{1-\sigma}) f \left(\frac{\varphi}{\varphi_d^*} \right)^{\sigma-1} - f - f_x$$

$$\frac{\partial \pi(\varphi)}{\partial \tau} = (1 - \sigma) f \varphi^{\sigma - 1} \varphi_d^{*-\sigma} \left(\tau^{-\sigma} \varphi_d^* + \tau^{1-\sigma} \frac{\partial \varphi_d^*}{\partial \tau} + \frac{\partial \varphi_d^*}{\partial \tau} \right) < 0$$

$$\Leftrightarrow \tau^{-\sigma} \varphi_d^* > -(1 + \tau^{1-\sigma}) \frac{\partial \varphi_d^*}{\partial \tau}.$$

Note that raising tariffs does in fact lower the threshold to domestic entry:

$$\frac{\partial \varphi_d^*}{\partial \tau} = -\left(\left(1 + \tau^{-k} \left(\frac{f}{f_x} \right)^{\frac{1+k-\sigma}{\sigma - 1}} \right) \frac{f}{\delta f_e} \left(\frac{\sigma - 1}{1 + k - \sigma} \right) \right)^{(1-k)/k} \varphi_{\min} \tau^{-k-1} \frac{f}{\delta f_e} \left(\frac{f}{f_x} \right)^{\frac{1+k-\sigma}{\sigma - 1}}.$$

Substituting in the partial derivative with respect to τ, we find sufficient conditions for a negative marginal effect of the tariff:

(A.11) $$\tau^{1-\sigma+k} \varphi_d^* > (1 + \tau^{1-\sigma}) \left(\left(1 + \tau^{-k} \left(\frac{f}{f_x} \right)^{\frac{1+k-\sigma}{\sigma - 1}} \right) \frac{f}{\delta f_e} \xi \right)^{(1-k)/k} \varphi_{\min} \frac{f}{\delta f_e} \xi \left(\frac{f}{f_x} \right)^{\frac{1+k-\sigma}{\sigma - 1}},$$

where $\xi \equiv (\sigma - 1)/(1 + k - \sigma)$. Equation (A.11) holds if and only if $\tau > (f/f_x)^{1/(\sigma-1)}$.

Notes

Chapter One

1. The Consumer Product Safety Commission governs product safety in the United States. However, prior to the CPSIA, it had only 100 field investigators and compliance personnel nationwide.

2. The term *children's product* is defined in section 3(a)(2) of the 1972 Consumer Product Safety Act (15 U.S.C. 2052[a][2]) as a consumer product designed or intended primarily for children 12 years of age or younger.

3. At the time of passage, it was not even clear that proving compliance with this new limit was technically feasible.

4. Mattel reported that the typical level of lead on the recalled products was about 10,000 parts per million, but some products had tested as high as 110,000 parts per million (Olesen 2007).

5. Representative Joe Barton quoted Rush as saying, "God himself at Mount Horeb where He gave the Ten Commandments to Moses, that may have been the only holy ground in the world that would have met this standard," during the passage of the CPSIA (Congress 2011, p. 36235).

6. One set of activists staged a "national bankruptcy day" to protest the effects of the legislation on small firms.

7. Statistics of US Businesses Annual Data Tables by Establishment Industry, NAICS code 33993 Commodity number 4021. The estimates presented are based on data from the 2007 and 2012 Commodity Flow Survey. The latter estimates only cover businesses with paid employees.

8. Selecta Spielzeug, a producer of wooden toys, ceased US distribution after the 2008 Christmas season, citing CPSIA's requirements as cost prohibitive (Playthings staff 2008).

9. In 2008, retail sales of toys generated $21.64 billion, of which Mattel accounted for $3.02 billion (NPD 2009). See also Huang (2011).

10. In addition, total profits earned by Chinese toy manufacturers declined by a quarter relative to the previous year (Donovan 2009).

11. In particular, large firms were able to source production abroad and so had lower manufacturing costs. Northup explains, "Large toy manufacturers have turned a corner to become supportive of the new regulations and clearly see the competitive advantage that the law gives them over their smaller competitors" (United States 2010).

12. These statistics are calculated as the sum of reported profits by large firms in the toy sector in 2009 and 2010 from China's National Statistical Bureau's annual Chinese Firm-Level Industrial Survey. Toys fall under China Industrial Classification code 2440.

13. Irwin (1992) identifies the similarities between mercantilist thought in the seventeenth century and strategic trade theory. In both cases, governments sought to capture the rents arising from imperfect competition at the expense of other nations. Neither anticipated governments would act to advance the interests of nonnational firms.

14. US exports of frozen swine offal amounted to $124 million in 2008.

15. The global movement toward democracy is theorized to increase the representation of the median voter. In labor abundant societies, this has the effect of empowering political leaders to favor trade (Milner and Kubota 2005; Milner and Mukherjee 2009).

16. Average markups start to rise in 1980, from 18 percent above marginal cost to 67 percent in 2017 (Loecker and Eeckhout 2017).

17. In 1935, E. E. Schattschneider noted that opposition to American duties on sugar was driven by two firms, the Hershey Corporation and the Coca-Cola Company (Olson 1965; Schattschneider 1935).

18. The concentration is even more striking within the subset of trading firms. Of the 5.4 million firms in the 2000 data, 2,245 firms (the top 1 percent of trading firms, or less than half of a tenth of a percent [0.0005 percent] of all firms) are responsible for 81 percent of trade (Bernard, Jensen, and Schott 2009).

19. Data drawn from the Chinese Census of Manufacturers, reported by Gulotty and Li (2016).

20. Other explanations include delegation by the legislature to the internationalist President Eisenhower and a postwar environment that initially excluded Germany and Japan (Bailey, Goldstein, and Weingast 1997; Goldstein and Gulotty 2014b).

21. The authors commissioned the National Opinion Research Center to administer a survey that asked, among other things, the following: "Taking everything into consideration, would you favor raising most tariffs, reducing most tariffs, or leaving most tariffs at their present level?" (Bauer, de Sola Pool, and Dexter 1963, 113). There are a number of issues with the measurement under-

lying this result. Economically speaking, it is not clear that any firm should embrace raising most tariffs, as that firm only benefits materially from tariffs on their product (Rho and Tomz 2017). Therefore, asking an executive whether most tariffs should be raised would primarily pick up sociotropic concerns and less the particular economic interests that could motivate political engagement (Mansfield and Mutz 2009).

22. In the 1958 census, 2,981,431 firms reported fewer than 20 employees and 143,746 firms between 20 and 99 employees.

23. Irwin (1996) traces these ideas to the writings of Robert Torrens in the early nineteenth century.

24. A complementary approach focuses on the use of trade agreements to resolve domestic institutional challenges. For example, trade agreements offer governments a mechanism to commit to domestic political actors when facing a time-inconsistency problem. Governments set policy after producers make irreversible investment decisions. See Staiger and Tabellini (1987). This domestic commitment model offers a substantive complement to the market-access motivation for trade agreements. Instead of allowing the mutual reduction of tariffs, a trade agreement offers an enforcement mechanism, which allows governments to overcome their own limitations in the face of powerful lobbies.

25. One of the interesting features of trade today is that the share of intra-firm trade has not changed, even as multinational production and FDI has risen so quickly. Thibault Fally (2011) argues that this may be a consequence of the importance of technologies that shift value added toward industries closer to final demand, particularly in rich countries. Research and development and marketing play an important role in this shift, decreasing the relative value of manufacturing inputs added upstream in the supply chain. Strikingly, the 700 largest MNCs make up half of world's research and development spending. Additionally, complicated production processes are often difficult to coordinate across plants, or are extremely time sensitive, encouraging firms to keep high-value production tasks close to consumers. It is therefore important to distinguish trade in intermediates from the location of value added: declining trade costs promote offshoring, while technological changes may decrease the value-weighted length of the supply chain. This leads conventional measures of globalization to underreport the changes in the value of global production processes. Therefore, I emphasize the technical characteristics of production rather than the distribution of the value of goods to measure the extent of global production.

26. Interestingly, this new logic of competition for foreign production alone does not fundamentally change the rationale of trade agreements (Bagwell and Staiger 2012). Instead, even in the presence of profit shifting or other consequences of imperfect competition, the rationale for trade agreements remains

the same, as the effects of the foreign policies on local prices can be offset by domestic policies.

27. However, some regulatory measures affect both fixed and variable costs; for example, a requirement to label a product as meeting a requirement has the fixed cost of reconfiguring the product to meet the standard, plus the cost of labeling each unit. Another prototypical mixed example is automotive emission requirements, where the manufacturer must now pay the cost of redesigning the vehicle to satisfy the standard and that of using platinum or other rare metals in the catalytic converter. Moreover, some nontariff barriers are economically near equivalent to tariffs: for example, quotas and countervailing duties.

28. These results are drawn from Evenett (2013).

29. Membership in trade treaties appears to not be a deterrent; in fact, regulatory barriers may be facilitated by regional agreements. For example, it was only after joining the Eurasian Customs Union that Kazakhstan and Belarus adopted Russian technical barriers to trade (Ferrantino, Gillson, and Schmidt 2016).

30. Small foreign domestic firms' preferences are driven by general equilibrium effects. Those that are unable to export under the lax policy would prefer strict regulatory barriers abroad. This is because international trade raises labor costs and domestic firms are better off not having to compete with exporters for workers. This effect is described in detail in the appendix and by Melitz (2003).

31. This notion of "liberal peace" is an endemic feature of American foreign policy. One farmer summed up the interdependence theory for congressional testimony: "I think we should trade with the Soviets. I think the world has gotten so small that you can't pick your customers and pick your friends. In fact, you don't shoot people as a rule that you trade with. That is the cause of most of your disturbances, lack of trade between countries" (United States 1956, 2050).

32. Leftist political economy scholarship is also skeptical of multinationals, albeit for different reasons. Dependency theorists argued that multinationals support foreign affiliates that are either too small and inefficient or so productive and capital intensive as to only benefit a small slice of the population (Evans 1979).

33. Robert Gilpin (1973) argues that the United States ought to consider discouraging outward foreign direct investment to avoid creating a network of foreign affiliates that would substitute for American exports.

34. Unlike the reciprocity norm, nondiscrimination is not dependent on a measure of trade volume; there is no guarantee that any third party enjoy an increase in trade after the agreement. According to econometric evidence from the Reciprocal Trade Agreements Act (RTAA) agreements, governments have limited the market access advantages granted to third parties (Gowa and Hicks 2018).

35. There are important exceptions: nonreciprocal agreements have been adopted by many developing countries, particularly between former colonial

relations, and all preferential agreements violate the principle of nondiscrimination.

Chapter Two

1. In the Heckscher-Ohlin model of trade, "international trade necessarily lowers the real wage of the scarce factor expressed in terms of any good" (Stolper and Samuelson 1941, 66). To avoid these losses, the scarce-factor owners mobilize for protection, while abundant-factor owners press for lower tariffs (Alt and Gilligan 1994; Milner and Kubota 2005; Rogowski 1989).

2. For example, Chinese customs data from 2005 show that among 410 thousand private exporting firms in 97 industries, the median industry has 37 percent of exports attributable to the top 1 percent of companies; this number rises when considering trade by state-owned enterprise (Gulotty et al. 2017).

3. Other work has motivated differential firm-level interests in trade barriers with per-unit costs of trade; see Osgood (2016).

4. In 1996, US firms that engaged in FDI had a 15 percent labor productivity advantage over exporters who did not engage in FDI, and the latter had a 39 percent labor productivity advantage over firms who engaged in neither export nor FDI (Helpman, Melitz, and Yeaple 2004).

5. See Lawless (2010); Dutt, Mihov, and Van Zandt (2013).

6. Fixed costs can rise with higher capital demands, increasing investment risks, or labor costs for certification and compliance (Leone 1986).

7. Dutt, Mihov, and Van Zandt (2013) identify "a small countervailing general equilibrium effect: Keeping fixed the firms in the market, a reduction in their fixed costs increases their profit and hence worldwide income, including the income of the destination country."

8. This is the contrapositive of the argument advanced in Blanchard and Matschke (2015).

9. For the political consequences of product differentiation on tariff policymaking, see Kim (2017).

10. Since 1947, the national-treatment provisions of the GATT require that the government treat products uniformly upon entry into a domestic market. For the purposes of evaluating challenges beyond open protectionism, this chapter limits attention to regulations that impose costs equally. Formally, regulations imply some level of $\eta > 0$, which is added to both the foreign and the domestic firm's fixed costs rather than independently chosen levels of regulations on domestic and foreign products, f and $f^*_{\exp}$.

11. Note that these costs are paid in local wages, but I assume that each country is the same size and that wages are set equal to 1: $w = w^* = 1$.

12. In order to ensure that the marginal firm productivity is at least as productive as the minimum $f/(\delta f_e) \geq (1 + k - \sigma)/(\sigma - 1)$.

13. The analytic benefit of this distribution also has negative consequences, as it ensures that, conditional on the fixed costs, all variation in trade arises through the extensive margin (Fernandes et al. 2016).

14. In general, average productivity is increasing in the cutoff φ^*:

$$\frac{\partial \varphi(\varphi^*)}{\partial \varphi^*} = \frac{1}{\sigma - 1}[\varphi(\varphi^*)]^{2-\sigma}\left[\frac{g(\varphi^*)(\int_{\varphi^*}^{\infty} \varphi^{\sigma-1}g(\varphi)d\varphi - \int_{\varphi^*}^{\infty} \varphi^{*\sigma-1}g(\varphi)d\varphi)}{(1 - G(\varphi^*))^2}\right] > 0.$$

This is because $\forall \varphi^* > 0$ and for any density function g,

$$\int_{\varphi^*}^{\infty}\left(\frac{\varphi}{\varphi^*}\right)^{\sigma-1} g(\varphi)d\varphi > \int_{\varphi^*}^{\infty} g(\varphi)d\varphi$$

$$\Leftrightarrow \frac{\partial \varphi(\varphi^*)}{\partial \varphi^*} > 0$$

15. Proof in appendix.

16. Taking the cross partial, we can verify that the most productive firms benefit the most from an increase in the fixed cost:

$$\frac{\partial^2 \pi(\varphi)}{\partial f \partial \varphi} = (\sigma - 1)\frac{1 + k - \sigma}{k} f^{(1-\sigma)/k}\varphi^{\sigma-2}\left[\left[\frac{1}{\delta f_e}\left(\frac{\sigma - 1}{1 + k - \sigma}\right)\right]^{1/k} \varphi_{min}\right]^{1-\sigma} > 0.$$

17. According to Novak (2013), this was first identified by Huntington (1952) in a study of the United States Interstate Commerce Commission. Subsequent analysis has shown that even nongovernment institutions, including unions, are responsive to firm interests. One prominent example is the manipulation of wage rates as a barrier to entry in mining (Williamson 1968).

18. "Regulate Us Now Please," *Economist*, January 8, 1994.

19. See de Mesquita et al. (2005); North, Wallis, and Weingast (2009); Acemoglu, Antràs, and Helpman (2007).

20. As Aggarwal and Evenett (2013) put it, "Policies don't have to slash trade to distort it, misallocate resources, and reduce living standards."

21. Host governments can impose taxes on foreign enterprises through tariffs, but local affiliates are subject to a variety of other taxes, from land taxes where the facility is based to corporate income taxes.

22. Wealthy countries are generally insulated from tax competition (Mutti 2003).

23. MNCs avoid paying taxes on a substantial portion of their profits by shifting taxable income to jurisdictions with low corporate tax rates. Microdata from Denmark revealed that multinationals artificially reduced the unit values of their exports between 5.7 and 9.1 percent to take advantage of lower foreign taxes.

24. The question then arises why a deal cannot be struck between the two nations. In chapter 7, I consider a stochastic weight on the consumption externality and consider the problem of government commitment to such a scheme.

25. A similar coalition is described in Vogel (2012).

Chapter Three

1. Technical measures define the characteristics of goods, prescribe a particular method of production, or create administrative provisions to enforce a product characteristic or production method. The fact that the TBT Agreement now covers regulations on process and production methods is the subject of some controversy (Durán 2015).

2. There is disagreement about the effects of these measures; Cadot and Gourdon (2016) estimate that on average, the prices per unit of traded goods are 5 percent higher than they would be otherwise because of technical barriers to trade.

3. One reason the costs are low is that WTO law generally grants any measure that has not been formally adjudicated with the presumption of legality. As a result, a government may raise an STC without risking escalation.

4. I thank a reviewer for this suggestion.

5. ISO 9001 is a quality-management system developed by the ISO. Certifications are obtained from a variety of accredited private organizations (Büthe and Milner 2011, 133).

6. The term is not used in the agreement except as an indirect reference to the Committee on Technical Barriers to Trade.

7. One such effort, and the principal database on nontariff measures, is the Trade Analysis and Information System developed by the United Nations Conference on Trade and Development. This measure includes a category for technical regulations, but these are drawn from the WTO's specific trade concerns and self-notifications.

8. A private survey firm sampled between 600 and 1,200 companies per sector, using phone interviews to screen for difficulties with NTMs. Companies that reported problems received detailed in-person follow-up surveys. The firms were asked about the nature of the barrier, the affected products, and the partner country.

9. This limitation is shared by more econometric techniques for estimating the presence of nontariff measures. For example, Kee, Nicita, and Olarreaga (2009) use observed trade flows and predictions from gravity models to estimate the extent to which nontariff measures, including technical barriers, limit trade. However, finding an ad valorem equivalent misses the distinguishing characteristic of regulatory barriers to trade: namely, that they act as a fixed cost. Recent

cross-sectional analyses of regulatory barriers using data from foreign affiliates of multinationals suggest that regulatory barriers have significant implications as entry barriers (Crivelli and Gröschl 2012). These analyses improve on those that depend on notifications, but modeling-based techniques have difficulty targeting particular barriers.

10. Prior research using these data include that of Fontagné et al. (2015) and Fontagné and Orefice (2016).

11. Specific trade concerns are subject to a form of selection—a government will likely only raise a specific trade concern if informal mechanisms do not work. Members sometimes request the WTO secretariat to put concerns on the agenda but withdraw them before they are presented to the committee, arguing that a bilateral arrangement has been found. Because of these selection effects, the World Trade Report 2012 suggests that specific trade concerns may provide a distorted picture of the trade-restrictive or trade-distorting effects of TBT and SPS measures (WTO 2012b). However, the selection effect is most severe if the target of analysis is to analyze all barriers to trade as opposed to just those that are a problem for international cooperation. To address the reporting bias—that is, that cases are only observed when the target state did not cut a deal—I focus analysis on variation in TBT use within a market and an industry.

12. These regulations often sought to limit the sale of air conditioners using chlorofluorocarbons, a chemical compound responsible for ozone depletion.

13. Sectors are defined using the US tariff schedule (WTO 2012b).

14. The most favored nation tariff rate is the tax firms must pay if there is no preferential agreement.

15. Because I assume that consumption has a constant elasticity of substitution, we can apply the estimates of Broda, Greenfield, and Weinstein (2017), who estimate this relationship as $\sigma = \nu C/M + \epsilon P/M$, where ν is the domestic elasticity of demand, ϵ is the domestic elasticity of supply, σ is the import elasticity of demand, C is domestic consumption, P is domestic production, and M is the import volume.

16. This measure has become common in the economics and political science literature; see Feenstra et al. (2012) and Carnegie (2014).

17. This analysis uses industry concordances from Feenstra (1996) that aggregated Rauch's measure to a four-digit SITC industry code.

18. The degree of contract intensity may interact with the elasticity of substitution used to evaluate the substitution argument. In principle, products with high contract intensity are likely to be differentiated, with a lower elasticity of substitution. Insofar, these are the products most likely to experience tariff protection, as varieties are more elastic when goods are more disaggregated and when they are traded on organized exchanges (Broda, Greenfield, and Weinstein 2017).

Chapter Four

1. Recent work on licensing, using data from Chile, shows that it will be more often chosen by less productive firms, the exact group that is likely to be affected by a fixed-cost regulation (Xie and Markusen 2011).

2. See, e.g., Baron (2016).

3. The European Commission proposes and implements legislation for the EU, along with the European Parliament and the European Council. See Council Directive 92/59/EEC.

4. The Scientific Committee of Toxicity, Ecotoxicity and the Environment (SCTEE) from September 28, 1999, found that phthalates—chemicals shown to be liable to cause liver, kidney, and testicular damage—are released in dangerous quantities when chewed on by children (EU Commission 1999).

5. Substances are defined in 67/548/EEC as chemical elements and their compounds, which together constitute all ordinary matter. The regulation offers a number of blanket exemptions. Food and feed, medicine, and certain chemicals that occur in nature (water, nitrogen, ores) are exempted. Additionally exempted substances include those that are produced in the storage or transport of otherwise registered products, as well as certain intermediates and agents, and incidentally transformed substances such as rust.

6. Resolution of the European Council of Nice, December 2000, on the precautionary principle that welcomes the Communication from the Commission on the precautionary principle, COM(2000)1, 2.2.2000.

7. Jonathan Blackie, Regional Director for the Government Office for the North East Comment 3205_public_en, from the archive of REACH commentary.

8. Office of Trade and Industry Information, Manufacturing and Services, International Trade Administration, 2013.

9. A firm enters this data if it reports at least one export shipment during the year valued at $2,501 or more.

10. If a company misrepresents or fails to substantiate its claim that it is an SME, the fines are calculated as 2.5 times the financial gain, or between €8,000 and €20,000.

11. See Prokes's (2015) table 3.6.2: "How has the competitive position of your firm vis-à-vis firms from outside the EU been affected?"

12. The SPI billed itself as having almost 1,000 members that employ 1.1 million workers, companies that "range from large from large multinational corporations to small and medium sized companies, many of which are family-owned businesses" (Pratt 2009). These workers are present in 17,600 facilities, a vast majority of whom work in small firms.

13. Commission of the European Communities, *Consultation Document* COMM/ENTR/E3, vol. 1, Title XV, Point 108.

14. The white paper that set out REACH cited a EUREX study of enforcement where 30 percent of companies could not identify whether a substance ought to have been registered, and an ex post study of chemical dyes found that of the new substances produced under a previous European directive, 37 percent were marketed illegally (CLEEN 1996).

15. The 50 largest chemical companies were calculated for 2004 for the Chemical and Engineering News of the American Chemical Society, available online at "U.S. Top 50 Chemical Companies," *Chemical and Engineering News*, 2019, http://cen.acs.org/us-top-50.html.

16. Cable from Secretary of State Colin Powell to US Diplomatic Posts, March 21, 2002, cited in Waxman (2004).

17. Subsidiarity is the principle that the EU does not take actions unless it is necessary to achieve the objectives of the treaty, instead leaving responsibility at the national, regional or local level. See COM:2003:644:FIN article 123.

18. Cited in Steingraber (2004).

19. For an expert analysis of parties prior to the European elections of June 2004, see McElroy and Benoit (2007).

20. UK Greens member Caroline Lucas, quoted in Rettman (2006).

21. Quote taken from the Dow Corporate website, https://reach.dow.com/en-us, accessed April 2, 2019. For details on Dow Chemical's position on the regulation, see Daemmrich (2011).

22. While part of early lobbying on REACH, BASF denies changing its position; a senior manager claims that "BASF welcomed REACH already in 2006 when it was adopted and has not changed its position on REACH since then" (Simon 2012). However, by 2006, REACH had already undergone significant changes in its structure, including dropping the connection between punishments and worldwide turnover that would have disproportionately affected the largest firms.

23. This may also be a consequence of the technical capacity of the top firms, as companies innovate around technical restrictions (Marcoux and Urpelainen 2011).

24. Email correspondence, January 23, 2013.

25. Testimony of Equinox Chemicals' CEO Mark Grimaldi, *Promoting Innovation, Competition and Economic Growth*, House, 112th Cong. (2012). According to the company website, Equinox Chemicals has approximately 25 employees.

26. The 2010 registration numbers are taken from Janez Potocnik's remarks at the REACH Registration Conference, Brussels, Belgium, European Commissioner for Environment Speech 11/602, September 23, 2011.

27. Quoted in Simon (2012).

28. Restricting the survey sample to industry limits the power of any statisti-

cal test, but a two-sample *t*-test offers some statistical evidence for a difference between the two groups (*t*-statistic = 1.74, df = 64, *p*-value = 0.088).

29. In European countries, if an inventor is to ever get a patent, he or she must file prior to selling the product.

30. Uwe Wolfmeier, head of corporate product safety at Clariant, cited in Masson (2008).

31. One challenge with this and many other business and financial databases is that companies, particularly multinational corporations, are reported with varying abbreviations (*Pharm* vs. *Pharma*) or legal entity types (*BASF AG* vs. *BASF SE*) or names that reflect acquisitions and mergers (*Glaxo-SmithKline*). To correct this, I automatically correct the company names by removing common endings, spaces, and other formatting issues. Rerunning the analysis with only companies with a four-letter code obtains similar results.

32. Trade statistics calculated from the Japan Ministry of Finance Trade Statistics of Japan.

33. Because every user must register their substance, substances are registered hundreds of times. For example, as of 2016, calcium dihydroxide (pickling lime) has been registered 457 times (European Chemicals Agency 2016).

34. There does appear to be a spike in patent activity in 2006, which is primarily driven by a dip in the overall number of patents filed in the EPO by labeled firms, a change that does not occur in the overall EPO patent statistics.

35. A two-sample *t*-test finds statistically significant evidence against the null of no difference from before and after REACH (*t*-statistic = 2.6, df = 10, *p*-value = 0.025).

36. See the European Chemical Industry Council's 2016 "Facts and Figures," http://www.cefic.org/Documents/FactsAndFigures/2016/FullDataCefic-Facts -and-Figures-2016.xlsx.

Chapter Five

1. Congressional Record November 18, 2010: S8015.

2. Congressional Record November 18, 2010: S8015.

3. This has analogies to the analysis of "regulatory capture," a concept developed in economics to describe the interaction between monopoly rents and government regulations. Carpenter and Moss (2013) point out that such regulatory capture is routinely overdiagnosed and can produce regulatory outcomes with lower regulatory costs (corrosive regulation).

4. The opacity of nontariff measures is one of their attractive features as protectionist instruments, according to Kono (2006).

5. This is one of the main shortcomings of much of the literature on regulatory capture (Carpenter and Moss 2013).

6. Potatoes reached 257 million hundredweight (cwt) in 1960 and 424 million cwt in 2005. Corn production was 100 million metric tons (4 billion bushels) in 1960 and 370 million metric tons (14 billion bushels) in 2017 (USDA 2018).

7. Trade facts from US trade representative.

8. Judith Goldstein cites the United States' insistence on agricultural protectionism as evidence against theories that connect hegemonic rise with liberal policies (Goldstein 1989; Krasner 1976).

9. The boundaries are not just along pescatarian lines. The FDA regulates bagel-dogs (a product composed of a hotdog wrapped in bagel dough that is then baked), while the USDA monitors corn dogs (a product composed of a hotdog coated in corn batter and fried; Goetz 2010). The FSIS claims (incorrectly) that the bagel-dog is a "closed-face" sandwich and is thus excluded from FSIS jurisdiction. See Derfler (2005); Hodgman (2014).

10. The full title of the act is Public Law 107-188, *Public Health Security and Bioterrorism Preparedness and Response Act of 2002.*

11. The Senate version of the bill also included provisions to exempt countermeasure developers in the pharmaceutical industry from antitrust law for three years, a provision dropped at the insistence of Senator Wellstone (Congressional Record, December 20, 2001: S13903).

12. The FDA notification window closes at eight hours to arrival for ocean shipments, four hours to arrival for air and rail traffic, and two hours to the border or by truck.

13. For example, advocates for the amendment included the American Goat Society but not the larger American Dairy Goat Association.

14. Congressional Record, November 17, 2010: S7929.

15. Congressional Record, November 17, 2010: S7930.

16. Congressional Record, November 17, 2010: S7930.

17. Senator John Barrasso (R-WY), November 30, 2010: S510.

18. The Senate bill was substituted for H.R. 2751—the Consumer Assistance to Recycle and Save Act, an unrelated voucher program to encourage the replacement of polluting vehicles.

19. Representative Joe Pitts (R-PA), Representative Frank Lucas (R-OK), December 21, 2010: H8885.

20. Representative Frank Lucas (R-OK), December 21, 2010: H8886.

21. Representative Henry Waxman, December 21, 2010: H8887.

22. Agriculture accounted for 1.4 percent of the US workforce in 2014.

23. This may be because of a generous agricultural use exemption to local and state taxes; see Levine (2011).

24. Note that while Delaware has many productive poultry farms, with broilers making up 74 percent of its agricultural sales, poultry is regulated for the most part by the USDA.

25. S 510, roll call vote no. 257, November 30, 2010.

26. The bootstrapped 95 percent confidence interval for the difference is (0.5, 9.6).

27. The regression with party suffers from complete separability—all Democrats voted in favor of the legislation, making the standard MLE estimator inappropriate. Instead, these estimates use a Bayesian generalized linear model with Student's t priors on the coefficients, implemented following Gelman et al. (2008).

28. Put another way, party and ideology are posttreatment.

29. These are crops, fruits, peas, vegetables, hay, milk, greenhouse products, and seafood.

30. FDA-2011-N-0920-0001.

31. For context, the smallest threshold would qualify an additional 34,000 processing facilities, more than twice the number of McDonald's restaurants in the United States.

32. September 2014, FDA-2011-N-0920-1553.

33. FDA-2011-N-0920-0011.

34. Exempt or "qualified" firms are required to satisfy sections 1.502, 1.503, and 1.509 of title 21 of the Code of Federal Regulations, which state that a qualified individual must have the education, training, or experience (or a combination thereof) necessary to perform their assigned activities and must be able to read and understand the language of any records that must be reviewed in performing an activity.

35. See sections 1.504 through 1.508 or section 1.510 of title 21 of the Code of Federal Regulations.

36. These definitions are in title 21, chapter I, subchapter A, part 1, subpart L, section 1.512.

37. While comments are not required to be signed, only one comment was anonymous, allowing individual identification of submissions.

38. FDA-2011-N-0143-0334.

39. FDA-2011-N-0143-0284.

40. FDA-2011-N-0143-0241.

41. FDA-2011-N-0143-0335.

42. FDA-2011-N-0143-0314.

43. FDA-2011-N-0143-0369.

44. FDA-2011-N-0143-0142.

45. FDA-2011-N-0143-0317.

46. FDA-2011-N-0920-0221.

47. FDA-2011-N-0143-0166.

48. FDA-2011-N-0143-0370.

49. FDA-2011-N-0143-0370.

50. FDA-2011-N-0143-0370.

51. See, e.g., the extension of comments, FDA-2011-N-0143-0037.

52. This chapter uses the Regulations.gov data API, which is neither endorsed nor certified by Regulations.gov. Regulations.gov and the federal government cannot verify and are not responsible for the accuracy or authenticity of the data or analyses derived from the data after they have been retrieved from Regulations.gov. For more on the API, see http://api.data.gov.

53. While there are tens of thousands of comments, many are by individuals. To limit the coding burden, all titles with more than two comments are coded, without reference to whether the comment was processed. Extant machine-learning efforts to classify stakeholders in public comment data miss 40 percent of hand-coded entities (Arguello and Callan 2007).

54. This strategy follows Roberts et al. (2013).

55. See FDA-2011-N-0144-0044. The voluntary qualified importer program preapproves importers; the AFFI reasoned that "if the fees varied, companies would not know their share upfront and this would present challenges when determining whether to apply for participation."

56. Concerns about the Food Safety Modernization Act were raised by Mexico (WTO 2011a, paras. 127–30). Concerns about REACH were raised by Argentina, Australia, Botswana, Brazil, Canada, Chile, China, Colombia, Costa Rica, Cuba, the Dominican Republic, Ecuador, Egypt, El Salvador, India, Indonesia, Israel, Japan, the Kingdom of Saudi Arabia, Kuwait, Malaysia, Mexico, Pakistan, the Philippines, Qatar, the Russian Federation, Singapore, South Africa, South Korea, Switzerland, Taiwan, Thailand, the United States, and Uruguay (e.g., WTO 2003, paras. 49–62).

57. According to the World Bank's and OECD's national accounts data files, final consumption expenditures in 2015 in constant 2010 USD were as follows: EU, $13,725,895,220; US, $13,796,294,900; world, $55,141,126,020.

Chapter Six

1. This reasoning follows Bagwell and Staiger (1997, 2001).

2. Despite its name, the RTAA act did not explicitly require reciprocity; the Committee for Reciprocity Information and the Interdepartmental Committee on Trade Agreements were formed to ensure that a given reduction in tariff rates would result in concessions abroad that expand exports in a way that created a net improvement in industrial activity and employment (Berglund 1935).

3. See Gilligan (1997); Bagwell and Staiger (2001). Cf. Regan (2015).

4. As I show in chapter 2, firms charge a constant markup over marginal costs.

5. See WTO document MTN/3C/1, 15–16.

6. See WTO document MTN.TNC/W/113. Note that these sectors are subject to substantial regulation.

7. The text of the agreement specifies that governments are obligated to offer

conditions "not less" favorable to trade. Governments are free to make unilateral concessions.

8. These data are among the first systematic bilateral trade data collected by any organization and are published by country. These data are found in the publications for Cuba, Belgium, Sweden, Canada, Brazil, Netherlands, France, Colombia, and Finland (League of Nations 1921–38).

9. Germany imported $867 million worth of soybeans from the US in 2012.

10. Government choices to unilaterally lower tariffs, in theory, represent a change in the politically optimal tariff level. If local political preferences or institutions are shaped by the international forces that led the US to liberalize, then the instrument is invalid.

11. The Limão (2006) result is robust to two-digit industry-level controls, as well as a battery of alternative specifications.

12. For an extensive analysis of NTM policy substitution, see WTO (2012).

13. There are a variety of ways in which host states benefit from foreign investment, but all depend on retaining, and not just attracting, profits. See Pandya (2014).

14. However, recent empirical work finds that TBT and SPS measures are no more prevalent on intermediate products (WTO 2012).

15. From an efficiency perspective, any use of nontariff measures poses a puzzle, especially when tariffs are unbound (Limão and Tovar 2011). Regulatory barriers and other nontariff measures are imperfect substitutes for tariffs but can generate distortions that benefit certain firms.

Chapter Seven

1. In particular, the dispute-settlement system enables an international equivalent to "breach and pay," where violators compensate the harmed party to maintain reciprocity (Koremenos 2001, 2005; Koremenos, Lipson, and Snidal 2001; Sykes 2001).

2. For a formal analysis of escape clauses, see Rosendorff and Milner (2001); Kucik and Reinhardt (2008); Johns (2014); Busch and Pelc (2014). For analysis of the relationship between depth and flexibility in PTAs, see Baccini, Dür, and Elsig (2015).

3. Specifically, the trade effects of regulations that meet a relevant international standard, including those developed by the Codex Alimentarius Commission, the World Organization for Animal Health and the Secretariat of the International Plant Protection Convention, are given legal presumption against challenge. These international standards are themselves functions of national political processes and industry influence; see Büthe and Mattli (2011).

4. The TBT Agreement operates in a similar fashion, but allows for a wider

set of justifications, including "fundamental technological problems or geographical factors."

5. Cited in Howse (2016, 57). Daniel Drezner argues that scientific evidence played little or no role in the US-EU GMO disputes (2007).

6. For examples in American politics, see Calvert, McCubbins, and Weingast (1989); Gilligan and Krehbiel (1987, 1989); Krishna and Morgan (2001).

7. In particular, national treatment allows exporters in rich countries to take advantage of poor countries' low standards while maintaining high standards at home. The intuition is that the rich country gets to maintain its high, nondiscriminatory quality standard to limit some consumption externality that has a de facto trade-restrictive effect. Because the poor country has less efficient technology or a higher marginal utility to income relative to the consumption externality, it will set more lenient standards.

8. The profit of a high-cost producer i is $\pi_{Hi} = (\alpha - q_L - (N-1)^*q_{H-i} - q_{Hi})^*q_{Hi} - q_{Hi}^*c_{Hi} - F$, which is maximized at $q_{Hi}^*(q_L) = [\alpha - (N-1)^*q_{H-i} - q_L - c_{Hi}]/2$. Taking all N high-cost firms as identical, this equation simplifies to $q_H^*(q_L) = (\alpha - q_L - c_H)/(N^\dagger + 1)$. Substituting the conjectured quantities generates the following quantities for high- and low-cost firms as a function of $N^\dagger$:

$$q_H^* = \frac{\alpha + c_L - 2c_H}{N^\dagger + 2},$$

$$q_L^* = \frac{\alpha - c_L}{2} - \left(\frac{\alpha + c_L - 2c_H}{2}\right) * \frac{N^\dagger}{N^\dagger + 2}.$$

9. Although technically $N^{\dagger*}$ is an integer count of the number of firms, for tractability, I later assume $N^{\dagger*}$ as a positive real number.

10. Under linear demand, profits simplify to $\pi_H = q_H^2 - F$.

11. Note that this equation creates an upper bound on F that allows positive entry: namely, $((\alpha + c_L - 2c_H)/2)^2 \geq F$. I later assume there is some lower bound on F to ensure that entry is not infinite.

12. This result arises naturally with an additional fixed cost to engage in foreign sourcing (Antràs 2003).

13. Specifically, Rogerson (1984) shows that under linear demand $p = \alpha - \beta q$, marginal costs c and fixed costs F, an increase in fixed costs raises the dominant firm's profits if and only if $F < (\alpha - c)/25\beta$.

14. This means that $V''(F) + B''(F) < 0$, and $(V''(F) + B''(F))/(B''(F)) > 1/2$.

15. In this formulation, we assume that the pdf of the regulatory demand g is nondecreasing, for $\gamma_1 < \gamma_2, g(\gamma_1) \leq g(\gamma_2)$.

16. Formally, for $B''(F) < 0\beta > (\alpha - c_H)/(2(c_H - c_L))$. In order for $V''(F) + B''(F) \leq 0$, it must be that F is not too small relative to β:

$$\beta > \frac{\alpha - c_H - \sqrt{F}}{2(c_H - c_L)} + \frac{3(\alpha + c_L - 2c_H)}{2F(c_H - c_L)}.$$

17. This escape clause remains highly inefficient, as the cost paid does not depend on the political demands for protection.

18. Buyse, cited in Richardson (2008).

19. For example, the Treaty with British Merchants of 1700 between British merchants and the magistrates of St. Ander, confirmed by a treaty of commerce between Great Britain and Spain in 1715 (Hertslet 1878).

20. One stark example of the question of national-treatment flexibility was at issue in the Canada–European Communities (EC) asbestos dispute. As GATT/WTO members, Canada and the European Communities are mutually obligated to provide equal treatment for imports and domestic goods. On these grounds, Canada challenged a 1996 French ban on imported cement construction materials containing asbestos, which came, in part, from Canada. Canada argued that cement construction material that contained asbestos was "like" other domestically produced substitutes from the perspective of the market—consumers did not distinguish between asbestos and other cement additives. While the WTO panel ruled in favor of the EC, upholding the ban, it was on the grounds that despite the fact that the EC violated national treatment, this violation was justified under Article XX(b) of the GATT as "necessary" for the protection of human health. By contrast, the appellate body ruled that the health concerns of the government could be used as a basis for determining whether two products were "like" but did not allow the health concern to be directly considered (Howse and Türk 2001). The tension between the appellate body and the panel reveals one of the serious issues with the national-treatment provisions in the GATT and one of the grounds for introducing supplementary codes and rules as the institution matured.

21. For a formalization of this logic, see Battigalli and Maggi (2003).

22. Previous to the Tokyo Round, there were no GATT provisions that included an appeal to scientific evidence. Even as late as 1970, a working group on standards acting as barriers to trade made no mention of scientific evidence.

23. Despite the regulatory threat, Swiss "footwear with soles of leather/rubber/plastic" (SITC rev. 1. 85102) sales rose from a little less than $2 million USD in 1985 to over $3 and $4 million in 1986 and 1987 respectively according to the COMTRADE data in the World Integrated Trade Solutions database (see http://www.wits.worldbank.org). This point has been overshadowed by the fact that the standard was not formally withdrawn until the "1986/87 ski sales season was effectively over" (Büthe and Mattli 2011, 135).

24. Group of Negotiations on Goods Negotiating Group on Agriculture, "A Discussion Paper on Issues Related to the Negotiations Submitted by the United States," MTN.GNG/NG5/W/44 22 (1988).

25. Finding a rational relationship is a low barrier but seems to have helped deter regulatory behavior in some cases.

26. This is not to say there is no value in general studies of international organizations. Governments do not design organizations in response to what would be optimal but rather from prior experiences and practices (Goldstein and Gulotty 2014a).

Chapter Eight

1. Freund and Pierola (2015) find that in a sample of 32 countries, the top five firms are together responsible for 30 percent of trade.

2. Right-wing populist parties have gained standing following the 2008 and 2010 global financial crises but are inconsistently opposed to globalization. Advocates for Brexit argued not only that the UK would retain its existing trade with Europe but that trade would rise with the rest of the world. The 2015 UKIP manifesto claims, "You do not have to be in political union with a nation in order to trade with that nation" (http://www.ukip.org). While opposed to immigration and existing trade agreements, the 2016 US Republican Party platform called for a new "worldwide multilateral agreement among nations committed to the principles of open markets" (GOP 2016, 2).

3. When asked, "Turning now to trade, generally speaking, do you think US trade policy should have more restrictions on imported foreign goods to protect American jobs, or have fewer restrictions to enable American consumers to have the most choices and the lowest prices?" 65 ± 3 percent of Americans reported support for more restrictions (Bloomberg Politics Poll conducted by Selzer & Company, March 19–22, 2016).

Appendix

1. In order to ensure that the marginal firm productivity is at least as productive as the minimum productivity, $f/(\delta f_e) \geq (1 + k - \sigma)/(\sigma - 1)$.

2. In addition, the top producers also benefit increasingly from fixed cost to export: $(\partial^2 \pi(\varphi))/(\partial f_x \partial \varphi) > 0$.

References

Acemoglu, Daron, Pol Antràs, and Elhanan Helpman. 2007. "Contracts and Technology Adoption." *American Economic Review* 97 (3): 916–43.

Aggarwal, Vinod K., and Simon J. Evenett. 2013. "A Fragmenting Global Economy: A Weakened WTO, Mega FTAs, and Murky Protectionism." *Swiss Political Science Review* 19 (4): 550–57.

Alt, James E., and Michael Gilligan. 1994. "The Political Economy of Trading States: Factor Specificity, Collective Action Problems and Domestic Political Institutions." *Journal of Political Philosophy* 2 (2): 165–92.

Amador, Manuel, and Kyle Bagwell. 2012. "Tariff Revenue and Tariff Caps." *American Economic Review* 102 (3): 459–65.

———. 2013. "The Theory of Optimal Delegation with an Application to Tariff Caps." *Econometrica* 81 (4): 1541–99.

Antràs, Pol. 2003. "Firms, Contracts, and Trade Structure." *Quarterly Journal of Economics* 118 (4): 1375–418.

Antràs, Pol, and Elhanan Helpman. 2008. "Contractual Frictions and Global Sourcing." In *The Organization of Firms in a Global Economy*, edited by Elhanan Helpman, Dalia Marin, and Thierry Verdier, 9–54. Cambridge: Harvard University Press, 2008.

Antràs, Pol, and Robert W. Staiger. 2012. "Offshoring and the Role of Trade Agreements." *American Economic Review* 102 (7): 3140–83.

Arguello, Jaime, and Jamie Callan. 2007. "A Bootstrapping Approach for Identifying Stakeholders in Public-Comment Corpora." In *Proceedings of the 8th Annual International Conference on Digital Government Research: Bridging Disciplines and Domains*, 92–101. Philadelphia: Digital Government Society of North America, 2007.

Arkolakis, Costas, Svetlana Demidova, Peter J. Klenow, and Andrés Rodríguez-Clare. 2008. "Endogenous Variety and the Gains from Trade." *American Economic Review* 98 (2): 444–50.

Ashley, Percy. 1910. *Modern Tariff History: Germany—United States—France.* London: J. Murray.

Baccini, Leonardo, Andreas Dür, and Manfred Elsig. 2015. "The Politics of Trade Agreement Design: Revisiting the Depth–Flexibility Nexus." *International Studies Quarterly* 59 (4): 765–75.

Baccini, Leonardo, Pablo Pinto, and Stephen Weymouth. 2017. "The Distributional Consequences of Preferential Trade Liberalization: Firm-Level Evidence." *International Organization* 71 (2): 373–95.

Bagwell, Kyle. 2009. *Self-Enforcing Trade Agreements and Private Information.* Technical Report, National Bureau of Economic Research.

Bagwell, Kyle, Petros C. Mavroidis, and Robert W. Staiger. 2002. "It's a Question of Market Access." *American Journal of International Law* 96 (1): 56–76.

Bagwell, Kyle, and Robert W. Staiger. 1997. "Reciprocity, Non-discrimination and Preferential Agreements in the Multilateral Trading System." Working Paper no. 5932, National Bureau of Economic Research.

———. 1999. "An Economic Theory of GATT." *American Economic Review* 89 (1): 215–48.

———. 2001. "Domestic Policies, National Sovereignty, and International Economic Institutions." *Quarterly Journal of Economics* 116 (2): 519–62.

———. 2002a. "Economic Theory and the Interpretation of GATT/WTO." *American Economist* 46 (2): 3–19.

———. 2002b. *The Economics of the World Trading System.* Cambridge: MIT Press.

———. 2012. "Profit Shifting and Trade Agreements in Imperfectly Competitive Markets." *International Economic Review* 53 (4): 1067–1104.

Bailey, Michael, Judith Goldstein, and Barry R. Weingast. 1997. "The Institutional Roots of American Trade Policy: Politics, Coalitions, and International Trade." *World Politics* 49 (3): 309–38.

Baldwin, Richard. 2016. *The Great Convergence.* Cambridge: Harvard University Press.

Baron, David P. 2016. "Self-Regulation and the Market for Activism." *Journal of Economics & Management Strategy* 25 (3): 584–607.

Baron, David P., and Daniel Diermeier. 2007. "Strategic Activism and Nonmarket Strategy." *Journal of Economics & Management Strategy* 16 (3): 599–634.

Battigalli, Pierpaolo, and Giovanni Maggi. 2003. *International Agreements on Product Standard: An Incomplete Contracting Theory.* Technical Report, National Bureau of Economic Research.

Bauer, Raymond A., Ithiel de Sola Pool, and Lewis Anthony Dexter. 1963. *American Business and Public Policy: The Politics of Foreign Trade.* New York: Atherton Press.

Beamish, Paul W., and Hari Bapuji. 2008. "Toy Recalls and China: Emotion vs. Evidence." *Management and Organization Review* 4 (2): 197–209.

Becker, William H. 1982. *The Dynamics of Business Government Relations.* Chicago: University of Chicago Press.

Berglund, Abraham. 1935. "The Reciprocal Trade Agreements Act of 1934." *American Economic Review* 25 (3): 411–25.

Bernard, Andrew B., Jonathan Eaton, J. Bradford Jensen, and Samuel Kortum. 2003. "Plants and Productivity in International Trade." *American Economic Review* 93 (4): 1268–90.

Bernard, Andrew B., J. Bradford Jensen, Stephen J. Redding, and Peter K. Schott. 2009. "The Margins of US Trade." *American Economic Review* 99 (2): 487–93.

Bernard, Andrew B., J. Bradford Jensen, and Peter K. Schott. 2009. "Importers, Exporters and Multinationals: A Portrait of Firms in the US That Trade Goods." In *Producer Dynamics: New Evidence from Micro Data*, edited by T. Dunne, J. B. Jensen, and M. J. Roberts, 513–52. Chicago: University of Chicago Press.

Blanchard, Emily J. 2007. "Foreign Direct Investment, Endogenous Tariffs, and Preferential Trade Agreements." *B. E. Journal of Economic Analysis and Policy* 7 (1): 1–52.

———. 2010. "Reevaluating the Role of Trade Agreements: Does Investment Globalization Make the WTO Obsolete?" *Journal of International Economics* 82 (1): 63–72.

Blanchard, Emily J., and Xenia Matschke. 2015. "US Multinationals and Preferential Market Access." *Review of Economics and Statistics* 97 (4): 839–54.

Bombardini, Matilde. 2008. "Firm Heterogeneity and Lobby Participation." *Journal of International Economics* 75 (2): 329–48.

Bombardini, Matilde, and Francesco Trebbi. 2012. "Competition and Political Organization: Together or Alone in Lobbying for Trade Policy?" *Journal of International Economics* 87 (1): 18–26.

Broda, Christian, Joshua Greenfield, and David Weinstein. 2017. "From Groundnuts to Globalization: A Structural Estimate of Trade and Growth." *Research in Economics* 71 (4): 759–83.

Bureau of the Census. 1963. *Enterprise Statistics, 1958: Based on Data Collected in the 1958 Census of Business, Manufactures, and Mineral Industries.* Washington, DC: US Government Printing Office.

Busch, Marc L., and Krzysztof J. Pelc. 2014. "Law, Politics, and the True Cost of Protectionism: The Choice of Trade Remedies or Binding Overhang." *World Trade Review* 13 (1): 39–64.

Büthe, Tim, and Walter Mattli. 2011. *The New Global Rulers: The Privatization of Regulation in the World Economy.* Princeton: Princeton University Press.

Büthe, Tim, and Helen Milner. 2011. "Institutional Diversity in Trade Agreements and Foreign Direct Investment: Credibility, Commitment, and Economic Flows in the Developing World, 1971–2007." Paper presented at the

Annual Meeting of the American Political Science Association, Seattle, WA, September 3, 2011.

Cadot, Olivier, and Julien Gourdon. 2016. "Non-tariff Measures, Preferential Trade Agreements, and Prices: New Evidence." *Review of World Economics* 152 (2): 227–49.

Calvert, Randall, Mathew D. McCubbins, and Barry R. Weingast. 1989. "A Theory of Political Control and Agency Discretion." *American Journal of Political Science* 33 (3): 588–611.

Carnegie, Allison. 2014. "States Held Hostage: Political Hold-Up Problems and the Effects of International Institutions." *American Political Science Review* 108 (1): 54–70.

Carney, Timothy P. 2009. "Washington Toy Story Shows Why Regulation Helps the Big Guys." *DC Examiner,* January 30, 2009.

Carpenter, Daniel, and David A. Moss. 2013. *Preventing Regulatory Capture: Special Interest Influence and How to Limit It.* New York: Cambridge University Press.

Chaney, Thomas. 2008. "Distorted Gravity: The Intensive and Extensive Margins of International Trade." *American Economic Review* 98 (4): 1707–21.

Chen, Shenjie, and Emily Yu. 2010. "Export Dynamics in Canada: Market Diversification in a Changing International Economic Environment." In *Trade Policy Research 2010: Exporter Dynamics and Productivity,* edited by Dan Ciuriak, 245–76. Ottawa: Minister of Public Works and Government Services Canada.

Cho, Sungjoon. 2007. "Doha's Development." *Berkeley Journal of International Law* 25:165.

CLEEN (Chemical Legislation European Enforcement Network). 1996. *European Inspection Project on the Notification of New Substances.* The Hague: Ministry of Housing Spatial Planning and Environment / Heidemij Avies.

Congress. 2011. *Congressional Record-House.* Vol. 153. Washington, DC: Government Printing Office.

Costinot, Arnaud. 2008. "A Comparative Institutional Analysis of Agreements on Product Standards." *Journal of International Economics* 75 (1): 197–213. https://ideas.repec.org/a/eee/inecon/v75y2008i1p197-213.html.

Crandall, Robert W. 1983. *Controlling Industrial Pollution.* Washington, DC: Brookings Institution Press.

Crichton, Michael. 1992. *Rising Sun.* New York: Alfred A. Knopf.

Crivelli, Pramila, and Jasmin Gröschl. 2012. "The Impact of Sanitary and Phytosanitary Measures on Market Entry and Trade Flows." IFO Working Paper Series 136.

Croome, John. 1996. *Reshaping the World Trading System: A History of the Uruguay Round.* Geneva: World Trade Organization.

Daemmrich, Arthur A. 2011. "International Lobbying and the Dow Chemical Company." Harvard Business School Case no. 710-027. November.

Davis, Christina L. 2004. "International Institutions and Issue Linkage: Building Support for Agricultural Trade Liberalization." *American Political Science Review* 98 (1): 153–69.

Davis, Christina L., and Meredith Wilf. 2017. "Joining the Club: Accession to the GATT/WTO." *Journal of Politics* 79 (3): 964–78.

Deise, Chuck. 2009. "Survey: How Leading Firms Manage Regulatory Change." *Chemical Week* 171 (26): 27.

De Loecker, Jan, and Jan Eeckhout. 2017. "The Rise of Market Power and the Macroeconomic Implications." Working Paper no. 23687, National Bureau of Economic Research.

de Mesquita, Bruce Bueno, Alastair Smith, Randolph M. Siverson, and James D. Morrow. 2005. *The Logic of Political Survival.* Cambridge: MIT Press.

Derfler, Philip S. 2005. "Meeting to Discuss Possible Changes to the Regulatory Jurisdiction of Certain Food Products Containing Meat and Poultry." *Federal Register* 70 (214): 67490–94.

Dimitri, Carolyn, Anne B. W. Effland, and Neilson Chase Conklin. 2005. *The 20th Century Transformation of US Agriculture and Farm Policy.* Report, Economic Information Bulletin no. 3, US Department of Agriculture.

Donovan, Joe. 2009. Telegram. "Hong Kong Toy Manufacturers Struggle with U.S. Product Safety Demands, Delayed Customer Orders." Public Library of US Diplomacy, WikiLeaks. April 7. https://wikileaks.org/plusd/cables/09HONGKONG649_a.html.

Drezner, Daniel W. 2007. *All Politics Is Global: Explaining International Regulatory Regimes.* Princeton: Princeton University Press.

Durán, Gracia Marín. 2015. "NTBs and the WTO Agreement on Technical Barriers to Trade: The Case of PPM-Based Measures Following US–Tuna II and EC–Seal Products." In *European Yearbook of International Economic Law 2015*, edited by Christoph Herrmann, Markus Krajewski, and Jörg Philipp Terhechte, 87–136. Berlin: Springer-Verlag.

Dutt, Pushan, Ilian Mihov, and Timothy Van Zandt. 2013. "The Effect of WTO on the Extensive and the Intensive Margins of Trade." *Journal of International Economics* 91 (2): 204–19.

Edelman, Peter B. 1987. "Japanese Product Standards as Non-tariff Trade Barriers: When Regulatory Policy Becomes a Trade Issue." *Stanford Journal of International Law* 24:389.

Ederington, Josh, and Michele Ruta. 2016. "Nontariff Measures and the World Trading System." In *Handbook of Commercial Policy*, vol. 1, part B, edited by Kyle Bagwell and Robert W. Staiger, 211–77. Amsterdam: North-Holland. https://www.sciencedirect.com/science/article/pii/S2214312216300102.

European Chemicals Agency. 2016. "Registration Statistics." https://echa.europa.eu/registration-statistics.

European Commission. 1999. *Ban of Phthalates in Childcare Articles and Toys: IP/99/829.* European Commission.

———. 2001. *Strategy for a Future Chemicals Policy: COM/2001/0088.* European Commission.

Evans, Peter B. 1979. *Dependent Development: The Alliance of Multinational, State, and Local Capital in Brazil.* Princeton: Princeton University Press.

Evenett, Simon J. 2013. *Protectionism's Quiet Return.* London: Centre for Economic Policy Research.

Fally, Thibault. 2011. "On the Fragmentation of Production in the US." Unpublished manuscript.

FDA (US Food and Drug Administration). 2013. *2013 Annual Report on Food Facilities, Food Imports, and FDA Foreign Offices.* Report to Congress. Archived at http://wayback.archive-it.org/7993/20171114122344/https://www.fda.gov/Food/GuidanceRegulation/FSMA/ucm376478.htm.

Feenstra, Robert C. 1996. "U.S. Imports, 1972–1994: Data and Concordances." Working Paper no. 5515, National Bureau of Economic Research.

Feenstra, Robert C., Chang Hong, Hong Ma, and Barbara J. Spencer. 2012. "Contractual versus Non-contractual Trade: The Role of Institutions in China." Working Paper no. 17728, National Bureau of Economic Research.

Fernandes, Ana M., Peter J. Klenow, Sergii Meleshchuk, Martha Denisse Pierola, and Andrés Rodríguez-Clare. 2016. "The Intensive Margin in Trade: Moving beyond Pareto." Working Paper no. 25195, National Bureau of Economic Research.

Ferrantino, Michael J., Ian Gillson, and Gabriela Schmidt. 2016. "Russian Federation, the World Trade Organization, and the Eurasian Customs Union." Working Paper no. 7748, World Bank Policy Research.

Finger, J. Michael, Ulrich Reincke, and Adriana Castro. 2002. "Market Access Bargaining in the Uruguay Round: How Tightly Does Reciprocity Constrain?" In *Going Alone*, edited by Jagdish Bhagwati, 111. Cambridge: MIT Press.

Fischer, Ronald, and Pablo Serra. 2000. "Standards and Protection." *Journal of International Economics* 52 (2): 377–400.

Fontagné, Lionel, and Gianluca Orefice. 2016. "Let's Try Next Door: Technical Barriers to Trade and Multi-destination Firms." *European Economic Review* 101:643–63.

Fontagné, Lionel, Gianluca Orefice, Roberta Piermartini, and Nadia Rocha. 2015. "Product Standards and Margins of Trade: Firm-Level Evidence." *Journal of International Economics* 97 (1): 29–44.

Freund, Caroline, and Martha Denisse Pierola. 2015. "Export Superstars." *Review of Economics and Statistics* 97 (5): 1023–32.

Gelman, Andrew, Aleks Jakulin, Maria Grazia Pittau, and Yu-Sung Su. 2008. "A Weakly Informative Default Prior Distribution for Logistic and Other Regression Models." *Annals of Applied Statistics* 2 (4): 1360–83.

Gilligan, Michael. 1997. *Empowering Exporters: Delegation, Reciprocity and Collective Action in Twentieth Century American Trade Policy.* Ann Arbor: University of Michigan Press.

Gilligan, Thomas W., and Keith Krehbiel. 1987. "Collective Decisionmaking and Standing Committees: An Informational Rationale for Restrictive Amendment Procedures." *Journal of Law, Economics, and Organization* 3:287.

———. 1989. "Asymmetric Information and Legislative Rules with a Heterogeneous Committee." *American Journal of Political Science* 33 (2): 459–90.

Gilpin, Robert. 1973. *The Multinational Corporation and the National Interest.* Technical Report, US Senate Committee on Labor and Public Welfare.

Goetz, Gretchen. 2010. "Who Inspects What? A Food Safety Scramble." *Food Safety News*, December 16, 2010.

Goldstein, Judith L. 1989. "The Impact of Ideas on Trade Policy: The Origins of US Agricultural and Manufacturing Policies." *International Organization* 43 (1): 31–71.

———. 1993. "Creating the GATT Rules: Politics, Institutions, and American Policy." In *Multilateralism Matters: The Theory and Praxis of an Institutional Form*, edited by John Gerard Ruggie, 201–31. New York: Columbia University Press.

Goldstein, Judith L., and Robert Gulotty. 2014a. "The Limits of Institutional Reform: America, Trade Liberalization and the GATT/WTO." In *Oxford Handbook on Historical Institutionalism*, edited by Orfeo Fioretos, Tulia G. Falleti, and Adam Sheingate. Oxford: Oxford University Press.

———. 2014b. "America and Trade Liberalization: The Limits of Institutional Reform." *International Organization* 68 (2): 263–95.

GOP. 2016. *2016 Republican Party Platform.* https://www.gop.com/platform/2016.

Gowa, Joanne, and Raymond Hicks. 2018. "Big Treaties, Small Effects: The RTAA Agreements." *World Politics* 70 (2): 165–93.

Gowa, Joanne, and Soo Yeon Kim. 2005. "An Exclusive Country Club: The Effects of the GATT on Trade, 1950–94." *World Politics* 57 (4): 453–78.

Grieco, Joseph. 1990. *Cooperation among Nations: Europe, America, and Nontariff Barriers to Trade.* Ithaca: Cornell University Press.

Gropp, Reint, and Kristina Kostial. 2000. *The Disappearing Tax Base: Is Foreign Direct Investment (FDI) Eroding Corporate Income Taxes?* Technical Report, International Monetary Fund.

Grossman, Gene M., and Elhanan Helpman. 1994. "Protection for Sale." *American Economic Review* 84 (4): 833–50.

————. 1995. "Trade Wars and Trade Talks." *Journal of Political Economy* 103 (4): 675–708.

Gulotty, Robert, and Xiaojun Li. 2019. "Anticipatory Responses to PTA Exclusion: Chinese Manufacturing Firms and the Trans-Pacific Partnership." Forthcoming in *Business and Politics.*

Gulotty, Robert, Xiaojun Li, Wei Lin, and Lizhi Liu. 2017. *Regulatory Protection and the Geography of Trade: Evidence from Chinese Customs Data.* Technical Report, American Political Science Association.

Helpman, Elhanan. 2006. "Trade, FDI, and the Organization of Firms." *Journal of Economic Literature* 44 (3): 589–630.

Helpman, Elhanan, Oleg Itskhoki, Marc-Andreas Muendler, and Stephen J. Redding. 2017. "Trade and Inequality: From Theory to Estimation." *Review of Economic Studies* 84 (1): 357–405.

Helpman, Elhanan, Marc J. Melitz, and Stephen R. Yeaple. 2004. "Export versus FDI with Heterogeneous Firms." *American Economic Review* 94 (1): 300–316.

Hertslet, Edward. 1878. *Treaties and Tariffs Regulating the Trade between Great Britain and Foreign Nations.* London: Butterworths.

Hiscox, Michael J. 1999. "The Magic Bullet? The RTAA, Institutional Reform, and Trade Liberalization." *International Organization* 53 (4): 669–98.

Hodgman, John. 2014. "Dunkin' Corn Pone." *New York Times Magazine,* May 2, 2014.

Horn, Henrik. 2006. "National Treatment in the GATT." *American Economic Review* 96 (1): 394–404.

Howse, Robert. 2016. "The World Trade Organization 20 Years On: Global Governance by Judiciary." *European Journal of International Law* 27 (1): 9–77.

Howse, Robert, and Elisabeth Türk. 2001. "The WTO Impact on Internal Regulations—a Case Study of the Canada-EC Asbestos Dispute." In *The EU and the WTO: Legal and Constitutional Issues,* edited by Gráinne de Búrca and Joanne Scott, 283. Oxford: Hart.

Huang, Wenguang. 2011. "No Joy This Season for China's Toymakers." *Fortune Magazine,* December 14, 2011.

Hudec, Robert E. 2003. "Science and Post-discriminatory WTO Law." *Boston College International & Comparative Law Review* 26:185.

Huntington, Samuel P. 1952. "The Marasmus of the ICC: The Commission, the Railroads, and the Public Interest." *Yale Law Journal* 61:467.

Irwin, Douglas A. 1992. "Strategic Trade Policy and Mercantilist Trade Rivalries." *American Economic Review* 82 (2): 134–39.

————. 1996. *Against the Tide: An Intellectual History of Free Trade.* Princeton: Princeton University Press.

Jensen, J. B., Dennis P. Quinn, and Stephen Weymouth. 2015. "The Influence of

Firm Global Supply Chains and Foreign Currency Undervaluations on US Trade Disputes." *International Organization* 69 (4): 913–47.

Johns, Leslie. 2014. "Depth versus Rigidity in the Design of International Trade Agreements." *Journal of Theoretical Politics* 26 (3): 468–95.

Johnson, Harry G. 1953. "Optimum Tariffs and Retaliation." *Review of Economic Studies* 21 (2): 142–53.

Johnson, Renée. 2010. *The Federal Food Safety System: A Primer.* Congressional Research Service.

Kee, Hiau Looi, Alessandro Nicita, and Marcelo Olarreaga. 2009. "Estimating Trade Restrictiveness Indices." *Economic Journal* 119 (534): 172–99.

Keohane, Robert O., and Van Doorn Ooms. 1972. "The Multinational Enterprise and World Political Economy." *International Organization* 26 (1): 84–120.

Kim, In Song. 2017. "Political Cleavages within Industry: Firm Level Lobbying for Trade Liberalization." *American Political Science Review* 111 (1): 1–20.

Kindleberger, Charles P. 1969. "American Business Abroad." *International Executive* 11 (2): 11–12.

Kono, Daniel Yuichi. 2006. "Optimal Obfuscation: Democracy and Trade Policy Transparency." *American Political Science Review* 100 (3): 369.

———. 2009. "Market Structure, Electoral Institutions, and Trade Policy." *International Studies Quarterly* 53 (4): 885–906.

Koremenos, Barbara. 2001. "Loosening the Ties That Bind: A Learning Model of Agreement Flexibility." *International Organization* 55 (2): 289–325.

———. 2005. "Contracting around International Uncertainty." *American Political Science Review* 99 (4): 549.

Koremenos, Barbara, Charles Lipson, and Duncan Snidal. 2001. "The Rational Design of International Institutions." *International Organization* 55 (4): 761–99.

Krasner, Stephen D. 1976. "State Power and the Structure of International Trade." *World Politics* 28 (3): 317–47.

Krishna, Vijay, and John Morgan. 2001. "A Model of Expertise." *Quarterly Journal of Economics* 116 (2): 747–75.

Krugman, Paul R. 1997. "What Should Trade Negotiators Negotiate About?" *Journal of Economic Literature* 35:113–20.

Kucik, Jeffrey, and Eric Reinhardt. 2008. "Does Flexibility Promote Cooperation? An Application to the Global Trade Regime." *International Organization* 62 (3): 477–505.

Lake, David A. 2009. "Open Economy Politics: A Critical Review." *Review of International Organizations* 4 (3): 219–44.

Lamy, Pascal. 2012. "The Multilateral Trading System and Regional Economic Cooperation." WTO speech given at the University of International Business and Economics, Beijing. https://www.wto.org/english/news_e/sppl_e/sppl246 _e.htm.

Lawless, Martina. 2010. "Déconstruction de la gravité: Coûts du commerce et marges extensive et intensive." *Canadian Journal of Economics / Revue canadienne d'économique* 43 (4): 1149–72.

League of Nations. 1921–38. *International Trade Statistics*. Geneva: League of Nations.

Leone, Robert A. 1986. *Who Profits?* New York: Basic Books.

Levine, Yasha. 2011. "This Tax Day, 'Farms' Owned by the Rich Provide Massive Tax Shelter." *The Nation*, April 14, 2011.

Lewis, Jeffrey B., and Keith T. Poole. 2004. "Measuring Bias and Uncertainty in Ideal Point Estimates via the Parametric Bootstrap." *Political Analysis* 12 (2): 105–27.

Limão, Nuno. 2006. "Preferential Trade Agreements as Stumbling Blocks for Multilateral Trade Liberalization: Evidence for the United States." *American Economic Review* 96 (3): 896–914.

Limão, Nuno, and Patricia Tovar. 2011. "Policy Choice: Theory and Evidence from Commitment via International Trade Agreements." *Journal of International Economics* 85 (2): 186–205.

Lindgren, Karl-Oskar, and Thomas Persson. 2008. "The Structure of Conflict over EU Chemicals Policy." *European Union Politics* 9 (1): 31–58.

Lindsey, Brink, and Steven Teles. 2017. *The Captured Economy: How the Powerful Enrich Themselves, Slow down Growth, and Increase Inequality*. New York: Oxford University Press.

Low, Patrick, and Roy Santana. 2009. "Trade Liberalization in Manufactures: What Is Left after the Doha Round?" *Journal of International Trade and Diplomacy* 3 (1): 63–126.

Mansfield, Edward D., and Diana C. Mutz. 2009. "Support for Free Trade: Self-Interest, Sociotropic Politics, and Out-Group Anxiety." *International Organization* 63 (3): 425–57.

Marcoux, Christopher, and Johannes Urpelainen. 2011. "Profitable Participation: Technology Innovation as an Influence on the Ratification of Regulatory Treaties." *British Journal of Political Science* 44 (4): 1–34.

Marette, Stéphan, and John Beghin. 2010. "Are Standards Always Protectionist?" *Review of International Economics* 18 (1): 179–92.

Masson, Fanny. 2008. "Confidential Business Information (CBI) within the Framework of REACH." Master's thesis, ETH Zurich.

McElroy, Gail, and Kenneth Benoit. 2007. "Party Groups and Policy Positions in the European Parliament." *Party Politics* 13(1): 5–28.

Melitz, Marc J. 2003. "The Impact of Trade on Intra-industry Reallocations and Aggregate Industry Productivity." *Econometrica* 71 (6): 1695–725.

Melitz, Marc J., and Stephen J. Redding. 2015. "Heterogeneous Firms and Trade." *Handbook of International Economics* 4:1.

Milner, Helen V. 1988a. *Resisting Protectionism: Global Industries and the Politics of International Trade.* Princeton: Princeton University Press.

———. 1988b. "Trading Places: Industries for Free Trade." *World Politics* 40 (3): 350–76.

Milner, Helen V., and Keiko Kubota. 2005. "Why the Move to Free Trade? Democracy and Trade Policy in the Developing Countries." *International Organization* 59 (1): 107–43.

Milner, Helen V., and Bumba Mukherjee. 2009. "Democratization and Economic Globalization." *Annual Review of Political Science* 12:163–81.

Monroe, James. 1822. Negotiations and Treaty with France of June 24, 1822. In *Foreign Relations.* Department of State.

Moravcsik, Andrew. 1997. "Taking Preferences Seriously: A Liberal Theory of International Politics." *International Organization* 51 (4): 513–53.

Mutti, John H. 2003. *Foreign Direct Investment and Tax Competition.* Washington, DC: Peterson Institute for International Economics.

North, Douglass C., John Joseph Wallis, and Barry R. Weingast. 2009. *Violence and Social Orders: A Conceptual Framework for Interpreting Recorded Human History.* New York: Cambridge University Press.

Novak, William J. 2013. "A Revisionist History of Regulatory Capture." In *Preventing Regulatory Capture: Special Interest Influence and How to Limit It,* 25–48. New York: Cambridge University Press.

NPD Group. 2009. "U.S. Toy Industry Sales Generate $21.64 Billion in 2008." http://www.npd.com.

Nunn, Nathan. 2007. "Relationship-Specificity, Incomplete Contracts, and the Pattern of Trade." *Quarterly Journal of Economics* 122 (2): 569–600.

Obama, Barack. 2009. "Statement by the President on House Passage of the Food Safety Enhancement Act of 2009." *White House Briefing Room Statements and Releases.* August 3.

Olesen, Alexa. 2007. "In Turnaround, Mattel Takes Blame for Toy Recalls." *New York Sun,* September 21.

Olson, Mancur. 1965. *The Logic of Collective Action: Public Goods and the Theory of Groups.* Cambridge: Harvard University Press.

Osgood, Iain. 2016. "Differentiated Products, Divided Industries: Firm Preferences over Trade Liberalization." *Economics & Politics* 28 (2): 161–80.

Osgood, Iain, Dustin Tingley, Thomas Bernauer, In Song Kim, Helen V. Milner, and Gabriele Spilker. 2017. "The Charmed Life of Superstar Exporters: Survey Evidence on Firms and Trade Policy." *Journal of Politics* 79 (1): 133–52.

Ossa, Ralph. 2011. "A 'New Trade' Theory of GATT/WTO Negotiations." *Journal of Political Economy* 119 (1): 122–52.

Oster, Sharon. 1982. "Intraindustry Structure and the Ease of Strategic Change." *Review of Economics and Statistics* 64 (3): 376–83.

Pandya, Sonal S. 2014. *Trading Spaces Foreign Direct Investment Regulation, 1970–2000*. New York: Cambridge University Press.

Piketty, Thomas. 2014. *Capital in the 21st Century*. Cambridge: Harvard University Press.

Playthings staff. 2008. "Selecta Exits U.S. Market over Cost Concerns." *Gifts & Decorative Accessories*, December 5, 2008. http://www.giftsanddec.com/article/353219-selecta-exits-us-market-over-cost-concerns.

Prajogo, Daniel, and Amrik Sohal. 2006. *The Implementation of ISO 9000 in Australian Organisations: A Comparison between 1994 and the 2000 Versions*. Technical Report, Australian Supply Chain Management Research Unit, Monash University.

Pratt, Neil. 2009. *Comments on Standards-Related Foreign Trade Barriers in the European Union (USTR-2009-0032-0048)*. Technical Report, Society of the Plastics Industry.

Prokes, Pavel. 2015. *Monitoring the Impacts of REACH on Innovation, Competitiveness and SMEs*. Luxembourg: Publication Office of the European Union.

Ramsey, Frank P. 1927. "A Contribution to the Theory of Taxation." *Economic Journal* 37 (145): 47–61.

Rapoport, Carla. 1992. "The Rights and Wrongs of Rising Sun." *Fortune Magazine*, March 23, 1992.

Rauch, James E. 1999. "Networks versus Markets in International Trade." *Journal of International Economics* 48 (1): 7–35.

Redhead, C. Stephan, and Donna U. Vogt. 2002. *Public Health Security and Bioterrorist Preparedness Response Act (PL 107-188): Provisions and Changes to Preexisting Law*. Report RL31263, Congressional Research Service.

Regan, Donald H. 2015. "Explaining Trade Agreements: The Practitioners' Story and the Standard Model." *World Trade Review* 14 (3): 391–417.

Rettman, Andrew. 2006. "Champagne Corks Fly as EU Gives Birth to Chemicals Law." *EUobserver*, December 13, 2006.

Rho, Sungmin, and Michael Tomz. 2017. "Why Don't Trade Preferences Reflect Economic Self-Interest?" *International Organization* 71 (S1): S85–S108.

Richardson, Gary. 2001. "A Tale of Two Theories: Monopolies and Craft Guilds in Medieval England and Modern Imagination." *Journal of the History of Economic Thought* 23 (2): 217–42.

———. 2008. "Brand Names before the Industrial Revolution." Working Paper no. 13930, National Bureau of Economic Research.

Roberts, Margaret E., Brandon M. Stewart, Dustin Tingley, and Edoardo M. Airoldi. 2013. "The Structural Topic Model and Applied Social Science." In *Advances in Neural Information Processing Systems Workshop on Topic Models: Computation, Application, and Evaluation*. http://goo.gl/uHkXAQ.

Roberts, Margaret E., Brandon M. Stewart, Dustin Tingley, Christopher Lucas, Jetson Leder-Luis, Shana Kushner Gadarian, Bethany Albertson, and David G. Rand. 2014. "Structural Topic Models for Open-Ended Survey Responses." *American Journal of Political Science* 58 (4): 1064–82.

Rodrik, Dani. 1997. *Has Globalization Gone Too Far?* Washington, DC: Peterson Institute for International Economics.

Rogerson, William P. 1984. "A Note on the Incentive for a Monopolist to Increase Fixed Costs as a Barrier to Entry." *Quarterly Journal of Economics* 99 (2): 399–402.

Rogowski, Ronald. 1987. "Trade and the Variety of Democratic Institutions." *International Organization* 41 (2): 203–23.

———. 1989. *Commerce and Coalitions: How Trade Affects Domestic Political Alignments.* Princeton: Princeton University Press.

Rosendorff, B. Peter, and Helen V. Milner. 2001. "The Optimal Design of International Trade Institutions: Uncertainty and Escape." *International Organization* 55 (4): 829–57.

Schattschneider, Elmer Eric. 1935. *Politics, Pressures and the Tariff.* New York: Prentice-Hall.

Scott, Alex. 2008. "Survey: North Americans Are Least Prepared for REACH." *Chemical Week*, March 17, 2008.

Setser, Vernon G. 1937. "The Commercial Reciprocity Policy of the United States 1774–1829." PhD thesis, University of Pennsylvania.

Simon, Frédéric. 2012. *REACH Chemical Law "Worth the Money in the End," Says BASF.* Technical Report, EurActiv.

Song, Jae, David J. Price, Fatih Guvenen, Nicholas Bloom, and Till von Wachter. 2015. "Firming Up Inequality." Working Paper no. 21199, National Bureau of Economic Research.

Staiger, Robert W. 2012. *Non-tariff Measures and the WTO.* Technical Report ERSD-2012-01, World Trade Organization.

Staiger, Robert W., and Alan O. Sykes. 2011. "International Trade, National Treatment, and Domestic Regulation." *Journal of Legal Studies* 40 (1): 149–203.

Staiger, Robert W., and Guido Tabellini. 1987. "Discretionary Trade Policy and Excessive Protection." *American Economic Review* 77 (5): 823–37.

Steingraber, Sandra. 2004. "Report from Europe: Precaution Ascending." *Rachel's Democracy and Health News*, no. 786. https://web.archive.org/web/20160323025024/http://www.rachel.org/?q=en/node/6467.

Stigler, George J. 1971. "The Theory of Economic Regulation." *Bell Journal of Economics and Management Science* 2 (1): 3–21.

Stolper, Wolfgang F., and Paul A. Samuelson. 1941. "Protection and Real Wages." *Review of Economic Studies* 9 (1): 58–73.

Sundhar, Sindhu. 2014. "FDA Agrees to FSMA Rollout Deadline in Settlement." *Law360*, February 20, 2014. http://www.law360.com/publicpolicy/articles/511920.

Suwa-Eisenmann, Akiko, and Thierry Verdier. 2002. "Reciprocity and the Political Economy of Harmonization and Mutual Recognition of Regulatory Measures." *CEPR Discussion Paper*, no. 3147. https://ssrn.com/abstract=299418.

Swann, G. M. Peter. 2010. "International Standards and Trade: A Review of the Empirical Literature." *OECD Trade Policy Papers* 97.

Sykes, Alan O. 1995. *Product Standards for Internationally Integrated Goods Markets*. Washington, DC: Brookings Institution Press.

———. 2001. "Efficient Protection through WTO Rulemaking." In *Efficiency, Equity, and Legitimacy: The Multilateral Trading System at the Millennium*, edited by Roger B. Porter, Pierre Sauvé, Arvind Subramanian, and Americo Beviglia Zampetti, 114–41. Washington, DC: Brookings Institution Press.

Tsebelis, George. 2002. *Veto Players: How Political Institutions Work*. Princeton: Princeton University Press.

Tuncak, Baskut. 2014. "Driving Innovation: How Stronger Laws Help Bring Safer Chemicals to Market." *Sustainable Development Law and Policy* 14 (3): 4–11.

United States. 1956. *Price-Support Program: Hearings before the Committee on Agriculture and Forestry, United States Senate, Eighty-Fourth Congress, First [-second] Session, on Proposed Modifications of the General Farm Program*. Washington, DC: US Government Printing Office.

———. 2009a. *Keeping America's Families Safe: Reforming the Food Safety System. Hearing of the Committee on Health, Education, Labor, and Pensions*. 111th Congress, S. HRG. 111-1069 (statement of Senator Enzi).

———. 2009b. *Keeping America's Families Safe: Reforming the Food Safety System. Hearing of the Committee on Health, Education, Labor, and Pensions*. 111th Congress, S. HRG. 111-1069 (statement of Senator Isakson).

———. 2010. Oversight of the Consumer Product Safety Commission: Product Safety in the Holiday Season. *Hearing Before the US Senate Committee on Science, Commerce and Transportation Subcommittee on Consumer Protection, Product Safety and Insurance*. 111th Congress (December 2) (testimony of Commissioner Anne M. Northup).

USDA. 2018. *Crop Production Historical Track Records*. United States Department of Agriculture National Agricultural Statistics Service, April 2018.

Vaubel, Roland. 2006. "Principal-Agent Problems in International Organizations." *Review of International Organizations* 1 (2): 125–38.

Vogel, David. 1995. *Trading Up: Consumer and Environmental Regulation in a Global Economy*. Cambridge: Harvard University Press.

———. 2012. *The Politics of Precaution: Regulating Health, Safety, and Environ-*

mental Risks in Europe and the United States. Princeton: Princeton University Press.

Waxman, Henry A. 2004. "The Chemical Industry, the Bush Administration, and European Efforts to Regulate Chemicals." *US House of Representatives Committee on Government Reform.*

Westervelt, Robert. 2007. "An Opportunity to Reach Out." *Chemical Week,* May 30/June 6, 2007.

Weymouth, Stephen. 2012. "Firm Lobbying and Influence in Developing Countries: A Multilevel Approach." *Business and Politics* 14 (4): 1–26.

Williamson, Oliver E. 1968. "Economies as an Antitrust Defense: The Welfare Tradeoffs." *American Economic Review* 58 (1): 18–36.

Woldenberg, Rick. 2009. "CPSIA—If We Can Meet the Standards, Why Do I Still Hate This Law?" *CPSIA—Comments & Observations* (blog), March 25. https://learningresourcesinc.blogspot.com/2009/03/cpsia-if-we-can-meet-standards-why-do-i.html?m=0.

WTO (World Trade Organization). 2003. "G/TBT/M/30." *Committee on Technical Barriers to Trade.* Geneva: World Trade Organization.

———. 2007. *World Trade Report 2007.* Geneva: World Trade Organization.

———. 2009. "G/TBT/M/47." *Committee on Technical Barriers to Trade.* Geneva: World Trade Organization.

———. 2011a. "G/TBT/M/53." *Committee on Technical Barriers to Trade.* Geneva: World Trade Organization.

———. 2011b. *World Trade Report 2011.* Geneva: World Trade Organization.

———. 2012a. "G/TBT/N/SAU/478." *Committee on Technical Barriers to Trade.* Geneva: World Trade Organization.

———. 2012b. *World Trade Report 2012.* Geneva: World Trade Organization.

Xie, Yiqing, and James R. Markusen. 2011. *Exporting, Licensing, FDI and Productivity Choice: Theory and Evidence from Chilean Data.* Working Paper, Fudan University and University of Colorado at Boulder.

Index